Sport & Fitness Management
Career Strategies and Professional Content

Janet B. Parks, DA
Beverly R.K. Zanger, MEd
Bowling Green State University

Human Kinetics Books
Champaign, Illinois

Library of Congress Cataloging-in-Publication Data

Sport and fitness management : career strategies and professional content /
   editors, Janet B. Parks, Beverly R.K. Zanger.
        p.   cm.
     Includes bibliographical references and index.
     ISBN 0-87322-269-5
     1. Sports—Organization and administration.   2. Sports-
   -Organization and administration—Vocational guidance.   3. Sports
   facilities—Management.   4. Recreation centers—Management.
   5. Physical fitness centers—Management.   I. Parks, Janet B., 1942-
   . II. Zanger, Beverly K.
   GV713.S68   1990   67309
   796'.06'9023—dc20   89-71722
                                                          CIP

ISBN: 0-87322-269-5

Developmental Editor: June I. Decker, PhD
Copyeditor: Julie Anderson
Assistant Editors: Timothy Ryan, Valerie Hall, and Robert King
Proofreader: Laurie McGee
Photo Editor: Robert King
Indexer: Barbara Cohen
Production Director: Ernie Noa
Typesetter: Yvonne Winsor
Text Design: Keith Blomberg
Text Layout: Tara Welsch and Kimberlie Henris
Cover Design: Hunter Graphics
Illustrations: Instructional Media Services, Bowling Green State University
Printer: Versa Press

Printed in the United States of America

10 9 8 7 6 5 4 3 2 1

Human Kinetics Books
A Division of Human Kinetics Publishers, Inc.
Box 5076, Champaign, IL 61825-5076
1-800-747-4HKP

Especially for you . . .

Connelly and Nathan   Polly and Jack

Photo Credits

Photos in *Sport and Fitness Management* were used by permission of the following sources.

Photos on pages 1, 131, and 189 courtesy of CLEO Photography, St. Paul, Minnesota.

Photo on page 2 by Laslo Dornbush, Vero Beach, FL.

Photos on pages 9, 69, 75, 139, and 219 by Robert King, Champaign, Illinois

Photos on pages 18 (left) and 200 by Bill Boyle, courtesy of Reid Oslin, Boston College Athletic Association.

Photos on pages 18 (right) and 28 courtesy of Steven Hellyer, University of Oregon Sports Information.

Photos on pages 29 and 227 by Jim Mackey, courtesy of Bill Jamieson, Detroit Red Wings.

Photos on pages 35 and 37 courtesy of Michael Fragale, West Virginia University Sports Communications.

Photos on pages 45, 59, 67, 87, 89, 146, and 239 by Kimberlie Henris, Champaign, Illinois.

Photo on page 46 by Doug Filipov, courtesy of *The Daily Illini*, University of Illinois.

Photos of pages 54 and 246 by Stephen Warmowski, courtesy of *The Daily Illini*, University of Illinois.

Photos on pages 58, 83, and 216 by Steve Parker, Manlius, New York, courtesy of United States Field Hockey Association, Colorado Springs, Colorado.

Photo on page 86 courtesy of Tammy Frank, The University of Iowa Sports Information.

Photos on pages 95, 103, and 259 courtesy of Barry A. Franklin, PhD., William Beaumont Hospital—Cardiac Rehabilitation, Royal Oak, Michigan.

Photo on page 99 courtesy of *National Racquetball Magazine*, Clearwater, Florida.

Photo on page 106 by Mike Duda, courtesy of *The Daily Illini*, University of Illinois.

Photo on page 114 courtesy of Dr. Mitchell L. Feingold, Podiatrist, Ambulatory Foot Clinic of San Diego.

Photo on page 117 courtesy of Brian Sharkey, University of Montana.

Photo on page 121 by Bill Kahn, courtesy of *The Daily Illini*, University of Illinois.

Photo on page 155 by Phil Messersmith, courtesy of *The Daily Illini*, University of Illinois.

Photo on page 166 courtesy of Jack L. Groppel, Harry Hodman/Saddlebrook Resort, Wesley Chapel, Florida.

Photos on pages 177, 179, 180, 183, 185, and 237 courtesy of Champaign County Historical Archives, Urbana Free Library, Urbana, Illinois.

Photo on page 186 by Glen Spiering, Green Bay, Wisconsin.

Photo on page 188 by Tim Morse, courtesy of Reid Oslin, Boston College Athletic Association.

Photo on page 192 by Chance Brockway, Buckeye Lake, Ohio.

Photo on page 193 by Gary Eifert, courtesy of *The Daily Illini*, University of Illinois.

Photo on page 201 courtesy of Andrew A. Jacobs, PhD, The Winning Edge, Kansas City, Missouri.

Photo on page 202 by Lisa Davis, courtesy of *The Daily Illini*, University of Illinois.

Photo on page 225 by Mark Jones, The Tintype, Arthur, Illinois.

Photo on page 226 courtesy of American Coaching Effectiveness Program (ACEP), Champaign, Illinois.

Photo on page 230 by Pam Susemiehl, courtesy of *The Daily Illini*, University of Illinois.

Photo on page 260 by John Konstantaras, courtesy of *The Daily Illini*, University of Illinois.

Photos on pages 272-277 courtesy of the editors and authors.

Contents

Preface

As a future sport manager, you probably have many questions as you begin this course. What is sport and fitness management? What kinds of jobs are available to me? What skills will I need to be successful? *Sport and Fitness Management: Career Strategies and Professional Content* answers these questions and others you may have about sport and fitness management. The contributing authors are all leaders in the field, and their accumulated knowledge will greatly benefit you as you begin making your career decisions.

Chapter 1 gives you the definition and direction of sport and fitness management. Part I describes sport and fitness management careers and the many professional options available to you. Part II reviews fundamental skills that you need to be successful in sport and fitness management. Career planning, professional style, and coping skills are among the topics discussed. Part III summarizes the areas of professional content that make up sport management and fitness. Sport sociology, psychology, philosophy, and the modern history of both sport and management are presented in a holistic manner that places sport and fitness in the context of American culture. We encourage you to enhance your learning by participating in the suggested activities and discussions that conclude each chapter.

By the end of the semester, you will have learned the answers to many of your questions about sport and fitness management. We hope these answers lead you to a rewarding career.

Acknowledgments

We are grateful to the many individuals who contributed to the development of this book. Without their help and support, our task would have been insurmountable.

When we initiated this project, we selected a "round table of experts," a group of scholars with a wealth of knowledge and expertise to share. Their names and the content areas to which they contributed follow; we sincerely appreciate their efforts.

Dolores Black (Bowling Green State University), sports club management; Christine Brooks and Mike Palmisano (University of Michigan), sport marketing; Lynn Darby (Bowling Green State University), exercise physiology; Sue Hager (Bowling Green State University), facility management and campus recreation; Kathleen Hart and Carol O'Shea (Bowling Green State University), writing skills; Bernard Mullin (Pittsburgh Pirates Baseball), marketing and management theory; Patricia Peterson (Bowling Green State University), community recreation; Dean Purdy (Bowling Green State University), intercollegiate athletics; Cheryl Sokoll (Bowling Green State University), sports information; and Darrel Verney (Bowling Green State University), aquatics management.

We appreciate the financial support and the encouragement we received from administrators at Bowling Green State University: Roger Bennett (College of Education and Allied Professions) and Betty van der Smissen and Ronald Russell (School of Health, Physical Education and Recreation). Thank you for your confidence in this project.

Technical support was critical and we are grateful for the expertise and patience of Sherry Haskins, Judy Maxey, and Sheryl Sabo (word processing, Bowling Green State University), Lee Floro and Jack Ward (instructional media, Bowling Green State University); Gardner McLean (News Services, Bowling Green State University); Joanne Washburn (Washington State University); June Decker (Human Kinetics Publishers); and the anonymous reviewer. Your contributions made this a better book.

Finally, we wish to acknowledge the faculty and students of the Sport Management Division of the School of Health, Physical Education and Recreation at Bowling Green State University. The interaction we have been privileged to share with our faculty colleagues has enriched our professional lives, enhanced our knowledge, and enabled us to grow as professionals. Our students not only read portions of the manuscripts and suggested modifications but also provided us with the raison d'être for writing this book. Sincere thanks to all of you!

CHAPTER 1

Definition and Direction

Janet B. Parks and Beverly R.K. Zanger
Bowling Green State University

Sport/fitness management may be defined in two ways. It is an area of professional endeavor in which a wide variety of sport- and fitness-related careers exist, and it is an area of academic professional preparation—a major in higher education.

AN AREA OF PROFESSIONAL ENDEAVOR

Careers in sport management are found in, but not limited to, the following settings: school and college sport programs; professional sport; amateur sport organizations (e.g., United States Olympics, International Special Olympics, and the Amateur Athletic Union [AAU]); private club sport (e.g., tennis clubs, golf clubs, and racquetball clubs); commercial sport establishments (e.g., bowling alleys and ski resorts); sport arenas, coliseums, and stadia; community recreation sport programs; industrial sport programs; sport programs in social agencies (e.g., the Young Women's Christian Association [YWCA], the Young Men's Christian Association [YMCA], and the Jewish Community Center [JCC]; military sport programs; developmental programs for sport (e.g., the Athletic Institute, The Women's Sports Foundation, and

the National Golf Foundation); corporate sponsors (e.g., Volvo International Tennis Tournament); the sporting goods industry; and the sport news media, both print and broadcast (VanderZwaag, 1988). Discussions of careers in many of these settings are presented in subsequent chapters of this text.

Careers in sport management are not limited to school settings.

1

What Is Sport?

Most people know through experience and intuition what the word *sport* means. Sport is, of course, fun. It involves play and may include many participants, as in team sports; two participants, as in dual sports; or only one person, as in individual sports. What criteria qualify particular games or activities to be classified as sports? Is horse racing a sport? What about water skiing, pocket billiards, or chess and other board games? We know that football, basketball, ice and field hockey, tennis, golf, baseball, and softball are sports. Are they different from sailing or scuba diving?

Sport is defined many different ways. Snyder and Spreitzer (1989) define sport as competitive human physical activity that is governed by institutional rules. VanderZwaag (1988) elaborates on this definition: "Sport is a competitive physical activity, utilizing specialized equipment and facilities, with unique dimensions of time and space, in which the quest for records

is of high significance" (p. 3). Loy (1968) provides yet another perspective with his claim that sport should (a) be playlike in nature, (b) involve some element of competition, (c) be based on physical prowess, (d) involve elements of skill, strategy, and chance, and (e) have an uncertain outcome. These various interpretations of sport illustrate that a single definition is neither possible nor necessary. Using one or all of the definitions, we can create a workable concept of sport.

Fitness Management

The term *fitness* is generally understood and requires little explanation. The primary components of physical fitness are aerobic capacity, strength, cardiovascular endurance, and flexibility; physical fitness programs are designed to enhance these components. Settings that offer opportunities for fitness management careers include corporate fitness programs, commercial

Fitness activities are important for people of all ages.

health/fitness clubs, cardiac rehabilitation clinics, sports medicine clinics, social agencies, and amateur or professional sports teams.

Scope of Sport/Fitness Management

A discussion of the definitions of sport/fitness management is incomplete without a reference to the scope of such pursuits in society at large. Some sport and fitness programs (e.g., physical education programs) are limited to the school-age population. In a broader context, however, sport/fitness management includes sport and fitness activities that are pursued by participants of any age (i.e., children, adults, and senior citizens) and by individuals representing all segments of society (i.e., ethnic groups, the disabled population, and economically or culturally disadvantaged people).

Unique Aspects of Sport Management

Mullin (1980) provides insight into three unique aspects of sport management, and we may apply the same concepts to fitness management as well. According to Mullin, three aspects of sport management render it different from other business enterprises and, hence, justify it as a separate, distinct area of professional preparation. Those unique aspects are sport marketing, structure and financing of sport organizations, and career paths.

Marketing

Marketing of sport is unique because sport and fitness services are unlike other products purchased by consumers. Individuals providing the sport or fitness experience cannot predict the outcome, due to the spontaneous nature of the activity, the inconsistency of various events,

and the uncertainty surrounding the results. Marketers of sport and fitness, therefore, face unique challenges dictated by the very nature of the enterprise.

Financing

Most sport businesses and, to a great extent, fitness businesses are financed differently than the typical business. Typically, the sale of a product or service such as clothing, food, automobiles, or home cleaning finances the business. However, with the exception of sporting goods stores, sport enterprises earn a highly significant portion of revenue not from the sale of a service (e.g., game, workout, or 10K run) but from sources extraneous to the sale of the service (e.g., television rights, concessions, road game guarantees, parking, merchandise, and ancillary services). Intercollegiate athletics and municipal recreation sport/fitness programs may generate revenue from student or user fees, private donations, taxes, rentals, or licensing fees. Sport and fitness managers continually compete for the discretionary funds of consumers through the sale of items that may or may not be related to what appears to be the primary focus of the enterprise. One unique aspect of sport is that it invariably attracts consumers who spend more outside the sporting arena than they spend on the sport itself (e.g., travel, entertainment, souvenirs, and equipment). This unique financial base requires different practices within the sport/fitness setting.

Career Paths

Career paths associated with sport/fitness management are not as well defined as in other vocational areas. Traditionally, many sport management practitioners have been hired from very visible groups such as intercollegiate athletics or professional sport. An example of this phenomenon is the former basketball star who becomes a basketball coach and eventually an athletic director. Similar career advancement patterns may be found within municipal recreation programs, sports clubs, and professional sports teams. In many instances, employment might have depended less on *what* the applicant knew and perhaps more on *whom* the applicant knew and the nature of their relationship. Growing evidence shows that contemporary practice deviates from this tradition and that success in the sporting enterprise depends more and more on knowledge of finance, marketing, and management (Mullin, 1980). The current level of economic competition within sport and fitness enterprises mandates the consideration of sound business experience and expertise in employment practices.

CAREER CATEGORIES

Sport/fitness management careers can be categorized several ways. You could identify the different physical settings in which these careers exist (e.g., fitness clubs, sport clubs, intramural recreational programs, and universities) and describe each according to its setting. How many different sport or fitness settings can you think of? List them, noting whether each is unique or whether some share common characteristics.

You could identify numerous position titles associated with sport/fitness management (e.g., sport marketer, sport journalist, sports information director, general manager, and fitness instructor) and use the titles as a basis for categorization. Write down all the sport management position titles with which you are familiar. How do these titles interrelate with the physical settings you provided in the first list? Do these two lists help you understand sport management careers to a greater extent, or is something missing?

Although physical settings and position titles are important considerations in the classification of sport/fitness management careers, an additional factor allows us to classify the career areas into specific categories. This factor is a consideration of the day-to-day tasks involved with each of the careers. For example, what tasks do sport marketers perform that distinguish them from physical fitness directors or athletic trainers? How do prospective fitness instructors prepare for their careers differently than do prospective sport journalists?

Task Analysis

Respondents to a national survey of sport management practitioners provided extensive information about duties and responsibilities of personnel in a wide variety of sport/fitness organizations (Parks, Quain, Chopra, & Alguindigue, 1987). An analysis of these duties and responsibilities revealed that four groups of tasks are related to sport management careers (see Figure 1.1).

General tasks are associated with duties and responsibilities that are common to all sport/fitness management careers. Competencies in these areas are transferable skills. For example, regardless of whether you work in a sports club, a fitness spa, a sports medicine clinic, or an intercollegiate athletic department, you need to know something about marketing, sales, public speaking, and the other general tasks shown in the figure. Expectations in these areas are constant, and wise aspirants to sport management will equip themselves with knowledge and competencies in these areas.

The tasks delineated within each of the three clusters that branch out from the general tasks reflect distinctions that can be made among sport/fitness management career groups. For instance, leadership and management skills are necessary for the performance of tasks listed in the *organization management* cluster. Sport organization managers will likely be concerned with tasks such as planning, organizing, leading, and evaluating within a sport enterprise (Chelladurai, 1986). Careers in organization management may be found at the community

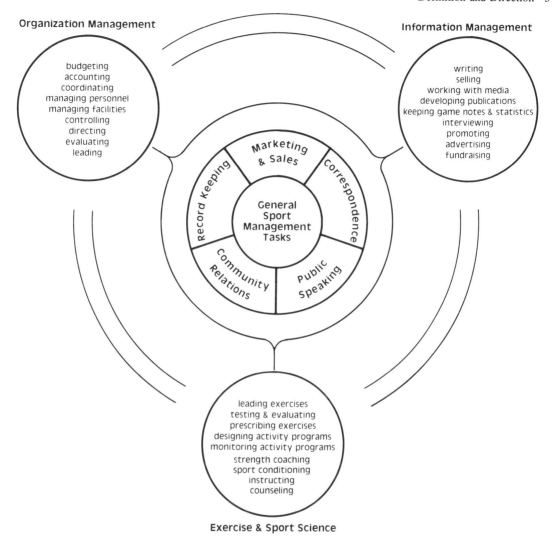

Figure 1.1 Sport management task clusters.

level (e.g., sports clubs, municipal recreation programs, or sport associations for specific populations such as seniors or the disabled), in intercollegiate athletics, in professional sport, and in the business aspect of any sport- or fitness-related enterprise.

In the *information management* cluster, writing and communication skills are of paramount importance. Practitioners in this area acquire,

organize, analyze, synthesize, store, retrieve, and disseminate information regarding sport and fitness (Meltzer, 1967). Examples of professional positions in this area are sport marketing director, sports information director, and sport journalist.

The tasks presented in the *exercise and sport science* cluster require an extensive base of scientific knowledge. Careers in this area are found in exercise leadership, cardiac rehabilitation, sport conditioning, athletic training, aquatics settings (e.g., camps, resorts, agencies, and municipal recreation), campus recreation programs, and the physical fitness industry.

AN AREA OF PROFESSIONAL PREPARATION

Sport management as an area of professional preparation in universities and colleges was recommended in 1957 by Walter O'Malley, owner of the Los Angeles Dodgers (Mason, Higgins, & Wilkinson, 1981). Although O'Malley's original suggestions referred to the management of traditional sport settings (e.g., marinas, race tracks, and ski resorts), the concept has since expanded to include settings for fitness activities as well. Consequently, university and college major programs designed to prepare students for careers in both sport and fitness management are frequently housed within the same academic unit. Because management of both sport and fitness activities involves an understanding and application of similar management concepts, this arrangement ensures that students receive consistent, accurate information and experiences. This text, therefore, uses the term *sport/fitness management* in acknowledgment of the trend to include fitness management in the total concept of sport management.

Sport Versus Sports

Why are many professional preparation programs titled *sport* management whereas others are called *sports* management? *Sports* implies a collection of separate activities such as golf, soccer, hockey, volleyball, softball, and gymnastics—items in a series that can be counted. *Sport*, however, is a collective noun that includes all activities that meet the criteria, not just a few that may be placed on a list. *Sports* may be considered singular in nature, whereas *sport* is a more all-encompassing concept. The North American Society for Sport Management (NASSM), a professional association composed of university academicians and scholars, has chosen the collective noun "sport" and encourages its use.

Management Versus Administration

Some confusion exists regarding the titles *manager* and *administrator*. Frequently the terms are used interchangeably, and the differences between them are not always clear. Mullin (1980), drawing from the work of Duncan, attempted to provide this distinction through the information in Table 1.1.

A careful analysis of this table reveals that sport organizations may be classified into either the public or the private sector. In most situations, however, the duties of practitioners involved with sport and fitness fall under the title *manager* rather than *administrator*. With the exception of high school athletic directors and some not-for-profit organizations that rely heavily on donations for support (e.g., YMCA, YWCA, and JCC), sport and fitness organizations are typically required to generate income, cater to the consumer, market extensively, and produce a return on the investment. For these reasons, the faculty of many of the programs that prepare individuals for positions in sport or fitness settings have chosen to designate the area as *sport* (or *fitness*) *management* rather than *sport administration*. However, this distinction is not universally accepted, and there are excellent academic programs titled *sport administration*, particularly at the graduate level. So investigate all curricula carefully, and do not rely on the titles of programs to make decisions regarding your academic career.

Management Defined

Management may be defined in a variety of ways. Chelladurai (1986) suggested a reason-

Table 1.1   Comparison of Administrators and Managers

	Administrator	Manager
Location	Usually public sector	Usually private sector
Financial base	Revenue generated through • tax dollars • student fees • grants	Revenue generated through • sale of product • sale of a service
Resource allocation	Expenditures monitored against budgeted figures	Assets generated as well as expended; revenues, assets, and owner equity important
Relationship with consumer	Indirect; consumer satisfaction important but not top priority	Direct; to ignore a consumer is to reduce revenue
Marketing	Not a significant function	Paramount to success
Perspective	Internal to organization	Internal to organization and external to consumer needs and societal trends
Objectives	Maintenance of status quo • avoidance of controversy • minimization of conflict	Growth • market penetration • return on investment

Note. Concepts from "Sport Management: The Nature and Utility of the Concept" by B.J. Mullin, 1980, *Arena Review,* (**4**), 3, 3-4. Adapted by permission.

able alternative to selecting a single definition from the many concepts of management that exist in current literature. His approach is to explore the functions that managers perform and, hence, arrive at a clearer picture of what is really involved in the management process. From Chelladurai's perspective, the four managerial functions that emerge as most significant to sport/fitness managers are planning, organizing, leading, and evaluating.

Planning

Filley, House, and Kerr (cited in Chelladurai, 1986) defined *planning* as "the specification of means necessary to achieve a prescribed end *before action toward that end takes place*" (p. 45). Planning involves setting goals and objectives

and then determining how those goals and objectives will be reached. According to Robbins (cited in Chelladurai, 1986), most objectives "will relate to one or more of the following: profitability, growth, market share, productivity/ efficiency, leadership, client satisfaction, and social awareness" (p. 45).

Examples of objectives that may be established for sport- and fitness-related enterprises include (a) determining the profit margin desired for a professional team, (b) deciding on the optimum number of patrons necessary to keep a health club operational, (c) establishing goals for the percentage of athletes who should graduate from a university, or (d) developing a marketing plan that includes socially responsible objectives such as purchasing signage promoting only safe and healthful products. Goals and objectives reflect the philosophy of the organization and must be developed thoughtfully and carefully to ensure compatibility with the desired image.

Attempting to manage a sport or fitness enterprise without sufficient attention to the planning phase is tantamount to sailing into uncharted waters. The time that is spent in planning will be rewarded by a smoother operation and a greater probability of success. However, planning is not enough. Action is imperative, and implementation of the plan is critical.

Organizing

Organizing is concerned with "breaking down the total work specified in the planning process into specific jobs, and then establishing a formal relationship among these jobs, and among the individuals assigned to carry them out. While the planning process specifies what should be done and how, the organizing process elaborates on who should do it" (Chelladurai, 1986, p. 6).

Organization can be explained by examining the structure of any team sport in which each participant has a role. Coaches are the managers, and each player has a responsibility unique to a particular position. In football, tackles protect the quarterback, and wide receivers catch passes; in softball, the pitcher delivers the ball to the batter, and the outfielders catch balls and throw them to the infield; in soccer, players cover a specific area of the field. Players and coaches understand and respect the concept of playing a position as well as the need to adjust and cover another person's position when necessary. The same concept holds true for organizations: The managers are in charge, and each of the team members has specific responsibilities and reports to particular persons in the hierarchy. For example, in intercollegiate athletics, the business manager and the marketing manager may report to the associate athletic director, whereas the athletic director may report directly to the vice-president or president. Organizational charts are helpful in interpreting re-lationships among tasks, individuals, and vertical and lateral communications.

Leading

If one managerial function could be singled out as most critical to the success of the organization, it is *leadership*. According to Barrow (cited in Chelladurai, 1986) leading is the "interpersonal process of influencing members toward organizational goals" (p. 7). Leadership is central to the implementation of plans. A good leader creates a climate in which members of the organization are motivated to work at optimum levels of efficiency and productivity. Effective leaders understand human nature and possess good interpersonal skills. A productive staff is usually composed of employees who feel appreciated, respected, and rewarded; consequently, they work toward the goals of the organization. Knowledge of psychological and sociological principles will help sport and fitness managers understand human nature in business situations.

In sport/fitness enterprises, managers can demonstrate leadership by setting good examples in their personal health habits, offering financial incentives to employees who enlist a given number of new members, asking for and listening to employees' ideas, and managing in an open, positive style. Creating a climate in which members are encouraged to contribute to the organization is a first step toward the development of good leadership qualities.

Evaluating

Evaluation involves "assessing the degree to which the organization is a whole, and various units and individuals have accomplished what they set out to do" (Chelladurai, 1986, p. 7). In evaluation, managers compare results with previously established objectives. This function is critical because the information gained through the evaluation process reveals the effectiveness of the planning, organizing, and leading processes. These data may then be used to maintain, adjust, or discontinue certain procedures, programs, and performances.

In sport/fitness enterprises, evaluation techniques may include (a) the distribution of a survey instrument to measure the level of patron satisfaction at a golf club, (b) a comparison of actual attendance figures with those projected at the beginning of basketball season, (c) a report on the number of student athletes who maintained academic eligibility, or (d) a comparison of the number of new patrons at a water park each year.

WHERE ARE YOU GOING IN SPORT AND FITNESS MANAGEMENT?

As a future sport/fitness manager, you are justifiably concerned about your professional goals and how you are going to achieve them. The first

Thoroughly investigate your options before making decisions about your sport and fitness management career.

step in establishing a career in sport management is to select a college or university that offers a sound curriculum. If you are already enrolled in a sport/fitness management program or if you are contemplating enrolling in one, the following discussion should help you evaluate your current program or select a program that is compatible with your needs.

Professional Preparation

Most sport/fitness management curricula are organized into the following components: general education courses, major courses, and field experiences (van der Smissen, 1984). Although the terminology may vary among institutions, these three components represent the critical elements in all sport/fitness management professional preparation programs.

General Education

You will be required to take a significant number of general education courses as you work toward your undergraduate degree. This aspect of your education is vital because graduates of universities should demonstrate understandings and capabilities different from those developed through technical training.

Among these differences, you should demonstrate a maturity and capability that comes from being aware of an assortment of aspects of your culture and other cultures. You should understand and appreciate art, music, language, writing, drama, history, political science, dance, behavioral and physical sciences, human movement, and other cultural domains. You should also be able to utilize *critical thinking skills* in concert with a wide range of knowledges in order to generate original ideas and creative solutions to a broad spectrum of societal and global concerns. As sport management majors, you are not being *trained* for careers in sport management; you are being *educated* for lives in which you hope to enjoy professional positions in sport. If your vocational goal does not become a reality, you should, nevertheless, be knowledgeable, intellectual, imaginative citizens who will contribute to society in a variety of ways.

Major Curriculum

The sport/fitness management major curriculum provides career information and opportunities for skill development that will prepare you to make valuable contributions within sport/fitness management settings. The curriculum is career specific by design and is geared toward preparation for the world of work. According to Quain (1984), "a truly essential requirement of any sport management program must be to enhance or help develop the 'heart for sport' along with the tools necessary to succeed in the business world" (p. 72). Mullin adds that "an understanding of the unique aspects of sport is essential—merely 'loving sport' or having been a sport participant are not enough" (Mullin, personal communication, February 28, 1989). The sport/fitness major curriculum is the source of the information that will allow you to develop that intellectual understanding.

Although major curricula in sport/fitness management vary greatly, basic courses and experiences should be included in all of them. The National Association for Sport and Physical Education (NASPE) Task Force on Sport Management Curricula (Brassie, 1989) suggests that the following courses are critical to an undergraduate sport management program: management, marketing, economics, accounting, finance, computer science, sport foundations (e.g., sport sociology, sport history, women in sport), sport law, sport economics, sport marketing/promotion, sport administration, and field experiences. NASPE (1986) also suggests that fitness management curricula include a foundational core (e.g., anatomy and physiology), instruction in exercise prescription for normal and special populations, course work in wellness and health promotion, theory and practice in teaching methodology, training in ad-

ministrative tasks, information about human relations, experiences in professional development, and practical experience. In addition, Mullin suggests that

> individuals who aspire to careers in the fitness industry must be aware that management and marketing skills are also important in that area. Many health and fitness enterprises are quite small, and entry-level employees invariably are assigned management and marketing responsibilities. Knowing only the scientific base to the exclusion of the business aspect is insufficient for success in the fitness industry. (Mullin, personal communication, February 28, 1989)

Field Experiences

Field experiences consist of two components: part-time work experiences, usually called *practica*, and full-time work experiences, usually called *internships* (Brassie, 1989). When you engage in these experiences, you go into the workplace and "practice" the types of jobs you think you might like to pursue after graduation. A site supervisor and a campus supervisor usually oversee these experiences. Close supervision and appropriate performance evaluation procedures are critical to the success of the practicum or internship.

With respect to the value of field experience in the professional preparation curriculum, Sidwell (1984) states,

> These experiences benefit students by allowing them to explore career options, observe professionals at work, develop a better understanding of how selected businesses and agencies operate, and gain valuable supervised work experience. Field experiences also afford students opportunities to have their work evaluated on a regular basis, to evaluate themselves as pre-professionals, and to become even more committed to their chosen field of study. (p. 79)

Washburn (1984) suggests that three constituencies benefit from sport/fitness management field experiences. The intern benefits by learning "the necessity of taking orders or receiving directions, the undertaking of responsibility, and the sense of fulfillment in having been responsible and productive" (p. 55). The cooperating organization gains from the intern's time and energy, enjoys the opportunity to observe a potential employee in a meaningful situation, and benefits from the intern's contributions in the areas of finance and public relations. The university benefits through having doors opened for future interns, through enhanced prestige and reputation in the eyes of the organization, and (if the intern is pleased with the experience) through future alumni support in either a recruiting or monetary sense.

Fieldwork also might provide a springboard into a permanent position at the sponsoring agency or institution. Although this phenomenon has occurred and is a compliment to both the intern and to the university, it is not a legitimate reason for participating in a practicum or internship. Don't assume that an internship will lead to permanent employment.

Graduate School

When you graduate from college, you will know only portions of what you need to know professionally; you have many years left to pursue continued professional development and advanced degrees. A primary focus of undergraduate programs is to develop an appreciation of the need to continue to learn and an understanding of the processes whereby this learning may occur. The concept of continued education is the cornerstone upon which future professional development is built.

After receiving the baccalaureate degree, you may choose to pursue the master's degree in an area of particular interest. This experience may directly follow undergraduate school, or you may wish to work for several years before returning to school. If you consider graduate school, seek advice from your adviser concerning the most judicious course of action.

Many sport-related careers require the master's degree as a prerequisite to obtaining employment. Parks and Quain (1984) found that a high percentage of practitioners in physical fitness, intramural/recreational sport directing, and sport organization management held a master's degree. Reasons for this phenomenon may be that the science base in fitness is complex and requires additional study and that many positions in intramural/recreational sport directing and sport organization management exist in a school or university setting where a master's degree is imperative.

Although undergraduate education is "preparation for life," graduate level education allows you to concentrate on expanding your knowledge in specific areas of interest. Programs offered by graduate schools are quite diverse, and institutions offer curricula that reflect their unique missions and philosophies. When you contemplate graduate school, investigate several graduate schools so that you will be able to take full advantage of the variety of curricula available. Again, sound advice from professors and mentors is recommended.

At this stage of your academic career, the thought of earning a master's degree may seem like only a dim possibility. The undergraduate years will go by quickly, however, and early planning for advanced degrees is critical. Even at these beginning stages, you can give some thought to a doctoral degree. If you aspire to become a university athletic director or a professor in sport/fitness management or other discipline, you should begin now to plan for your doctorate, which is a prerequisite for obtaining a position in many colleges and universities.

The pursuit of lifelong learning and an understanding of the value of continuous professional development are distinguishing characteristics of truly committed sport management practitioners, educators, and students. Knowledge is power, and the pursuit of knowledge is a source of great pleasure and satisfaction.

LEARNING ACTIVITIES

1. Define sport management and explain why are you majoring in this field.

2. Interview current practitioners about the four functions of management and how each applies in sport or fitness settings.

3. If your university has access to *ExSport 1*, microcomputer software designed to help you make career choices in sport management, run the program and compare your printout with those of your classmates.

4. Interview individuals who managed sport or fitness activities 15 to 20 years ago. Document the differences between then and now.

5. Interview a practitioner in a career in which you are interested. Share the results of the interview with your classmates.

6. Outline your career goals and your plan for achieving them.

7. Read articles on sport/fitness management and report the content of the articles to your classmates.

REFERENCES

Brassie, P.S. (1987). Guidelines for programs preparing undergraduate and graduate students for careers in sport management. *Journal of Sport Management, 3*(2), 158-164.

Chelladurai, P. (1986). *Sport management: Macro-perspectives*. London, ON: Sports Dynamics.

Loy, J.W. (1968). The nature of sport: A definitional effort. *Quest, 10*, 1-15.

Mason, J.G., Higgins, C.R., & Wilkinson, O.J. (1981). Sports administration education 15 years later. *Athletic Purchasing and Facilities, 5*(1), 44-45.

Meltzer, M.F. (1967). *The information center: Management's hidden asset*. New York: American Management Association.

Mullin, B.J. (1980). Sport management: The nature and utility of the concept. *Arena Review, 4*(3), 1-11.

National Association for Sport and Physical Education. (1986). *Standards for programs preparing undergraduate students for careers in fitness*. (Available from the National Association for Sport and Physical Education, 1900 Association Drive, Reston, VA 22091)

Parks, J.B., & Quain, R.J. (1984). *Survey of sport management practitioners*. Unpublished raw data, Bowling Green State University, School of Health, Physical Education and Recreation, Bowling Green, OH.

Parks, J.B., Quain, R.J., Chopra, P.S., & Alguindigue, I.E. (1987, May). *ExSport 1: Computerized sport management career interest system*. Paper presented at the meeting of the North American Society for Sport Management, University of Windsor, Canada.

Quain, R.J. (1984). The REM statement. In B.K. Zanger & J.B. Parks (Eds.), *Sport management curricula: The business and education nexus* (pp. 71-75). Bowling Green, OH: Bowling Green State University, School of Health, Physical Education and Recreation.

Sidwell, M.J. (1984). The sport management field experience profile at Bowling Green State University. In B.K. Zanger & J.B. Parks (Eds.), *Sport management curricula: The business and education nexus* (pp. 79-83). Bowling Green, OH: Bowling Green State University, School of Health, Physical Education and Recreation.

Snyder, E.E., & Spreitzer, E.A. (1989). *Social aspects of sport*. Englewood Cliffs, NJ: Prentice-Hall.

van der Smissen, B. (1984). A process for success: Sport management curricula—an idea whose time has come! In B.K. Zanger & J.B. Parks (Eds.), *Sport management curricula: The business and education nexus* (pp. 5-18). Bowling Green, OH: Bowling Green State University, School of Health, Physical Education and Recreation.

VanderZwaag, H.J. (1988). *Policy development in sport management*. Indianapolis, IN: Benchmark Press.

Washburn, J.R. (1984). What does academe need from business/agencies? Supervision: A participatory activity. In B.K. Zanger & J.B. Parks (Eds.), *Sport management curricula: The business and education nexus* (pp. 53-57). Bowling Green, OH: Bowling Green State University, School of Health, Physical Education and Recreation.

SUGGESTED READINGS

Hager, S. (1984). Curricular questions confronting sport management: A summary. In B.K. Zanger & J.B. Parks (Eds.), *Sport management curricula: The business and education nexus*. Bowling Green State University, School of Health, Physical Education and Recreation.

Kjeldsen, E. (1980). Sport management: An emerging profession. *Arena Review*, **4**(3), i-ii.

Koontz, J.L. (1984). Sport management—A profession. In B.K. Zanger & J.B. Parks (Eds.), *Sport management curricula: The business and education nexus*. Bowling Green State University: School of Health, Physical Education and Recreation.

Lewis, G. (1980). The sports enterprise. *Arena Review*, **4**(3), 12-17.

Lewis, G., & Appenzeller, H. (1985). *Successful sport management*. Charlottesville, VA: Michie.

Parkhouse, B.L. (1978, May). Professional preparation in athletic administration and sport management. Graduate programs in the United States. *Journal of Physical Education and Recreation*, **49**(5), 22-27.

Parkhouse, B.L. (1987, July). Sport management curricula: Current status and design implications for future development. *Journal of Sport Management*, **1**(2), 93-128.

Parkhouse, B.L. (1984, September). Shaping up to climb a new corporate ladder . . . sport management. *Journal of Physical Education, Recreation, and Dance*, **55**(6), 12-14.

Parkhouse, B.L., & Ulrich, D.O. (1979). Sport management as a potential cross-discipline: A paradigm for theoretical development, scientific inquiry, and professional application. *Quest*, **31**(2), 264-276.

Parks, J.B., & Quain, R.J. (1986, April). Sport management survey: Curriculum perspectives. *Journal of Physical Education, Recreation and Dance*, **57**(4), 22-26.

Quain, R.J., & Parks, J.B. (1986, April). Sport management survey: Employment perspectives. *Journal of Physical Education, Recreation and Dance*, **57**(4), 18-21.

Sandomir, R. (1987, November). GNSP: The gross national sports product. *Sports, Inc.*, pp. 14-16, 18.

Ulrich, D.O., & Parkhouse, B.L. (1982). An alumni oriented approach to sport management curriculum design using performance ratings and a regression model. *Research*

Quarterly for Exercise and Sport, **53**(1), 64-72.

VanderZwaag, H.J. (1980). Preparation of the sport manager of the future. *Arena Review*, **4**(3), 22-27.

PART I

SPORT AND FITNESS MANAGEMENT CAREERS

CHAPTER 2

Intercollegiate Athletics and Professional Sport

James W. Lessig
Mid-American Conference

William L. Alsop
West Virginia University

In the United States, sport seems to generate more interest and enthusiasm than just about any other area of endeavor, and this interest is particularly evident at the intercollegiate and professional levels. The tremendous enthusiasm surrounding intercollegiate athletics and professional sport prompts many people to pursue careers in these areas.

Career opportunities in intercollegiate athletics and professional sport are numerous, but the number of applicants for positions is equally great, and the job market is extremely competitive. Your chances for entering either field will be greatly enhanced if you understand similarities and differences between the two fields, the settings in which the jobs exist, the titles of the positions, and the duties or tasks involved in each. In addition, an understanding of the personal sacrifices and emotional challenges that frequently accompany positions in athletics and professional sport is critical to your decision regarding entering these dynamic fields.

INTERCOLLEGIATE ATHLETIC SETTINGS

Positions associated with intercollegiate athletics may be found primarily in three settings: on university or college campuses and, to a lesser extent, in national governing bodies and in conference offices. The following discussion provides overviews of each of these settings.

University or College Campus

A wide variety of positions and job titles exists within a university or college athletic program. Although the job titles may remain somewhat constant from one school to the next, the responsibilities of the positions vary greatly. The size and scope of each athletic program determines in large measure the extent of these differences in responsibilities. For example, individuals who work in large athletic programs in all likelihood have very defined duties and are responsible for specific areas. These people devote almost all of their concentration and time to a single aspect of the athletic program. It is not unusual to find major athletic programs with well over 200 employees, each of whom is assigned to a rather narrow area of responsibility (see Figure 2.1).

On the other hand, individuals who work at smaller schools may find that although they have specific titles, they are probably expected to assume a variety of duties, because the number of staff members at these institutions is considerably smaller. In some of the smaller institutions, athletic department staff also teach in an academic area relating to athletics, such as sport management, coaching, health, physical education, or recreation (see Figure 2.2).

In order to understand the various positions available in intercollegiate athletics, we must consider some of the major differences among the levels of competition in intercollegiate athletics. In most instances, these levels of competition are determined by the national governing body with which each school is affiliated. These governing bodies are the National Collegiate Athletic Association (NCAA), the National Association for Intercollegiate Athletics (NAIA), and the National Junior College Athletic Association (NJCAA).

National Collegiate Athletic Association

The NCAA is the governing body for most university and college athletic programs in the United States. This organization uses a three-division structure to differentiate among the levels of the over 900 schools within the NCAA. Figure 2.3 illustrates the NCAA's executive structure.

Division I. Members of Division I strive for regional and national excellence and prominence in their athletic programs. Accordingly, recruitment of student athletes and emphasis on and support for the athletic programs are regional and national in scope. Members of Division I

College athletic programs provide a variety of sport management jobs.

Division I schools offer full athletic scholarships to qualified student athletes.

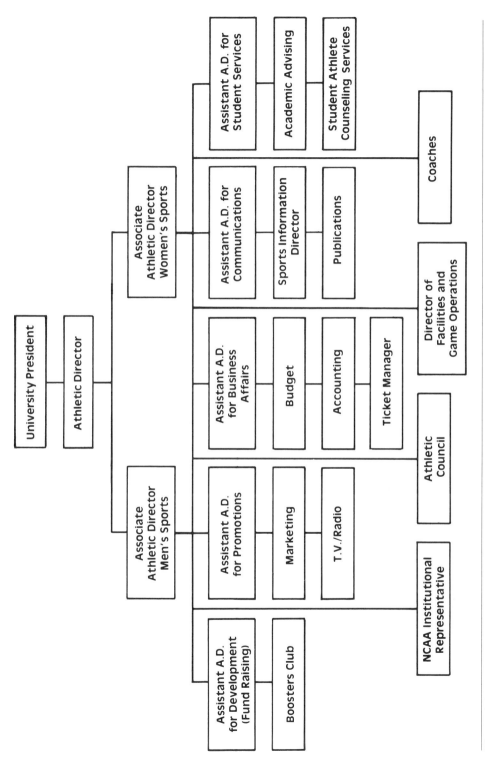

Figure 2.1   Organizational chart: NCAA Division I athletic department.

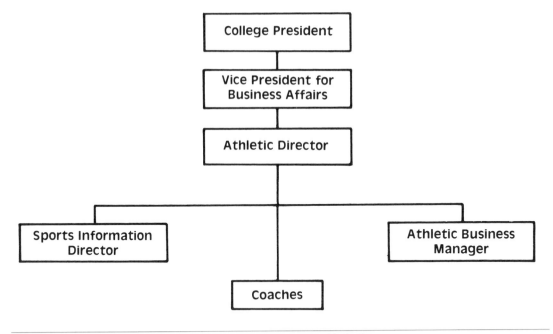

Figure 2.2   Organizational chart: NCAA Division II or NAIA athletic department.

also recognize the dual objectives in the athletic programs. Division I programs strive to serve the university (including the student body, faculty, staff, and graduates) as well as the general public (including the community, area, state, and nation).

Division I members believe in offering the highest feasible levels of intercollegiate competition in football and men's basketball, the traditional spectator sports on most American college campuses. These sports also generate the greatest amount of revenue and, on some campuses, enable the other teams to exist. Division I schools also offer full athletic grants-in-aid to student athletes who are academically qualified and who demonstrate the ability to perform at high levels in their sports.

Division II.   Division II schools subscribe to many of the philosophies supported by Division I. The major difference is that Division II seeks recognition on the regional rather than

national level. Schedules of Division II teams reflect the philosophy that Division II institutions should compete against other Division II institutions. Although Division II schools do grant financial aid for the athletic talents of selected student athletes, these schools do so on a much more modest basis than is permitted in Division I.

Division III.   Division III differs considerably from Divisions I and II. Division III schools primarily emphasize athletes and their participation. As a rule, Division III schools are not interested in generating income through gate receipts, fund raising, or television. These schools are more concerned with providing maximum participation opportunities for their students and do not view their athletic programs as a form of entertainment.

A basic Division III philosophy is that student athletes should be treated as all other students are treated. This philosophy covers admission

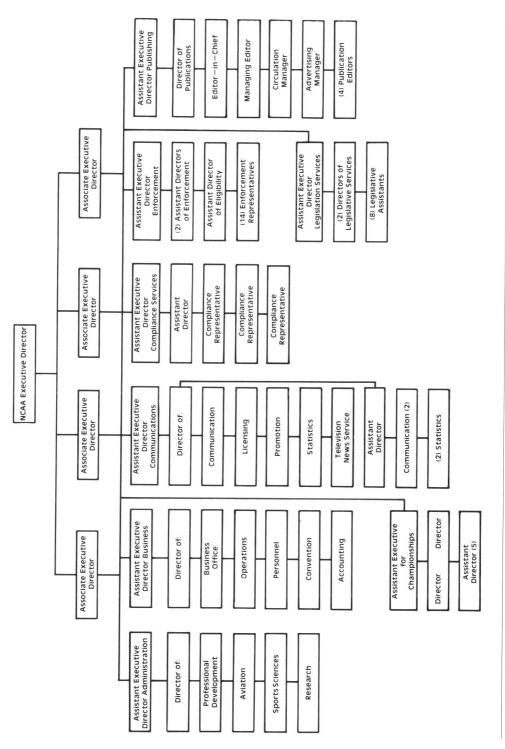

Figure 2.3 Organizational chart: NCAA.

policies, academic advisement, and scholarship opportunities. Financial aid in Division III is based entirely on academic performance and financial need criteria, never on the student's athletic ability.

National Association of Intercollegiate Athletics and National Junior College Athletic Association

Although the majority of schools belong to the NCAA, a sizable number of institutions align themselves with the NAIA or the NJCAA. See Figures 2.4 and 2.5 for the structures of these organizations.

For the most part, NAIA schools follow philosophies similar to the Division II philosophy. Philosophies at the junior/community college level vary so much from one institution to another that it is impossible to state a general philosophy for these schools. Both NAIA and NJCAA institutions represent settings in which you may wish to pursue a career associated with intercollegiate athletics.

Many of the positions identified in the NCAA, NAIA, NJCAA, and athletic conference organizational charts are institutional representatives. Many positions (e.g., NCAA representatives, executive board members, and eligibility officers) are elected or appointed positions from college and university administrators and faculty.

Position Descriptions

Job opportunities exist in all levels of intercollegiate athletics. Several of the positions outlined in this chapter are found at all three NCAA levels as well as at NAIA and NJCAA institutions. Others will probably be found only at the NCAA Division I level. The sheer number of different position titles and descriptions precludes the possibility of discussing each of them in detail.

Athletic Director

All athletic departments, regardless of the level of competition, have an athletic director or someone with a similar title who is in charge of the overall athletic program. In most cases, this is a full-time job, although at the Division III level this person could also take on other responsibilities at the college or university.

Until fairly recently, most athletic directors were retired coaches who became athletic directors at the institutions where they had coached. This is no longer the case. Today, athletic directors come from a variety of backgrounds and experiences and are very much like executives or people in managerial positions with any major corporation. As Williams and Miller (1983) indicate, administering an athletic program may not be essentially different from running a business. At the Division I level, athletic directors administer multifaceted programs that include responsibilities in finance, fund raising, scheduling, contract negotiations, hiring and firing of staff members, coordination of the athletic program with other departments on campus, and public relations. Most athletic directors at the Division I level deal with annual budgets that range from $3 million to over $15 million per year.

The majority of universities in all divisions have a conference affiliation. Figure 2.6 shows a conference organizational flow chart. Athletic directors have the added responsibilities of working with the conference office and the other institutions within the conference to ensure that their programs and the entire conference are promoted in a positive way. Athletic directors must also thoroughly understand the rules and regulations of the national and conference-level governing bodies with which they are affiliated. Frequently, the athletic director will have a staff member whose major responsibility is rules interpretation.

Although the responsibilities of athletic directors may vary depending upon the sizes of

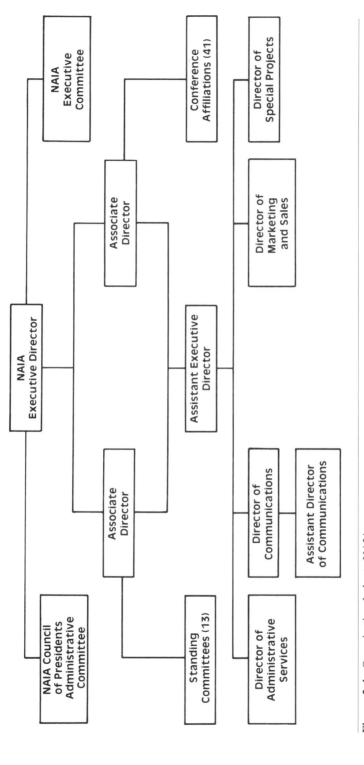

Figure 2.4   Organizational chart: NAIA.

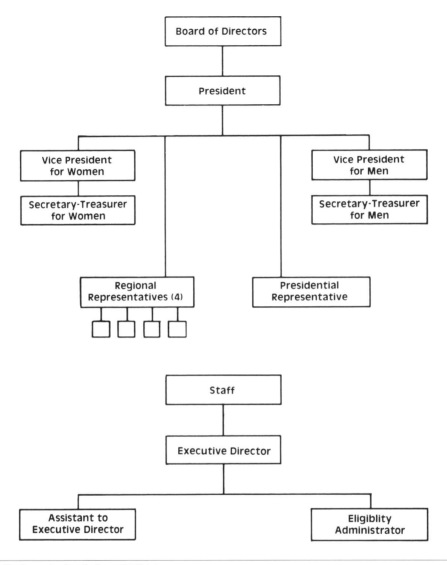

Figure 2.5 Organizational chart: NJCAA.

institutions, the qualities that athletic directors must possess are fairly constant. First and foremost, they must be managers who can relate to a variety of publics, including athletic staff, the faculty and staff of the university, the alumni of the university, the community and the fans, and all other individuals who support the athletic program. Athletic directors who are able

to hire qualified individuals with potential for success and who can manage those individuals will probably enjoy success.

Athletic directors at major institutions often answer directly to the president of that institution or, if not, are responsible to the president through a vice-president. Before accepting any job as an athletic director, you should have a

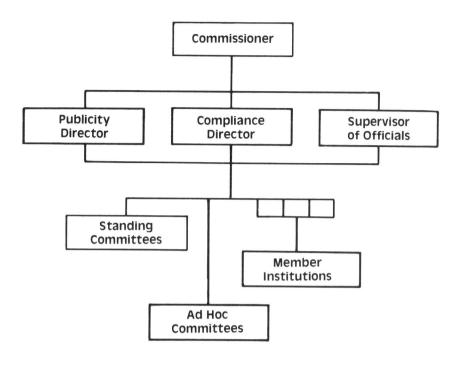

Figure 2.6   Organizational chart: A Division I athletic conference.

clear understanding of the chain of command and a realistic view of your access to the president of the university (see Figures 2.1 and 2.2).

Although athletic directors come from a variety of backgrounds and experiences, many athletic directors at major universities are hired after they have had extensive experience in athletic fund raising or financial management. This is because most major universities must generate income through gate receipts, private donations, and television broadcasts. This income is necessary to cover the expenses of the athletic program, not only for the revenue-producing sports such as football and men's basketball but also for the nonrevenue sports. To ensure this income, universities seek athletic directors who have educational backgrounds and proven records in private fund raising or who have sound business backgrounds (Cuneen, 1988).

Additionally, more and more universities seek athletic directors who have at least master's degrees and preferably doctorates. Many university administrators believe that graduate degrees are essential in enabling the athletic director to relate to faculty and other academic departments on campus. In some situations, athletic directors need some experience in the coaching arena so they can understand and deal with the problems faced by coaches. In their study of intercollegiate athletic administration, Williams and Miller (1983) presented, in rank order of importance, 15 responsibilities typically associated with athletic administration: budget management, eligibility review, policy development, representation of department to governing organization, attendance at athletic contests, personnel recruitment and management, public relations, events/facilities scheduling, record keeping, report writing, financial aid management, game/contest management, equipment ordering, fund raising/promotion, and travel arrangements.

Associate/Assistant Athletic Director

Most athletic departments have at least one associate or assistant athletic director. These individuals are usually staff members who are designated as associate or assistant athletic directors for fund raising, promotions, or facility management and who have major responsibilities in those specific areas.

It is also quite common to have an associate athletic director for women's athletics. This individual, sometimes known as the primary woman administrator (PWA), coordinates the women's athletic program and integrates it with the men's athletic program. Some universities have separate athletic directors for men's and women's athletics, with each having equal responsibility and both reporting to the president or to the same vice-president. Still other universities have an athletic director for revenue-generating sports and an associate athletic director for all other sports, both men's and women's.

In major athletic programs, the athletic directors are assisted by a staff of individuals who are responsible for specific areas within the program. The ability to select competent people for these positions is critical to the success of the athletic director and the athletic program. Many graduates of sport management programs find initial employment at this assistant level.

Director of Athletic Fund Raising

The position of director of athletic fund raising, particularly at the Division I level, has become second in importance only to the athletic director. Most major universities need to solicit private funds to meet their athletic budgets. Although income from gate receipts and television may be substantial, money raised from private donors allows athletic programs to meet financial obligations. To do this, programs must set up a wide network of fund raising. This network is composed of alumni, fans, and other interested persons and is usually administered through some type of an athletic booster organization that carries the nickname of the institution (e.g., the Sun Devil Club or the Tiger Boosters).

People interested in entering the fund raising field should have the ability and the desire to interact with people and must be willing to ask for financial contributions. Some people find this easy; others find this extremely difficult. This position normally involves a great deal of travel and includes speaking before large booster organizations and convincing the members to support the athletic program. A background in public relations, communications, and fund raising is extremely helpful to an individual seeking such a position. The following responsibilities are usually associated with the position of director of athletic fund raising.

- Plan, coordinate, and service all athletic fund-raising events.
- Identify and solicit potential contributors.
- Continuously cultivate and recognize existing donors.
- Solicit and close on major gifts of personal and real property through wills, trusts, insurance, and other means of planned giving.
- Establish and promote a viable plan for the solicitation of endowment funds for the support of the athletic department programs.
- Prepare fund-raising brochures and literature for distribution to alumni and contributors.
- Maintain donor records and individual and club memberships.
- Prepare the fund-raising budget.
- Keep abreast of current pending tax laws relative to charitable and deferred (planned) giving.
- Assign season priority seating for football and basketball.

Promotions Director

The promotions director's major responsibility is to ensure that capacity crowds attend the revenue-producing sporting events and to promote athletic events in a way that will gain maximum public exposure. The promotions director must be imaginative and able to invent unique programs and ideas that will encourage people to attend athletic events. These ideas must go beyond the normal athletic contest. The promotions director must constantly create special giveaways and promotions for children, youth, high school students, adults, and special interest groups.

Depending on the size of the staff, the promotions director may also serve as a liaison with local television and radio stations, particularly to help promote the athletic program. Responsibilities usually associated with the position of director of promotions are as follows.

- Promote advertising and sales in all media markets (television, radio, and the printed press).
- Supervise all public relations efforts, and oversee all media policies.
- Coordinate all special media projects (e.g., television packages and national radio network broadcasts).
- Develop revenue sources related to television packages.
- Coordinate marketing of ticket sales.
- Prepare promotional messages for all media.

Director of Athletic Facilities

The individual in this position must ensure that the athletic facilities are maintained in first-class condition. Facilities under his or her auspices include practice areas, stadia, basketball arenas, soccer fields, baseball diamonds, golf courses, locker rooms, weight training facilities, and all other physical facilities used by the athletic program.

The director of athletic facilities is frequently responsible for game staging, also known as contest management. In this capacity, he or she looks after such things as security at games; hiring, training, and supervision of ushers; marking and lining of fields and courts; arrangements for ticket sellers and ticket takers; management of the time schedule for the game, including such things as the National Anthem, bands, and half-time shows; and attendance to the needs of game officials. Anything that relates to the successful staging of a home athletic contest normally falls under this person's jurisdiction.

Obviously, the facility director must have a thorough understanding of the operations of the athletic department. Perhaps more than anyone else on the staff, this person must be able to work with the coaches and other athletic administrators, because the job responsibilities of the facilities manager touch on all aspects of the department and are of vital importance to each coach, player, and administrator. Success in this position depends upon patience, ability to listen, and willingness to work long and demanding hours.

Director of Academic Affairs

During recent years, the public has given a great deal of attention to the level of academic achievement of collegiate student athletes. Due to legislation such as NCAA Proposals 48 and 42, many collegiate athletic departments have added staff members—variously titled director of academic affairs, athletic adviser, or eligibility counselor—who are responsible for academic concerns of the student athlete.

Examples of responsibilities of the director of academic affairs are as follows.

- Understand all conference and national governing body eligibility regulations.
- Submit to the appropriate offices the eligibility forms for all student athletes.
- Monitor and report grades and progress reports.
- Encourage student athletes to work with their academic department advisers and

other counseling and support staff available on campus.

- Keep records of the student athletes' academic progress.
- Serve as a liaison with the other offices on campus that are related to academic performance of student athletes (e.g., admissions, registrar, and bursar).

In most instances, the director of academic affairs for student athletes is not responsible for helping students determine their class schedules. That function is within the purview of the academic department in which the student athlete is enrolled, and athletic department personnel usually encourage student athletes to maintain close ties with those departments.

Most college athletic departments have an academic advisor to help players coordinate sports and study.

Athletic Department Staff

Most of the previously described personnel may have one or more assistants who support and help in that particular facet of the athletic operation. As previously indicated, most entry-level positions, particularly in the Division I institutions, are as assistants in one of the areas described.

Professional Organizations

National Association for Collegiate Directors of Athletics (NACDA)
National Association for Athletics, Marketing, and Development Directors (NAAMDD)
International Association of Auditorium Managers (IAAM)

Professional Publications

Athletic Administration
Auditorium News
NCAA News
The Chronicle of Higher Education

CAREERS IN PROFESSIONAL SPORT

A number of opportunities are available for employment in professional sport. However, the available positions are considerably fewer than those found in intercollegiate athletics, because collegiate teams outnumber professional teams in the United States. Consequently, the job market in professional sport is even more competitive than at the intercollegiate level.

In considering career possibilities in professional sport, you should not limit yourself, at least initially, to the "glamour" leagues such as the National Basketball Association (NBA), Major League Baseball (MLB), the National Football League (NFL), or the National Hockey

League (NHL). These organizations are at the very top of professional sport, and job opportunities are severely limited, particularly at the entry level. Anyone aspiring to work in professional athletics should thoroughly research the opportunities available in the many so-called minor professional leagues throughout the country. Professional baseball has an extensive minor league system, and each organization within it requires administrative personnel. Professional basketball and football also have minor leagues. Additional professional opportunities exist in the Major Indoor Soccer League; in professional automobile racing, tennis, and golf; and the new areas of volleyball and arena football. The experience gained in some of these organizations may be your stepping-stone to one of the major professional organizations. Limiting yourself to those three or four best-known leagues is doing yourself a great disservice.

An entry-level position with a professional sport organization will likely pay a very low salary, because professional sport organizations know they can get young, talented people who are eager for such a position, regardless of salary. Many people believe that working at the professional sport level is a very glamorous style of life, and there are many applicants for position vacancies. Consequently, salary schedules reflect the overabundance of applicant supply as compared with demand.

Positions in professional sport are somewhat difficult to define because the job titles and responsibilities tend to change from one sport to another and from one team to another. For example, most professional sports teams are privately owned, and therefore the president of the organization is frequently the owner, although this is not always the case. The president's responsibilities, then, will differ vastly from one organization to another depending upon whether she or he owns the team. This same principle of different titles and duties exists throughout the organizational charts of professional teams. Therefore, when investigating various positions, you should study the job descriptions to be cer-

tain you understand what duties the positions entail (see Figure 2.7).

General Manager

The general manager, a person employed in almost all professional sport organizations, is similar to the athletic director in intercollegiate athletics. Hatfield, Wrenn, and Bretting (1987) conducted a study that compared the job responsibilities of athletic directors and general managers. The authors developed a 50-item inventory related to job responsibilities, which were then grouped into six major areas: labor relations, marketing, financial management, administration, personnel evaluation, and public relations. The general managers rated labor relations and personnel evaluation as more important, whereas the athletic directors assigned higher ratings to all other categories. The study further indicated an important concern that appears to be important to general managers: the responsibility for and skill in assessing player talent.

Professional athletes often work their way into management positions after their playing days are over.

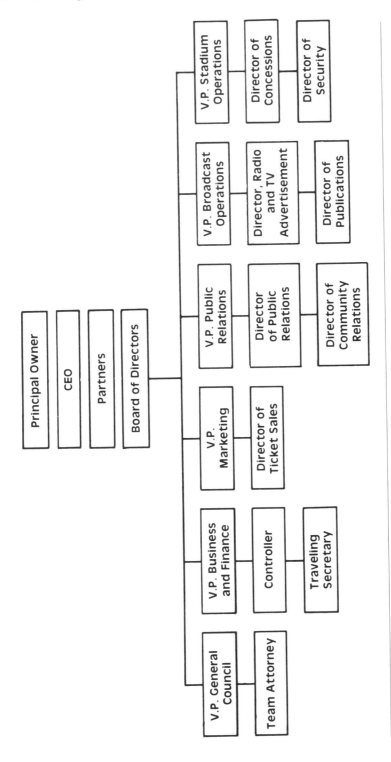

Figure 2.7   Organizational chart: Professional sports team.

The general manager must ensure that the team is run in a successful, efficient, and profitable manner. General managers of almost all professional sports teams have a long history in that sport. Many times they are former players or coaches who have worked their way up from being a general manager in the minor leagues to the same position with a major league organization. There is no fast way to become a general manager. You can attain this position only through years of experience and hard work associated with a variety of jobs within the organization.

Director of Promotions

As is the case with the general manager, the duties of the director of promotions in professional sport are quite similar to those of the corresponding position in intercollegiate athletics. This individual must generate home game crowds beyond what might be expected by the ability and record of the team. Directors of promotions constantly look for special ideas and ways to draw fans into the site of the competition. At the professional level, more than at the intercollegiate level, the director of promotions works with private industry in sponsoring special days. Companies often have giveaways at certain games where products like T-shirts, visors, coolers, sunglasses—almost anything you can imagine—are given to fans as they enter the arena or ball park. Such promotions as ''bat day'' in baseball and ''basketball day'' in professional basketball are popular and seem to draw large crowds.

Individuals such as ''San Diego Chicken'' have developed lucrative professions from working with promotions directors and being hired to entertain at their games. The Chicken has proven that he alone as an entertainment device can draw thousands of people into the ball park, regardless of how well the team may be playing at that particular time.

Because they work with many different attendance incentives and gimmicks, promotions directors need a thorough understanding of marketing techniques and market analysis strategies. It is not enough for promotions directors to know how to get the Chicken to come to the ball park; they must also be able to accurately assess the impact of his appearance on attendance. This may appear to be a simple process, but in reality it is very complicated and requires specific skills.

Public Relations Director

The director of public relations is charged with maintaining a positive relationship between the team and the local community. This person must also give special attention to the press, the fans, the city officials, and others who work with the team. The director of public relations does a great deal of public speaking and makes numerous appearances throughout the community and state. Public relations people must have consistently positive attitudes, regardless of the win/loss record of the team!

Ticket Director

The ticket director's responsibilities at the professional level are usually more extensive and more complicated than at the intercollegiate level. This is because the professional teams play so many more games and the demand for tickets is usually extremely high. Also, most professional teams maintain ticket outlets throughout a wide area of the region, and the ticket director must keep account of all tickets for all games and ensure accuracy of financial audits and ticket accountings for each game. Ticket managers in professional sport usually have a large staff because of the magnitude of the work. Someone with a sound business background who likes to work with numbers and has an eye for detail may be suited for a position as a ticket manager.

Traveling Secretary

Some professional teams employ a person known as the traveling secretary, who makes all of the travel arrangements for the team, including flights, ground transportation, hotel reservations, and meals. When working with a baseball team that plays 162 games a year and continually flies from one city to another, the traveling secretary has an extremely difficult and responsible position. In other professional sports in which travel is more restricted, another member of the staff, such as the director of public relations, may handle travel arrangements. Obviously, traveling secretaries have to accept the facts that they are going to be away from home a great deal of the time and will have to live out of a suitcase.

Sports Information Director

Most professional teams employ an individual quite similar to the sports information director in intercollegiate athletics. This person is responsible for maintaining the statistics of the team and working closely with the press in releasing team stories, facts, and highlights that provide interesting reading in the newspaper. This individual may also be responsible for developing the preseason press guide as well as the game programs and any special publications that the team might sell to the public. A person who works in this area of professional sport has probably had experience in sports information at the intercollegiate level.

PERSONAL ASPECTS OF CAREERS IN INTERCOLLEGIATE ATHLETICS AND PROFESSIONAL SPORT

If you seek a career in intercollegiate athletics or professional sport, be aware that this type of work is extremely exciting and unpredictable. You will encounter the emotional highs and lows that come with the territory. As many athletic administrators and sport managers like to say, "You must be able to ride the roller coaster if you are going to survive." No matter how hard you may work or how successful you may be, the bottom line is usually the success of the team and its ability to win a majority of its games. You might be on cloud nine one weekend because of a great athletic victory and be down in the dumps the next weekend because of a loss. So, before you decide to pursue a career in intercollegiate athletics or professional sport, you must be convinced that you possess the personal skills to cope with these situations; you must also be able to accept the fact that much of your success or failure will depend upon the performance of the athletes, a factor over which you have no control. The other side of the coin, however, is that although the roller coaster may provide you with some challenging ups and downs, the exhilaration of success is worth a great deal.

A WORD TO THE WISE

A multitude of exciting opportunities exist in intercollegiate athletics and professional sport. The competition for these jobs, particularly the good ones, is extremely fierce because so many people in this country want to be associated with sport. Read as much as you possibly can about the various positions in both intercollegiate athletics and professional sport. Also, visit with professionals currently working in these fields. Most people employed in intercollegiate and professional sport will be happy to discuss with you their impressions of the future in their particular career areas. They may also give you some valuable information concerning how you might pursue your path toward such a job.

You will have discouraging moments. You may find it difficult to get that first interview, and you may have to apply for several positions. Eventually, though, the first interview will come, and you must be totally prepared to present yourself and your qualifications in a professional manner.

Don't aim too high for your first job opportunity. No one is going to start out as an athletic director at a Division I institution or as a general manager of a professional team. You have to start in a position that allows you to learn the business from the ground up. Once you do that and apply yourself, you will be able to climb the administrative ladder and experience the thrills and disappointments that come with the territory.

LEARNING ACTIVITIES

1. Invite guest speakers from the fields of intercollegiate athletics and professional sport to lecture on career opportunities and current issues (e.g., NCAA Propositions 48 and 42 or free agency).

2. Analyze organizational charts obtained (or developed) from various professional teams, intercollegiate athletic departments, and conferences; determine similarities and differences in job titles, positions, job responsibilities, chains of command, and general administration of the organizations. For example, compare and contrast the organizational structure of two professional baseball teams. Or compare intercollegiate athletic departments in Division I, II, and III institutions.

3. Seek permission to attend athletic department meetings during the week prior to an athletic contest. Report on the responsibilities of each person (e.g., athletic director, director of facilities, and ticket manager) involved in the administration of the athletic event.

4. Attend, when possible, a local, regional, or national conference of athletic administrators, such as the National Association for Collegiate Directors of Athletics (NACDA), the National Association for Athletic, Marketing, and Development Directors (NAAMDD), the College Sports Information Directors of America (CoSIDA), or the International Association of Auditorium Managers (IAAM).

5. Meet with an athletic official who is in charge of a special event (e.g., hosting a conference tournament) and volunteer your services. Keep a log of your involvement in the event and conduct a discussion in class relating to your experiences.

REFERENCES

Cuneen, J. (1988). *A preparation model for NCAA Division I and II athletic administrators.* Unpublished doctoral dissertation, West Virginia University, Morgantown.

Hatfield, B.D., Wrenn, J., & Bretting, M. (1987). Comparison of job responsibilities of intercollegiate athletic directors and professional sport general managers. *Journal of Sport Management, 1*(2), 129-145.

Williams, J.M., & Miller, D.M. (1983). Intercollegiate athletic administration: Preparation patterns. *Research Quarterly for Exercise and Sport,* **54**, 398-406.

CHAPTER 3

Facility Management

David K. Stotlar
University of Northern Colorado

Sport facility management offers interesting, rewarding, and varied careers to sport management students. This chapter will concentrate on sports arenas and stadia and will not address facilities such as concert halls, convention centers, commercial recreation operations, amusement parks, or sports clubs.

THE CURRENT STATUS

Currently, the facility management profession is in a state of change. Building and maintenance costs have risen dramatically, and the owners and operators of these facilities are faced with limited avenues for raising funds. As a result of these changes, the facility that was once reserved solely for use as a sports arena is almost extinct. A few single-purpose facilities may remain, but they appear to be a dying breed. Primarily in response to increased financial pressures, owners now use sports arenas and stadia for events such as tractor pulls, rodeos, concerts, trade shows, flea markets, and professional wrestling exhibitions. Thus, negotiation skills are a necessity in facility management. Sport facility managers who have little previous experience with event promoters must take substantial care in these arrangements. Stories abound about novice facility managers who have

Sports facilities are often used for a variety of purposes.

been "taken to the cleaners" by slick promoters. Negotiations must produce terms and agreements that can provide financial benefits for both the facility and the promoter.

These programming changes, however, have not come about without controversy. The individual responsible for governing and managing the facility is the one who must interpret the philosophy and purpose of the facility. Implementation then follows through policy formation and administration. Sport facilities are constructed for a variety of purposes that must be articulated through the director. Some campus buildings are funded through student fees, and special attention is owed to the requirements of that group. In other situations, the athletic department may be a primary tenant and therefore has priority in use and scheduling. Some facilities are constructed and designed to serve the general community and may have constraints on commercial utilization. These factors often present difficult decisions for the facility manager.

PROFESSIONAL MANAGEMENT

Another trend over the last 10 years deserves the attention of a prospective facility manager: a move toward the utilization of professional management for sport facilities. Professional management means that a company specializing in sport facility management (as opposed to individuals employed by the city or college) is hired to independently manage and run the center. It has been estimated that 10 to 15 percent of the nation's sport facilities are currently operated by private companies. By the mid-1990s this figure is expected to approach 40 percent. Examples of the major companies in the facility management industry are Centre Management, Spectacor, Facility Management Group (FMG), and Ogden Allied.

In response to increased financial pressures and in an effort to attract major revenue events, many facilities in the secondary (small-town or reduced-seating) market have joined together to achieve more negotiating power. One such example is Tours West (originated by Jim Walczak, formerly of the Casper Events Center in Wyoming), which linked 22 small events centers, enabling them to obtain more high-caliber entertainment and sporting events.

PROFIT

Several aspects of hosting major sporting events are profitable. First, the money that spectators spend in a community can run into the millions of dollars. Second, the exposure that the facility and city (or state) get from television is extremely valuable. Finally, the clout gained by hosting a successful event can attract additional events. The economic gain that can be realized from major events has captured the attention of state and city governments. Many states and municipalities have formed sport authorities whose primary function is to attract major sporting events to their sites. These organizations are frequently involved in the construction, marketing, and possibly even the management of the local sport facility.

THE FACILITY MANAGEMENT INDUSTRY

The facility management industry operates in three sectors: private facilities, municipal facilities, and college and university facilities. Although many characteristics are shared by private, municipal, and college sectors, numerous differences are also apparent.

In marketing terms, each of the three sectors of the facility management industry is interested in increasing profit through a greater market share (i.e., getting more people to attend more events). In addition, all three sectors have enhanced their revenues through product diversification. This diversification includes auxiliary services such as parking, concessions, and especially souvenirs (merchandising).

Private Sport Facilities

The private sector emphasizes return on investment and profit; the sport facility must generate reasonable revenues in excess of expenses. Management of this type of building requires sophisticated business practices and excellent marketing and financial management skills. A manager's job security is often tied to the profit-and-loss statements that are generated on a quarterly basis. Putting people in the seats, events on the floor, and dollars in the stockholders' pockets is the name of the game.

Municipal Sport Facilities

The municipal sector requires significant political savvy, because the manager must be effective in dealing with elected politicians. The operating philosophy may be that the building is to serve a public function, regardless of the economic outcomes. These facilities often operate on a "run what the city brings you" level. However, a major trend in the management of municipal facilities encourages managers to operate facilities more like businesses and less like public service enterprises.

College and University Sport Facilities

Greater stability exists in the college and university setting than in either the private or municipal sectors. Traditionally, the manager in this

Some facilities are constructed for one primary purpose.

situation has acted as a liaison between the athletic director and the facility staff. Most arenas and stadia were designed to be used predominantly for the conduct of collegiate contests in football and basketball, with a few non-revenue sports thrown in for good measure. Today, however, the college/university sector is also moving toward insistence on financial solvency, and many managers must bring in more events that result in increased profit.

ORGANIZATIONAL STRUCTURE

The structure of the facility management business does not vary significantly across the three sectors. Most sport facilities have a director, an operations manager, a box office manager, a personnel manager, a stage manager, a concessions manager, a building engineer, and a general clerical support staff.

Facility Director

This individual is responsible for the total operation of the facility and reports directly to the designated superior, who (depending on the sector) can be the mayor, the city council, the corporate chief executive officer, or the college/university president. This position, therefore, requires a great deal of political and interpersonal skill. Long-range planning and the establishment of goals and objectives are often the director's tasks, as are budget presentation and management. This function may not be as straightforward as it seems, because some facilities have operational goals that go beyond profitability and encompass the philosophy of the organization. In addition, media management, contract negotiations, and labor relations are frequently part of the job. The director also makes programming, personnel, and budgeting decisions with input from subordinates.

Operations Manager

This person serves as the right hand to the director. Specific duties and responsibilities include event management, marketing, financial management, and personnel supervision. The operations manager is the "detail" person and often is called upon to manage the facility during events, a responsibility that frequently requires working the night shift. The coordination of details often involves working with agencies outside the organization, such as security and medical services. Consequently, the success or failure of an event usually depends on the skills of this individual.

Box Office Manager

The person in this position works closely with both the director and the operations manager. Tasks involved in this job begin as soon as the event is scheduled; the box office manager coordinates all ticketing operations, such as reporting to the operations manager and event promoters, supervising ticket takers and ushers, and accounting for all money received and expended for tickets and seat sales.

Personnel Manager

Depending on the size of the operation, this individual is usually responsible for hiring and training all part-time employees needed for efficient facility operation. The personnel manager often oversees setup and takedown of the performance area. Because this person deals with a great number of people from varied backgrounds, human relations skills are a priority. The abilities to calculate time frame requirements and to handle human resource planning are also skills necessary to succeed in this job.

Stage Manager

The responsibilities of this position often overlap those of a personnel manager. Such tasks as pre-event setup and managing the setup crew could be part of either position. Specialty aspects of this function can involve lighting, staging, and sound systems. This assignment calls for a person with both administrative skills and some artistic creativity.

Concessions Manager

The function of providing quality food and beverages to the customer is an enormous task. Many college and university facilities do not even attempt this task and instead hire independent companies to perform the service. However, many sport facilities successfully manage their own concessions operations. The concessions manager must be able to coordinate concession sales (and perhaps merchandise sales) in multiple locations, process the orders for all food and beverage items, maintain the concession areas and equipment, and supervise part-time employees. This job requires knowledge of financial management, health regulations, food services, and contractual agreements.

The teamwork required of all personnel is the essential ingredient for a well-managed sport facility. If any component is missing, the spectator is going to be unhappy. Knowing that the entire team worked together to make an event successful provides one of the greatest sources of satisfaction for everyone involved.

CAREER COMPETENCIES

The job skills that are most needed by an effective sport facility manager include personnel management, budgeting, financial analysis, and forecasting. Other general attributes that most managers believe are essential for success are planning and organizational abilities and public relations skills. Continual problem solving, critical thinking, and decision making are routine to facility managers.

You can best attain these skills through sport management courses in marketing, personnel management, finance, public relations, and administration.

SECURING EMPLOYMENT

The path to the facility management profession is usually paved by previous experience. Because the field is somewhat fragmented between the private, municipal, and college/university sectors, career paths in facility management are difficult to track. You will find it almost impossible to be hired at the director's level without having served as an operations manager or an assistant director. Serving in one of these capacities will give you valuable experience in dealing with promoters, performing artists, athletic directors, and television and radio representatives. The facility director often consults the operations manager in political and financial matters. This experience gives the operations manager valuable insight and skill in a relatively low-pressure way. In most facilities, the organizational structure places the operations manager in a position to supervise a great many people. This experience is essential prior to assuming the role of director.

Many people enjoy full and rewarding careers as operations managers without aspirations of becoming directors. The political entanglements and financial pressures that accompany the position of director create situations that some individuals prefer to avoid.

A network of colleagues, or word-of-mouth communication, is the best source for both recommendations and information about vacancies. As a new professional, you should cultivate relationships in the field and make a point of knowing fellow managers. You can accomplish this through attending local, regional, and national professional conferences sponsored by trade associations. Similarly, you can develop a network of professionals around the events themselves. This process will entail telephone conversations and written correspondence in regard to athletic contests and entertainment events.

Because personal networking is sometimes unproductive, you should also look to professional organizations for assistance. The IAAM publishes vacancy information in its newsletter. You should also join trade associations because of the personal networks and professional development that district and national conferences offer.

CAREER LADDER

Professionals in the industry can advance by moving from the directorship of a small facility to one with larger seating capacity and heavier events schedules. Many people feel that more prestige accompanies a position with a larger arena or stadium. In most cases such a position offers more attractive financial rewards as well. But prestige and money do not come without a price. The business pressures in larger facilities require proven skills in marketing, policy development, budgeting, and personnel management. Job security can also be more tenuous in these situations.

THE INTERNSHIP

An internship in facility management can be invaluable for getting a "hands-on" feel for the profession. You should try to get as many experiences as possible during your internship. Experience handling a variety of tasks and assignments will make you more valuable in the job market. You will also gain a significant advantage in managing one project from conception to production. This experience will demonstrate to potential employers that you can follow through on commitments and will illustrate your versatility. Select an internship site according to the type of setting in which you

would like to eventually work. Not only will the skills and abilities you learn during the internship be similar to those required on the job, but networking possibilities between your internship supervisor and prospective employers will be enhanced.

Professional Organizations

International Association of Auditorium Managers (IAAM)

Professional Publications

Athletic Business
Auditorium News
IAAM Newsletter

COMPENSATION

A common question asked by almost every student contemplating a specific profession is, "How much money am I going to make?" Table 3.1 shows average salaries in facility management.

A position in a smaller facility does not always correlate with a lower salary. Some facility managers have very profitable and enjoyable careers at facilities with a limited number of seats and events. However, most high-paying jobs are in facilities where the manager must put people in the seats and events on the schedule, which, in turn, dictates the economic benefits that the manager can achieve.

YOUR FUTURE IN FACILITY MANAGEMENT

Many students also ask, "What is the job market in the field of sport facility management?" Be-

Table 3.1 Facility Management Salaries

	Private	Municipal	College/university
Beginning	$18,000-28,000	$14,000-25,000	$16,000-20,000
Midcareer	$30,000-50,000	$30,000-45,000	$25,000-35,000
Later years	$50,000-150,000	$45,000-60,000	$40,000-50,000

cause only about 1,500 sport and entertainment facilities exist in the United States, the market is somewhat limited. Turnover, although moderate, does create jobs, and this is most common at the entry level. The trend in the business is clearly toward private management; thus, you may want to look closely at this area for the best employment opportunities. The increasing formation of city and state sport authorities and commissions is also an encouraging sign for employment.

LEARNING ACTIVITIES

1. The Virginia Slims Tennis Championships are scheduled for your facility. Prepare an event management plan for this event. Begin by listing all the activities that need to take place prior to the event. Include such items as reserving the facility, advertising, hotel accommodations, ticket printing and sales, and personnel scheduling. Next, place all of the activities in the sequence in which they must occur. Now, calculate the time needed to accomplish each task. Finally, place the items on a project calendar that shows each activity in sequence, the time required to complete it, and the overall chain of events.

2. Analyze the following case study and calculate the financial ramifications. A rock group is planning a concert in your facility. The group is scheduled to perform for two nights, Friday and Saturday, but because of ticket demand, you would like them to give a third performance on Sunday. The arrangement with the promoter is a fifty-fifty split of profits after expenses are paid. The group charges a $50,000 performance fee and requires that all meal and hotel expenses be paid for their 30-member traveling entourage. The labor and utility costs for your facility run about $5,000 per performance. The promoter informs you that the group is available but that *you* will have to pick up their expenses out of your share. You agree and sign the contract.

   In general, the show is a great success. The first two nights are sellouts. However, because advertising for the additional appearance was late, the arena is only 75% full (7,500 seats at an average of $10 per seat). Calculate your profits from this Sunday night performance. Be sure to add an extra $3,000 for increased ticket printing and advertising costs. Check with local hotels for single room rates and figure $40 per person per day for food. Remember to take into account the group's fee and to split the profits with the promoter *before* expenses. Did you make a good decision when you signed the contract for the extra performance? Did the promoter make a good decision?

SUGGESTED READINGS

A sport haven for the disabled. (1985, July). *Athletic Business*, 9(7), 70, 72-74.

A sporting place that doesn't live by sports alone. (1985, May). *Athletic Business*, 36-40.

American National Standards Institute (ANSI). (1982, September). Appendix I: Architectural and transportation barriers compliance board guidelines (Section 1190.40). Human Data.

Anderson, D.L. AIA. (1984, September). Sports facility checklist: A pre-design guide. *Athletic Business*, 84, 86.

Bahrke, T. et al. (1985, May/June). Video information systems for convention center management. *IAAM Newsletter*, 23(4), 16-17.

Bassi, R. (1981, December). How public assembly facility managers make facilities accessible to disabled. *IAAM Newsletter*, 19(12), 4-6.

Campane, J. (1982, September). Amendment IV: The Fourth Amendment at the rock concert. *IAAM Newsletter*, 20(9), 4-9.

Carlson, M. (1985, Fall). The 10 percent question. *Facility Manager*, 1(2), 20-23, 27.

Clement, A. (1988). *Law in sport and physical activity*. Indianapolis, IN: Benchmark Press.

Cooper, J. (1983). *Construction plan of "Cooper Clinic."* Dallas.

Danziger, G. (1984, December). Scheduling with computers: Reducing complexities to manageable problems. *Athletic Business*, 8(12), 78-81.

Dealer or direct? The changing face of athletic purchasing. (1985, October). *Athletic Business*, 9(10), 16, 18-20, 22.

Edwards, M.W. (1985, May). Fitness pays off in pool facility. *Athletic Business*, 30-34.

Ethiel, N. (1984, December). Private management/public management. *Auditorium News*, 22(12), 4-5.

From pit to palace. (1986, July). *Athletic Business*, 10(7).

Harrold, B. (1984, May). Product liability—A burning issue for auditorium managers. *Auditorium News*, 6.

Hirshfield, G. (1986, Fall). Development of a comprehensive weight training facility. *NIRSA Journal*.

Hunsaker, J. (1984, December). Aquatic maintenance: Don't confuse the urgent with the important. *Athletic Business*, 8(12), 46, 47.

Indoors or out—quality lighting needn't cost more. (1985, March). *Athletic Business*, 9(3), 42, 44-45.

Olson, J.R. (1985, October). Safety checklists: Does your facility measure up? *Athletic Business*, 9(10), 47, 48, 50, 51.

Olson, J.R. (1985, December). Safety checklist: How safe are your outdoor programs? *Athletic Business*, 48-59.

Smoke toxicity: Responsible solutions. (1985, May/June). *Auditorium News*, 23(4), 10-12.

Sol, N. (1985, April). To compete or cooperate. *Athletic Business*, 45.

Sports club design: Fitting facilities to program plans. (1985, April). *Athletic Business*, 22, 26, 28, 30.

Sports facility planning for the future. (1987, January). *Journal of Physical Education Recreation and Dance*, 58(1), 21-45.

The new locker room: Pampering the clientele. (1985, April). *Athletic Business*, 38, 40, 41.

Wilbur, C.W., & Johnson and Johnson. (1987, January). Working out at work. *The Runner*.

Williams, L. (1981, November). What you need to market your facility. *Auditorium News*, 4-8.

Williams, M.A. (1986, Summer). The small venues' blues. *Facility Manager*, II(1).

Williams, M.A. (1986, Summer). Understanding risk management. *Facility Manager*, **II**(1).

Wong, G., & Ensor, R. (1985, May). Torts and tailgates. *Athletic Business*, 46-49.

CHAPTER 4

Campus Recreation Programs

David O. Matthews
University of Illinois

Administrators of institutions of higher education have traditionally accepted responsibility for students' education and welfare (Matthews, 1984). The large numbers of curricular and extracurricular offerings in existence today stand as evidence of administrative commitment to this responsibility. A comprehensive campus recreation program is one way to meet this obligation. Such programs provide opportunities for students, faculty, and staff to release tensions and stresses, to combat the dangers of the sedentary academic existence, and to develop personal habits of regular involvement in physical activity. The campus recreation program can help individuals find a desirable balance between leisure and work through the relaxation that comes from pleasurable, vigorous participation.

PURPOSE OF CAMPUS RECREATION

At one time, campus recreation programs were called intramural programs. The term *intramurals* literally meant "within the walls" (Mitchell, 1939; Mueller & Reznik, 1979) and referred to activities, usually competitive sports, that took place within the confines of the campus property. In recent years, however, *intramurals* has taken on a different meaning because of the greatly expanded connotation of the word. Most

schools are developing programs that retain competitive intramurals while also including informal recreation, sports clubs, fitness, wellness, outdoor trips, dancing, music, table games, and special events. This emphasis on activities other than traditional competitive sports has caused many universities to rename their intramural departments *campus recreation*, a title that enables these departments to expand their programs to include recreational as well as competitive activities.

Campus recreation involves more than just competitive sports.

Philosophy of Campus Recreation

The philosophy of campus recreation is based on the concept that students should have freedom of choice, equality of opportunity, and responsibility for sharing, supervising, and administering their recreation programs. One of the most basic values of the campus recreation program is student involvement in directing and implementing a quality operation. Through active participation in conducting the program, students can acquire knowledge and techniques essential to the development of effective interpersonal relationships as well as leadership, management, and organizational skills. These skills are essential competencies for persons administering campus recreation programs.

ADMINISTRATION OF CAMPUS RECREATION

The location of campus recreation in the hierarchy of the university varies according to the geographic location of the school, student enrollment, number of staff, type and number of facilities, and school traditions. In addition, and perhaps more importantly, the chain of command is determined by the source of financial support, established priorities regarding use of facilities, and the degree of authority vested in the position of the director (Matthews, 1977). Because U.S. and Canadian colleges and universities use student fees extensively to support campus recreation programs and facilities, the best administrative hierarchy may be one in which the campus recreation director reports directly to a vice-president, or a vice-chancellor of student affairs/student services (see Figure 4.1).

The closer the director is in the chain of command to the person who ultimately makes the funding decisions, the better the chances are that the amounts of money the director requests in budget proposals will be approved. In addition to funding considerations, the campus recreation department should be in close proximity to upper administration so that the director can exert influence in the final determination of facility priorities.

Although exceptions to the type of administrative structure represented in Figure 4.1 are

Campus recreation is for everyone.

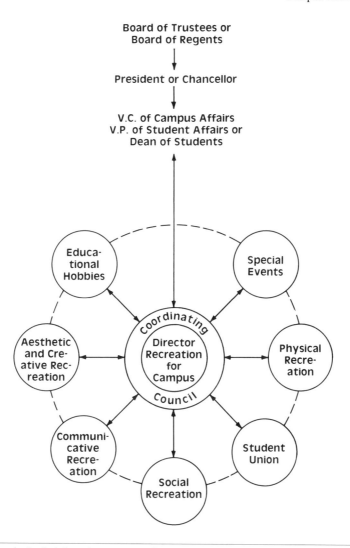

Figure 4.1 A theoretical administrative structure for a campus recreation program.

rare (Matthews, 1987), some campus recreation directors report to intermediate-level administrators such as the director of athletics, the director of the student union, the head of the physical education department, the head of the recreation department, or the dean of students. The organizational charts in Figures 4.2, 4.3, and 4.4 illustrate the diversity of possible administrative structures.

Just as organizational formats vary, so do the titles of the departments or divisions under whose auspices the campus recreation program is offered. Examples of existing unit titles are division of recreational sports, division of campus recreation, recreational services, campus-wide activities, university recreation and intramurals, intramural sports and recreative services, intramurals and extramurals, and intramurals and

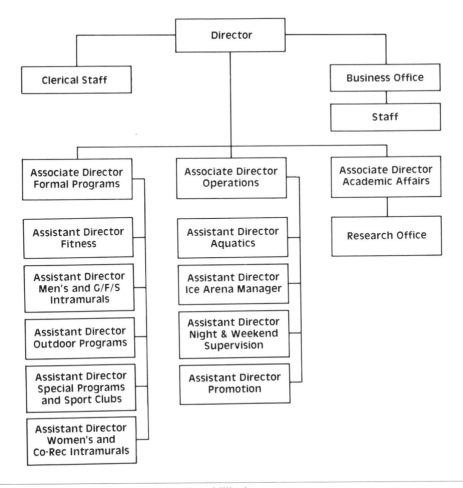

Figure 4.2 Campus recreation at the University of Illinois.

club sports (Matthews, 1987). The most inclusive title is department of campus recreation, because it permits sufficient latitude for the director to offer a wide variety of both competitive and noncompetitive activities.

DIRECTOR OF CAMPUS RECREATION

The director of campus recreation works with many constituencies in a variety of roles. Therefore, the responsibilities of the director are described by the duties, tasks, and competencies of this position.

Duties

The director of campus recreation must perform a variety of duties. The following list includes the major of these.

- Act as general adviser to the recreation coordinating council, a group of students, faculty, or staff appointed or elected to assist the director in the operation of the activity program (see Figure 4.1).

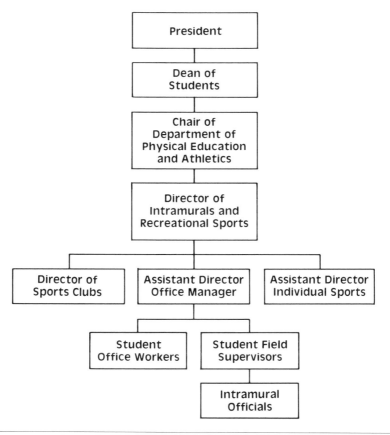

Figure 4.3 Campus recreation at the University of Chicago.

- Act as liaison with all organizations sponsoring student recreation programs and with all staff and faculty concerned with various phases of student recreation.
- Maintain continuity in matters related to the coordination of student recreation. A permanent director provides the guidance from year to year by virtue of a perspective obtained from a number of years of continuous administration.
- Provide professional leadership in program appraisal, program development, and recreation leadership training, to guarantee the prospect of an overall improved program.
- Accomplish the mandates of the recreation coordinating council.

Tasks

In addition to these duties, other major tasks include: educating; organizing the activities and staff to effect a good program; establishing a workable budget; administering personnel; scheduling facilities for the activities; planning a long-range program to meet growing and changing needs; and constantly evaluating the effectiveness of the program in meeting the stated objectives (Matthews, 1966).

Competencies

What competencies do you need to fulfill the duties of a responsible director? Communication

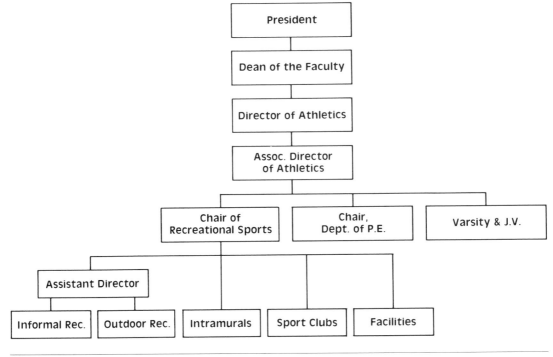

Figure 4.4   Campus recreation at Colgate University.

is primary, along with management skills specific to money, personnel, facility, schedule, and promotion. The competencies necessary for effective direction of campus recreation are described in Table 4.1.

CAREER OPPORTUNITIES IN CAMPUS RECREATION

If you intend to enter the field of campus recreation, you have several options from which to choose, including the generalist approach, the specialist approach, and a combination of the two. A generalist attempts to absorb a considerable amount of information about a lot of things and to develop skills and abilities in a number of areas. A specialist, on the other hand, concentrates on becoming an expert in one phase of the management of the program. The person who selects the combination approach seeks a balanced preparation, developing enough knowledge and skill in a number of areas to enter the job market as a generalist and then to progress toward the management level, which requires more specificity. The programmatic organizational chart presented in Figure 4.5 (p. 54) illustrates the range of general and specialized skills required in the operation of a campus recreation program.

If you were interested, for example, in the position of assistant director for fitness, then one or more advanced degrees in physiology would be your area of specialization. A master's degree is a prerequisite for most positions in campus recreation. What advanced study or kinds of specialization would some of the other positions indicated in Figure 4.5 require?

In a survey of 399 directors of campus recreation programs in the United States and Canada, Matthews (1986) discovered that out of 25 jobs identified as falling within campus

Table 4.1   Competencies Needed by a Campus Recreation Director

Communication skills
1. Writing
   a. Correspondence (letters, memos, and reports)
      (1) On-campus communications
         (a) Administrators (president, chancellors, deans, department heads, legal office, physical plant, campus recreation administrative staff)
         (b) Students
         (c) Nonacademic personnel
      (2) Off-campus communications
         (a) Parents
         (b) Public and private secondary and higher education institutions
         (c) Business and industrial firms
         (d) Publishing companies
         (e) Public agencies
   b. Articles for magazines and journals
   c. Written proceedings of conference presentations
   d. Written materials for books, monographs, and pamphlets
   e. Handbooks for the program policies and procedures
   f. Informational flyers, posters, and signs
   g. Rules and regulations for program activities
   h. Safety programs, procedures, policies, philosophy, and materials
2. Speaking
   a. Meetings with staff members, students, and administrators
   b. Conferences and workshops
   c. Presentations to potential donors and to alumni
   d. Meetings with business and industry

Money management
1. Collecting budget information
   a. Securing data related to the history of the departmental budgets
   b. Gathering current information
   c. Preparing income estimates from collected information
   d. Making comparative studies of preceding years
   e. Preparing a final draft of estimated incomes
2. Drafting the budget
   a. Checking requests and justifying proposals
   b. Consulting with staff members on budget requests/cuts
   c. Ensuring representation from all areas of the program
   d. Discussing with staff the final budget proposal
   e. Including all expense items in the draft
3. Adopting the budget—Forwarding budgets through the proper chain of command
4. Expending the budget
   a. Following the approved budget
   b. Prudently spending funds
   c. Keeping cash flow chart up to date

(Cont.)

Table 4.1   (Continued)

---

    d. Following all policies and procedures on expenditure of funds

    e. Identifying authorized person to expend funds

5. Appraising and accounting for the budget

    a. Preserving all records of transactions

    b. Retaining all records and receipts the required amount of time

    c. Keeping a current filing system for an immediate transactions and orders review (e.g., monthly account sheets)

    d. Financial accounting

        (1) Assigning account numbers for budget categories

        (2) Keeping an account journal

        (3) Preparing a monthly balance sheet

        (4) Assigning files for each account

        (5) Estimating income

        (6) Preparing an annual report

        (7) Retaining copies of transaction forms

Personnel Management

1. Hiring personnel

    a. Establishing goals, aims, purposes, and program components

        (1) Working with members of staff to determine department growth and development

        (2) Determining trends in campus recreation programming

        (3) Establishing priorities for program personnel

    b. Advertising new positions through

        (1) Professional journals

        (2) Educational periodicals

        (3) Campus media

        (4) Announcements to other colleges/universities and agencies

        (5) Personal calls to other directors

    c. Forming a personnel search committee to

        (1) Evaluate applicants' vitae

        (2) Determine top candidates

        (3) Invite candidate(s) for campus interviews

2. Assigning duties

    a. Outlining the responsibilities of the job

    b. Informing the employee of the immediate objectives and short-and long-range goals

    c. Orienting the employee to policies, philosophy, rules, and regulations of the department, college, and university

3. Evaluating the employee

    a. Informing the employee of the criteria for the evaluating process

    b. Keeping the rating system accurate and up to date. The rating system should be consistent with documents of the institution if merit raises, tenure, and promotion are a consideration

4. Rotating duties

    a. Administering employee reassignment

    b. Administering changes in staff responsibilities based on department needs and employee welfare

Facility management, planning of new facilities, repairing and remodeling of facilities

1. Determining facility needs for existing programs

2. Determining facility needs for expansion and/or improvement of activity program

3. Determining need to repair or remodel existing facilities

4. Hiring personnel to supervise facilities and program operation
5. Researching sources for information and assistance in facility management, planning, repair, and remodeling

Facilities scheduling
1. Establishing priorities for the use of facilities by all campus programs. Groups needing sport facilities would include:
   a. Intramural competitive teams
   b. Informal (drop-in) participants or users
   c. Varsity athletics
   d. Sports clubs
   e. Student organizations
   f. Faculty and staff, including spouses and families
   g. Community citizens
   h. Others
2. Keeping current, accurate records of facility scheduling

Promotion and advertising
1. Using verbal and written communication skills
2. Using interpersonal skills
3. Applying public relations and advertising knowledge
4. Demonstrating organizational skills to disseminate concise information for maximum readability
5. Using staff members and students to promote the program

Fund raising
1. Identifying present and future financial needs
2. Identifying sources of funds. These include:
   a. Student fees for program and facilities
   b. State or local funds
   c. Grants and gifts
   d. Sales
   e. Services and equipment rentals
   f. Fees and guarantees associated with sport participation
3. Utilizing publicity techniques to inform administrators, participants, faculty, and others of the financial needs of the program

Security control and risk management
1. Identifying the possible causes of injury in the activities presented to the participant
2. Instituting measures to alleviate or eliminate the possible causes of injury
3. Researching the various physical and electronic devices that can be used to safeguard persons and physical property from harm
4. Enforcing policies and procedures designed to protect the participant and property involved in the program
5. Working effectively with the various law enforcement agencies of the institution, community, state, and nation in the promotion of security

recreation departments, the top 15 that will be available within the next few years were (in rank order) intramural programmer, facility supervisor, sports club director, graduate student supervisor, informal recreational programmer, fitness programming director, aquatics director, outdoor recreation specialist, promotion/publicity coordinator, officials director, special events coordinator, grounds/fields keeper, sport camp manager, lifeguard service coordinator, and instructional skills coordinator. Each of these administrative positions requires competencies

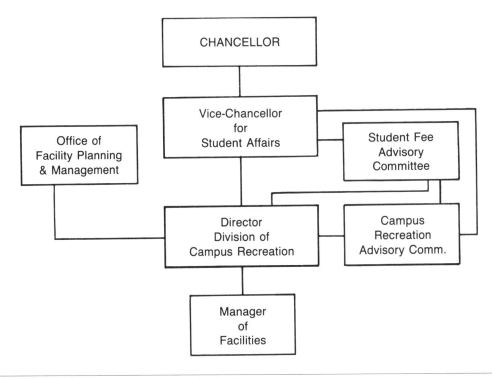

Figure 4.5   Sample campus recreation organizational chart.

Campus recreation programs provide jobs for hundreds of sport managers.

similar to those outlined for the director, as well as additional specialized skills, knowledge, and advanced degrees.

Aspiring campus recreation directors should become certified through the National Intramural–Recreational Sports Association (NIRSA). Although you can be hired without NIRSA certification, more and more schools require this credential for employment.

Thousands of campus recreation positions exist in universities and colleges in the United States and Canada. A 1987 survey revealed that approximately 200 to 300 schools were planning or were in the process of building new recreation buildings (Matthews, 1987). As a result of this construction, which will go on well into the 1990s, demand for persons to manage all of the many aspects of campus recreation programs will increase. Consequently, the outlook should be favorable well into the next century.

LEARNING ACTIVITIES

1. Identify the following elements of the campus recreation program at your university: (a) purpose, (b) philosophy, (c) financial base, (d) location in the hierarchy, (e) administrative structure, (f) programmatic organizational structure, and (g) role of coordinating council.

2. Invite the director or associate director of your campus recreation program to speak to your class about responsibilities of their positions.

3. Invite a member of the coordinating council to speak on the council's role in decision making for programs and space scheduling.

4. Interview a campus recreation program staff member for information on duties and responsibilities of the position.

Professional Organizations

National Intramural–Recreational Sports Association (NIRSA)

American Alliance for Health, Physical Education, Recreation and Dance (AAHPERD)

Canadian Intramural–Recreation Association (CIRA)

North American Society for Sport Management (NASSM)

Professional Publications

Journal of National Intramural–Recreational Sports Association

Journal of Physical Education, Recreation and Dance

Canadian Intramural–Recreation Association Journal

Journal of Sport Management

REFERENCES

Matthews, D.O. (1966). Intramural administrative principles. *The Athletic Journal*, **46**, 82.

Matthews, D.O. (1977). Campus recreation department of division. In J.A. Peterson & L.S. Preo (Eds.), *Intramural directors handbook* (pp. 7-10). Champaign, IL: Leisure Press.

Matthews, D.O. (1984). *Managing the intramural-recreational sports program*. Champaign, IL: Stipes.

Matthews, D.O. (1986). [Survey to determine job opportunities in the profession of campus recreation]. Unpublished raw data.

Matthews, D.O. (1987). [Survey to determine trends in campus recreation programs in institutions of higher education in the United States and Canada]. Unpublished raw data.

Mitchell, E.D. (1939). *Intramural sports*. New York: A.S. Barnes.

Mueller, C.E., & Reznik, J.W. (1979). *Intramural-recreational sports: Programming and administration*. New York: John Wiley and Sons.

CHAPTER 5

Community-Based Sport

Richard J. Quain

Bowling Green State University

The subject of sport management frequently conjures up images of careers in major sports such as professional football, basketball, and baseball, which most people associate with glamour. Lipsey (1987) notes that the mass media nurture and perpetuate the glamorization of major sports. Consider how the media cover sports. *USA Today* devotes 25 percent of its space to sports, and about 50 percent of the sports section deals with major sports. With this type of coverage, it is no wonder that people identify major, high-profile sports first when discussing careers in sport management. Although many fine careers are available in high-profile sport, community-based sport also has many excellent career opportunities that you should explore.

The term *community* implies that the individuals constituting this social unit have some common interests; frequently sport is the interest that binds the group together. An interest in sport is pandemic in the United States. The *1983 Miller Lite Report on American Attitudes Toward Sports* indicated that 98 percent of all Americans either participate in sport, read about sport, or watch sporting events on television at least once a week (Research & Forecasts, Inc., 1983). This overwhelming public involvement with sport is ample evidence of the need for competent sport managers at the community level.

Professional Organizations

American Alliance for Health, Physical Education, Recreation and Dance (AAHPERD)
National Recreation & Park Association (NRPA)
National Intramural–Recreational Sports Association (NIRSA)
Professional Golf Association
Association for Fitness in Business
Council for National Cooperation in Aquatics

Professional Publications

Journal of Physical Education, Recreation and Dance
Journal of National Intramural–Recreational Sports Association
Parks & Recreation

DIRECT AND INDIRECT PARTICIPATION

Discussions of community-based sport usually focus on actual physical participation in recreational pursuits within the community. In reality,

Youth recreation is a common community-based activity.

community-based sport is multifaceted and can provide numerous professional opportunities for individuals interested in sport management.

There are two types of participation in community sport: direct participation and indirect participation. Across the nation, communities have a vast array of sporting opportunities in one or both of these categories. Direct participation is the personal performance of an activity by a participant in an organized, structured setting. Examples of direct participation opportunities include Little League Baseball, coed volleyball leagues, aerobic dance classes, and locally sponsored road races. Indirect participation comes mainly in the forms of spectating at actual sporting events or through the use of electronic or print media. Examples of indirect participation include listening to games on the radio, reading news stories about sport, watching professional or collegiate sports teams on television, and cheering for family and friends at local ball games, swim meets, or boat races. Don't overlook indirect participation, because

it can be a significant area for career development. Community sporting events occur on a regular basis, and myriad opportunities are available for creative and competent sport management professionals who are able to recognize and meet the needs of the spectators at these events. Starting a small business venture in photographing action shots of community athletes is one way to serve interested spectators. Can you think of other businesses that would meet the needs of indirect participants?

Make a list of all the organized sport, recreation, and leisure activities you can think of in your home community. When the list is complete, write down the titles of all the people who are associated with each of the activities. Next to each title, write your estimate of the number of hours per week that person works with the sporting event or activity. Finally, indicate what you believe each person earns for his or her efforts.

Does your list include the people who maintain the facilities, transport people to activities, handle correspondence, coordinate and participate in fund raising, officiate the events, promote their organization or activity, or deal with finances? Possibly, you have overlooked some of the people who are vitally needed in your community to ensure that sport and leisure activities occur. This exercise should alert you to the number and variety of jobs available in community-based sport, which you can compare to the somewhat finite number of career opportunities found in professional sport. Next, take your list home with you and, through informational interviewing, investigate the accuracy of your estimates of hours worked, responsibilities, and compensation.

FINANCIAL BASE

Sport organizations have either public or private financial bases. Public agencies are designed to serve the public through city, state, or national governments. Because funding for public agencies is often tied to public money (e.g., tax revenues), the career growth potential in government-supported sport organizations fluctuates according to the changes in the local, state, national, and international economy (Lamb, 1987). For example, your community's own economy may be insulated from a recession that is affecting the rest of the country. However, the total funds available from the federal government to your community to provide sport opportunities could decrease due to the national situation, which would also decrease the number of personnel needed. Private businesses that rely on their own initiatives to generate revenue can better adapt to changing economic situations.

CAREER OPPORTUNITIES IN COMMUNITY SPORT

Direct and indirect participation opportunities that begin at the local community level may be

Private agencies often provide facilities for community-based sporting activities.

restricted to that level, or they may extend into state, regional, national, or international opportunities. Within most communities, individuals can find a level of competition commensurate with their skill levels and competitive drives. Communities can provide opportunities for everyone from the Sunday golfer to the elite amateur, and community programs need qualified professionals to conduct the events that will meet the needs of all of these individuals.

Local Career Opportunities

Local recreation agencies provide the organizational structure for competitive sporting activities within communities. Some examples include softball leagues, swimming programs, industrial recreation leagues, volleyball leagues, and basketball leagues. In these same communities, agencies such as the YMCA, YWCA, AAU, Catholic Youth Organization, Little League Baseball, Pop Warner Football, and Dixie Softball provide facilities and coordination for other community-based sporting activities. All of these organizations require personnel who can help ensure a well-managed, safe, and healthful environment for sport.

Many other forms of community-based sport offer variety to programs and may need special facilities. These opportunities create employment in specialty areas. For instance, community tennis courts can serve the public for lessons, court time, and tournaments, and the tennis specialist could be the pro, the manager, or the director. Other examples are community golf courses, swimming pools, archery ranges, miniature golf courses, batting cages, and cross-country ski trails. All of these examples can provide avenues through which residents may learn new activities and enjoy both direct and indirect participation; all of these activities need sport professionals as well.

Certain communities have ideal locations for marinas, ice arenas, and indoor aquatic centers. Complexes for community gymnastic clubs and fencing clubs can offer professionals opportunities to work with individuals who want specialized sports or have aspirations for Olympic competition.

Specialties and facilities need financing and support, and the community tax base and local employment picture are basic factors for growth. Communities that support specialty complexes and facilities can and do exist!

State, National, and International Career Opportunities

Lewis (1980) alluded to this component of extended sport career opportunities:

> Another part of the sports enterprise is one that provides support services for those sport operations that are directly involved with participant or spectator consumption. Among the units that perform in this capacity are the sporting goods industry, consulting firms (National Sport Management, Inc., Trigon, Sports Advisors), player associations, player agents, promotional and developmental organizations (Athletic Institute, American Sports Education Institute, National Golf Foundation), the academic sector (college and university programs in sport studies, sport management, physical education), and the media (both print and airways). (p. 16)

Additional organizations and associations offering extended opportunities and consequently career potential include Special Olympics, Little League Baseball, AAU, International Games for the Disabled, Pan American Games, Goodwill Games, and the United States Ski Association.

COMPETENCIES AND TASKS

In a national survey (Quain & Parks, 1986), sport management practitioners identified several competencies necessary for success in careers involving supervision and coordination of sporting activities at the community level. Human relations skills were rated most positively, and a knowledge of sport was a close second. Other competencies highly valued by practitioners were personnel management, money management, and time management.

Job-related tasks in community-based sport are extremely varied and reflect the need for competencies identified by this survey. Obviously, the setting in which each position exists and the job description associated with it will determine specific tasks; however, many responsibilities extend across all types of positions. Examples of some of the duties reported by practitioners include dealing with volunteers, coaches, and officials; scheduling and budgeting; writing reports; compiling statistics; organizing and supervising; planning, instructing, coordinating, and evaluating programs; coordinating competitions; complying with regulations; and managing facilities, equipment, and personnel (Parks & Quain, 1984).

LEARNING ACTIVITIES

1. Conduct library research to discover more opportunities in organizations such as Little League Baseball. *Sports Market Place* (1989) is an excellent reference with which to begin your search.

2. Which of the job-related tasks in community-based sport require good human relations skills? Why is a knowledge of sport necessary? Which tasks involve personnel management or money management? Why is time management important? Classify each task under one of the general management functions: planning, organizing, leading, and evaluating.

3. Investigate professional associations and publications in your campus or community library. The *Encyclopedia of Associations* (Koek & Martin, 1988) is a good place to start. Find the journals that are listed with the associations in the encyclopedia, and by scrutinizing the masthead of each, determine the sponsoring association, the target audience, the subscription rate, and the rate of publication. Additionally, read through the journals and note the types of articles (e.g., news, research, updates, and equipment and facility information). Through your research, decide which of these associations offer the most to individuals conducting sporting events at various levels.

REFERENCES

Koek, K.E., & Martin, S.B. (Eds.) (1988). *Encyclopedia of associations* (Vol. 1). Detroit: Gale Research.

Lamb, C.W., Jr. (1987, July-August). Public sector marketing is different. *Business Horizons*, **30**, 56-60.

Lewis, G. (1980). The sports enterprise. *Arena Review*, **4**(3), 12-17.

Lipsey, R.A. (Ed.) (1987). *Sports market place 1987*. Princeton, NJ: Sportguide.

Lipsey, R.A. (Ed.) (1989). *Sports market place 1988*. Princeton, NJ: Sportguide.

Parks, J., & Quain, R. (1984). *Survey of sport management practitioners*. Unpublished manuscript, Bowling Green State University, School of Health, Physical Education and Recreation, Bowling Green, OH.

Quain, R.J., & Parks, J.B. (1986). Sport management survey: Employment perspectives. *Journal of Physical Education, Recreation and Dance*, **57**(4), 18-21.

Research & Forecasts, Inc. (1983). *Miller Lite report on American attitudes toward sports*. Milwaukee: Miller Brewing Company.

CHAPTER 6

Sports Information

Allan Chamberlin
Mid-American Conference

Colleges and universities employ sports information directors to help publicize athletic programs. People with sports information backgrounds also work in a variety of sport-related settings such as national collegiate governing bodies, collegiate conference offices, and organizations such as AAU, the United States Olympic Committee (USOC), International Games for the Disabled, Pan American Games, Special Olympics, and professional sports teams.

In each of these settings, the publicists perform the same basic functions, though titles vary considerably. In collegiate athletics, an information director can have an alternate title such as sport media director, sport publicity director, director of athletic marketing and communication, assistant director of public relations for sport, or assistant athletic director for sports information. Some of the titles are synonymous, but in some cases they imply additional duties such as marketing and promotions. Because of the disparity in titles and duties, you should look beyond the position title to the specific job description to avoid being misled by a name.

UNIVERSITIES AND COLLEGES

The basic function of a sports information director in the college setting is to serve as a liaison between the news media and the school's athletic department. Although the size and scope of sports information offices vary tremendously in the more than 1,000 colleges and universities in the United States, each athletic department has someone who performs the duties of a sports information director.

All schools that sponsor intercollegiate athletics need a sports information director, whether they are small, private colleges, prestigious academic institutions, sprawling public schools, commuter schools, or anything in between.

The location of a sports information department in the organizational structure varies from school to school. At most NCAA Division I schools, the sports information department is a part of the athletic department; however, at a few of the major universities and many of the smaller schools, sports information is a branch of the university's public relations office. Sometimes the sports information office is physically located in the athletic department but reports to the public relations office.

Michigan State is an example of a school in which the sports information office is both physically and structurally part of the university relations department. The greatest advantage of this approach is access to other departments such as photo services and the publications office. The major disadvantage is lack of day-to-day contact with coaches and athletes.

Sports information offices at the most prominent athletic institutions have full-time staffs of five or more people and a suite of offices. At the other end of the spectrum in smaller schools, one person handles the sports information role on a part-time basis as part of a crowded public relations office.

In the 1960s, sports information was a relatively static field with many directors remaining in their positions until retirement. Although that is now the exception rather than the rule, some veterans are still in the field who have served for 30 to 40 years. The emergence of women's athletics and the accompanying increase in the sports information work load are at least partially responsible for this change in the lengths of careers in sports information. The information explosion and new computer technologies that allow incredible storage and retrieval capabilities have also impacted on the sports information work load and, consequently, on the longevity of sports information personnel.

NATIONAL GOVERNING BODIES

The majority of the colleges and universities that sponsor intercollegiate athletic programs are members of the NCAA. At the NCAA headquarters in Mission, KS, the staff, numbering over 100, interprets and enforces the association's regulations and administers championships. One of the branches of the national office is the NCAA Statistics Service, which compiles and publishes weekly national statistics in football and men's and women's basketball. The skills of a sports information director are essential for employees in the statistical operation.

The NAIA, a governing body for smaller colleges and universities, is located in Kansas City, MO. This association has statistical and informational functions similar to the NCAA.

CONFERENCE OFFICES

The conference office, a liaison between the institution and the national office, governs the athletic programs of member schools. Most NCAA institutions are members of regional conferences such as the Big Ten, the Southeastern Conference, the PAC-10, the Michigan Intercollegiate Athletic Association, and so forth.

Similarities run deep between the duties of a conference information director and those of the college sports information director. Like the college office, the conference office helps publicize athletics, but the conference information director publicizes the conference as a whole—all of the schools, teams, and athletes. Among the publications of a conference office are conference media guides, preseason polls, conference standings, statistics, all-conference teams, and players of the week. Almost all conference information directors begin their careers as sports information directors in campus settings.

ADDITIONAL SETTINGS

Public relations and information positions with organizations such as the USOC and the Special Olympics involve many of the same duties as those carried out by a sports information director. Major organizations such as the USOC and AAU do employ information personnel on a full-time basis, but opportunities at this level are very limited for inexperienced candidates.

The full-time staffs of these organizations count on volunteer assistance from aspiring information directors across the country during the Summer Olympic Festivals, Special Olympics, Pan American Games, and other events of this nature. Volunteer service is an excellent way for you to gain some invaluable experience and make contacts that could prove very beneficial in the future.

SPORTS INFORMATION SKILLS

The basic skills that all sports information directors must possess are writing abilities, computer skills, organizational skills, and attitudinal skills.

Writing Ability

The ability to write properly constructed sentences in an organized manner is a frequently overlooked skill that every sports information professional must possess. An organized, hard-working sports fanatic who gets along with everyone is well on the way to qualifying for a sports information position, but a lack of writing competence leaves a résumé incomplete.

"Brightening up" publications increases readership. An information professional must be able to write in a lively style and present information in an interesting manner. In a lecture at the 1987 College Sports Information Directors of America workshop, Professor Don Ranley of the University of Missouri School of Journalism pointed to the "seven Cs" of a good publication: Be correct, consistent, clear, concise, coherent, complete, and creative.

Effective writing ability includes being sensitive both in content and style. When a football team loses its seventh game in a row, the creative publicist emphasizes areas other than the team's record, such as individual accomplishments, areas of improvement, and other positive features.

A simple omission can offend a sensitive coach or administrator. Sports like football, ice hockey, softball, and wrestling do not need a gender reference, but for sports like swimming and track, the terms *men's* or *women's* must precede the name of the sport in order to accurately identify the team. The terms *boys* and *girls* are inappropriate for collegiate athletics.

Computer Skills

The computer age hit sports information in the early 1980s, permanently altering the course of the profession. Microcomputers calculate averages, print out statistics, store information, maintain mailing lists, and perform many other functions that assist in the operation of a sports information office. The larger offices have sophisticated computer setups with multiple terminals and one or more printers. At other schools, sports information offices can tie in with other phases of the athletic department or public relations department to share a computer system. With the aid of modems, computers can transmit and receive information over telephone lines. Computers continue to simplify the exchange of rosters, statistics, and other data and speed the distribution of information to the media. Eventually, computerization may make mailing news releases obsolete.

Computer technology is guaranteed to expand at a rapid pace, and if you are considering sports information as a career, you should learn as much as possible about computers.

Organizational Skills

No single trait is more important to a sports information director than organization. Requests pile up, deadlines near, and phone calls and meetings interrupt the production of material; all demand your ability to prioritize and organize.

A sports information office can quickly take on the look of a teenager's bedroom if file folders, publications, releases, and notebooks are strewn about. You can enhance your efficiency by spending the last few minutes of each day putting things back in their proper places and planning the start of the next day. Although interruptions are inevitable, outlining and prioritizing upcoming tasks increases your chances for a productive work day.

Having readily retrievable information in an organized filing system means you don't waste time finding what you need. A filing system that is complete yet not cumbersome allows you to keep track of current and former athletes and teams.

If space permits, a separate file folder on every current athlete is desirable. The file should include photos, information sheets filled out by the athlete, news releases about the athlete, and clips of published stories about the athlete. An important feature of an information sheet is a section in which the student athlete grants permission to release the information on the sheet; releasing any information without the student's permission is a violation of his or her rights. The majority of sports information offices are unable to maintain files on each athlete who ever played for the school, but an archives area that includes all of the letter winners, or at least all of the starters, limits wasted research.

Attitudinal Skills

A sports information specialist spends a lot of time dealing with people and must be able to get along with deadline-pressured members of the media, overworked administrators, anxious coaches, and verbose or reticent student athletes. It is stressful to have to deal with members of the print media who have to wait an extra 5 minutes to interview the star of the game because of a television or radio interview. Coaches may not understand that the media want to know why the coach disciplined the team's best player. Members of the media want to interview the best athletes, but this can create problems for the media if an athlete answers monosyllabically. Conversely, the athlete who fails to show restraint can make comments that give away a game plan or incite the opposition.

A listing of the functions of the sports information department and the tasks that an infor-mation specialist must perform tells only part of the story. It requires skill to write a thoughtful feature story or edit and lay out a brochure, but it requires something beyond skill to write the story or edit the brochure while being constantly interrupted by a ringing telephone, a curious athlete, or a nervous coach.

Sports information directors do not work from 9:00 a.m. to 5:00 p.m. five days a week. Games are played on week nights and weekends. The phone rings constantly during regular working hours, mandating the need to come to work very early or to stay late for quality time to complete projects.

SPORTS INFORMATION DUTIES

A simplified roster of some of the duties of a sports information director includes: writing news releases; updating hometown newspapers; writing feature stories; filing game reports; writing, editing, and laying out brochures; preparing game programs; selling advertising space; overseeing promotional activities; compiling records and statistics; organizing a photo file system; planning and conducting press conferences; answering requests from publications and organizations; managing a press box staff and managing the press box on game day; organizing a radio or television network; and any other duties assigned by the athletic director or other supervisor.

The scope and relative importance of these duties vary widely from one information office to another. The part-time sports information director at a small college is probably not concerned with television contracts or weekly telephonic press conferences, just as the Big 10 sports information director is not responsible for taking the team pictures. If you are interested in sports information, prepare yourself for a diversity of duties by developing knowledge and skills in a variety of areas.

Cooperating with local media is just one of a sports information director's many duties.

Weekly News Release

Nothing is more basic to the sports information profession than the weekly news release. An information specialist must decide which of the various forms of releases is most appropriate in his or her marketplace. Writing a three-page release in paragraph form would be a waste of time for the sports information director at a moderate-size urban school, because the sports editor of the local newspaper would not use it. This publicist would be better off writing an introductory paragraph and filling out the release with notes, quotes, and other pertinent data that could spawn a feature story or column idea. On the other hand, the sports information director at a school located in a small town might find four area newspapers in the 10,000 to 20,000 circulation range that would run verbatim the three-page release in paragraph form.

No matter what form the release takes, it should emphasize upcoming contests and events, not past events. What happened last Saturday is old news. The important facts are who your team is playing, the teams' records, and what the fan can expect to see. A detailed description of the previous week's action is inappropriate. Highlighting individual accomplishments does embellish the release, but the focal point must be the future.

Hometown Story

A time-consuming yet worthwhile form of news release is a hometown story. The 30,000-circulation paper 20 miles from your campus probably is not interested in the fact that Johnny Smith ran for 15 yards on three carries or that Susie Jones had three kills in the volleyball match, but the 7,000 circulation newspapers in Johnny's and Susie's hometowns want to know about it. A hometown story, or *hometowner*, should be sent out on every athlete on each team at least once a year. The hometowner can be a short release, or a full-length feature story with accompanying photos if appropriate. Hometowners are good projects to assign to student assistants or interns.

Media Guides

Much of the work done by the sports information office is behind the scenes, but media guides and game programs are visual reflections of the office's production. A media guide or brochure—the terms are usually used interchangeably in the profession—can be a folded 8-1/2″ × 11″ sheet of paper or it can be a 128-page, multicolor, bound book.

All Division I schools and many Division II and III schools produce brochures for football and men's basketball. If budget restrictions permit, the sports information office should produce a well-designed, factual brochure for all sports offered by the school. The number of pages is significant, but the quality of the piece is far more important than its size.

Most brochures serve a dual purpose: providing the news media with information and providing coaches with a recruiting tool. The largest variable is the size of the brochure. In determining the appropriate size, remember that producing a brochure that the coach wants as a recruiting tool should not compromise the inclusion of facts that the news media need.

Game Programs

Sports information directors can choose from a wide range of sizes and financial investments in producing game day programs. A simple photocopied roster can serve the purpose of a game program, and yet football programs at Division I schools often extend to 100 pages or more and often are printed in four colors.

The most significant difference between a brochure and a game program is the target audience. A brochure is printed for the media and as a recruiting tool, but a game program is printed for the fans. A 48-page program filled with stories and photos is a waste if an average of only 25 copies are sold per game. On the other hand, if distribution is sufficient you'll find no better place to tell your school's story to the public than in the game program. A news release must go through an editor to reach the public, and a brochure has a limited audience, but a game program is delivered directly to the hands of the public. Feature stories on the athletic teams, student athletes, and the university in general enhance a game program if time and space permit their inclusion.

Many schools have elected to increase the size of their football game programs by including a preprinted national supplement that has information on college football in general. These supplements add color to the program and greatly increase its size. The argument against using them is that they may take the focus away from the school's athletic and academic programs and accomplishments.

Advertising

At many schools, the task of selling advertising for game programs is under the jurisdiction of the sports information office. Selling advertising can provide a nice bonus if a sales commission is involved, but selling ads is a time-consuming task for what is in many cases an already overworked staffer. This assignment is frequently delegated to assistants or interns.

Statistics

Some information directors feel that statistics are the bane of the profession. Yet all recognize the importance of maintaining accurate and complete team and individual records. A fact-conscious sports editor or all-star team voter wants numbers, not vague adjectives. A fast football player has a best time for the 40-yard dash; a pole vaulter who has an off day clears a height a given number of inches or feet less than his personal best; a softball pitcher who is struggling with her control walks a specific number of batters or falls behind in the count a certain percentage of the time.

Photographs

At many of the smaller schools, the sports information director is responsible for taking photographs, both mug shots and action photos. Whether this task falls to the information director or is handled by the university photo service or a freelance photographer, the sports information office should have an organized photo

Maintaining accurate team and individual statistics is one responsibility of the sports information staff.

filing system so that photo requests can be filled in a timely manner.

Answering Requests

One of the simplest tasks, yet one that the information director often avoids, is filling out questionnaires. These requests forms come from regional and national publications, conference offices, opponents' schools, and other organizations affiliated with collegiate athletics.

An unanswered questionnaire can cause production problems for the person or organization sending out the form, but more importantly, it can diminish the positive publicity and visibility of the school. With rare exceptions, these questionnaires are easy to understand and do not require excessive time or effort to complete. The time spent on these can later prove to be time well spent. These questionnaires ask basic information such as the site of your school, the enrollment, the name of your coach and her or his record, and the number of returning letter winners. The questionnaires may also request more subjective information such as a brief outlook of your team.

Press Box Management

Properly staffing and managing a press box is an aspect of sports information that is both important and visible. Press box management can be divided into two basic functions: serving the media and setting up and running a statistical operation. Later parts of this chapter discuss the varying needs of the print and electronic media.

A good statistical crew in the press box is a major asset to the sports information operation. A stat crew can be as few as two people for a small college basketball game or 8 to 10 people for a Division I football game. The stat crew may consist of professionals, students, or a combination. An all-professional crew helps in terms of continuity, but information offices with a strong corps of student workers or budgetary restrictions frequently use students in the press box. The information director should convey to all workers the need to maintain a professional atmosphere; cheering has no place in a press box.

Game Reporting

Game reporting is a function of the sports information office at all schools. Game reporting may be a simple matter of calling the wire services with the game score. On the other hand, information specialists at small and medium-sized schools in rural areas may find it worth their time to write a game story for the local paper. This extra effort, although time consuming, can produce greater exposure than a phone call with the scoring summary.

Press Conferences

Like so many other aspects of the profession, the size and scope of press conferences vary tremendously between the division levels. Small schools usually hold press conferences only for special occasions: the hiring of a new athletic director, the announcement of plans to renovate the stadium, or some other one-time event.

At the other end of the spectrum, the sheer volume of requests to interview Division I football coaches mandates the need for press conferences on a regular basis. A 1-hour press conference, possibly with an electronic hookup for the opponent's local media, reduces the amount of time that the coach has to devote to interviews. The sports information director's responsibilities for press conferences include establishing a time and site convenient for the majority of the media, inviting and in some cases encouraging the media to attend, introducing the featured speakers, and coordinating one-on-one interviews.

The Media

News media are divided into two distinct groups: print and electronic. Radio and television broadcasters tell their stories as the game unfolds or immediately after with a live report from the site of the contest. A good sports information staff assists the electronic media by apprising broadcasters of records, pertinent statistics, and out-of-town scores. Representatives of the print media watch the game and tell their stories later, in tomorrow's paper or next week's magazine. Members of the print media have needs as the game progresses, but their needs are not as urgent from a time standpoint as those of the electronic media.

Some basic rules of conduct help in maintaining a symbiotic relationship with the media: Establish rapport with the sports editors and directors of local media outlets; understand the needs of the media; know the work schedules of key media personnel; be available to the media; be honest—never intentionally mislead the media; inform student athletes how to inter-

act with the media; never hold grudges against members of the media; never favor one member of the media over another; and keep communication lines open.

THE JOB MARKET

Twenty years ago, the prototype sports information director was an aging former star or frustrated athlete who excelled at telling stories in smoke-filled rooms. Sports information, not by decree but in practice, was an all-male profession. Currently, the profession is open to anyone who has the appropriate education, the required skills, and the positive attitude necessary to fulfill the duties of this demanding field.

Prior to the mid-1970s, the market for jobs in sports information was very limited. Even the largest schools rarely had more than two full-time sports information staff members, and these people usually stayed with the same job for a long period of time. In this setting, the "good ol' boy" network was self-perpetuating. That situation has changed dramatically. The growth of women's sports has increased the work load for a sports information office to the point that most large schools have three or more full-time staff members, and many moderate-sized schools have at least two full-time professionals. The turnover rate has also increased. These two phenomena have opened doors for more young people and more women to enter the profession.

Rosa Gatti was a pioneer in the field when she was hired at Villanova University in 1974. She was the first woman to hold the title of sports information director at a Division I school. Gatti, who later left the field to become a television executive, said in a panel discussion at the 1987 CoSIDA workshop, "It takes a long time to reverse attitudes that have been in existence for more than 100 years." Gatti said her concern for people with whom she worked and her willingness to confront problems when necessary were key factors in her successful career in sports information. "I liken my career to a tea bag," Gatti said. "It wasn't until I was in hot water that I realized my full strength."

Breaking into a profession is a matter of proper preparation and timing—being in the right place at the right time. Journalism, sport management, communications, and public relations are some of the academic majors that can lay the foundation for an aspiring sports information professional. No matter what major you choose, be sure to take writing and computer courses. Prior to the growth of sports information staffs in the late 1970s and early 1980s, newspaper writers provided the pool from which most sports information specialists were hired. Currently, the vast majority entering the profession come from within the ranks of the profession. Student assistants and interns become full-time assistants, and full-time assistants become directors.

Experience is more important than a specific academic major such as sport management or journalism. When hiring assistants, most directors will not even consider an applicant who has no sports information experience, regardless of his or her academic background. Volunteer service in a sports information office is an important first step. Volunteering for tasks such as stuffing envelopes, clipping newspaper articles, or working on the volleyball stats crew often leads to a paid position, which can lead to permanent employment.

Sports information positions are advertised in *NCAA News*, the weekly newspaper published by the NCAA, and in *CoSIDA Digest*, the association's monthly newsletter. In 1985, CoSIDA initiated a job placement service at the CoSIDA workshop. Job seekers as well as employers who are interested in hiring personnel register for the service, and interviews are held during the workshop. Although jobs are not usually offered on the spot, productive contacts are made, often leading to offers.

An exciting career awaits individuals who have the good fortune to enter the sports information profession. Yes, there are long hours, tight deadlines, unhappy coaches, and many other frustrations, but most sports information specialists look forward to going to work each morning, a claim not made by many!

LEARNING ACTIVITIES

1. Develop an athlete information sheet to be filled out by all varsity athletes at the school where you are the sports information director.

2. Write a sample news release to promote the men's and women's swimming meet to be held this weekend at your college. The meet will determine the conference champion in both the men's and women's divisions and represents the first time in school history that either team has finished higher than third place.

3. Over the next 6 weeks, develop a sample file for an athlete on your campus. You may include the athlete's information sheet, photos, stories you write about the athlete, and clips of published stories.

Professional Organizations

College Sports Information Directors of America (CoSIDA)

Football Writers Association of America (FWAA)

United States Basketball Writers Association (USBWA)

National College Baseball Writers Association (NCBWA)

Professional Publications

CoSIDA Digest
NCAA Public Relations and Promotion Manual
NCAA News
Athletic Administration
Chronicle of Higher Education

REFERENCES

Gatti, R. (1987). Panel discussion at the College Sports Information Directors Association workshop, Portland, OR.

Ranley, D. (1987). *Ranley revisited*. Lecture delivered at the College Sports Information Directors of America workshop, Portland, OR.

CHAPTER 7

Sport Marketing

Robert L. Callecod
Bowling Green Parks and Recreation

David K. Stotlar
University of Northern Colorado

Sport marketing is a relatively new and exciting career field that offers diverse entry-level opportunities with excellent potential for management-and-administrative career advancement. Although sport marketing is among the most dynamic and challenging specializations in sport management, it is also probably the least understood concentration in sport. This lack of understanding may be attributed to the fact that most people associate the field of marketing exclusively with the promotion and sale of products. Quiz questions found throughout this chapter will test your knowledge of various terms associated with sport marketing.

Θ Sport Marketing Quiz Question 1: What is Marketing?

_____ A. Sales

_____ B. Advertising and promotion

_____ C. Public relations

_____ D. Needs assessment

_____ E. Program development

_____ F. Pricing

_____ G. Scheduling and distribution

_____ H. All of the above

If you answered *H* to Question 1, you are more knowledgeable than 90 percent of college administrators polled in an American Marketing Association survey (Careers in Marketing, 1983). These administrators identified marketing with sales and promotion, nothing more.

SPORT MARKETING DEFINED

Virtually every book or article on basic marketing contains a different definition of marketing. The following definition includes the basic components of the marketing process.

Marketing is the process of (a) accomplishing objectives of the organization by means of a coordinated set of activities and (b) providing programs, products, and services that satisfy client needs. Let's break that definition down and discuss some of the critical components.

Coordinated Activities

Marketing is a process involving a coordinated set of activities. The activities normally included in the process are

- conducting research to determine customer needs and interests,

- putting together a research-based sport product or program package, which you hope will satisfy the identified needs and interests,
- pricing the product or program or developing a plan for raising money to finance the program,
- deciding when and where to conduct the program or distribute the product,
- developing and implementing a plan for informing the public about your program or product and convincing people to buy or attend, and
- selling your program or product.

Each of these activities represents a major area of professional opportunity within the field of sport marketing. Remember that you don't "do" marketing—rather, you perform some or all of the activities that make up the marketing process.

Four Ps of Marketing

The activities that make up the marketing process are often referred to as the four Ps of marketing: product, price, place, and promotion. Following is a brief description of these activities and their significance in sport management.

Product.   The sport product can be a tangible item such as a basketball; a program such as the Lakers versus the Celtics; a service such as a series of golf lessons; or a facility such as the Silverdome. A unique aspect of sport marketing is that we not only deal with core products such as these, but we also need to consider *product extensions*. Product extensions are additional programs, products, services, and facilities that are either essential or desirable in order to satisfy the needs of the customers. Examples of product extensions are food and beverage services, clubhouse facilities, program booklets, parking lots and parking lot attendants, and restroom facilities.

Price.   Management must determine the price of tickets to events, the charge for participation in a program, or the cost of a tangible product. Pricing should be based on a number of factors such as the cost of the product, the cost of getting the product to the public, the willingness of the public to pay for the product, and the amount of profit sought by management or the amount of subsidy the manager or administrator can generate for the program.

Place.   Place refers to the date and location of an event or to the date and location a product, program, or service is available.

Promotion.   This is probably the most common marketing term. The successful sport marketer utilizes four types of promotional activities: personal contact or word of mouth, advertising, publicity, and incentives. All representatives of an organization must make contact with influential people in the community and market area. Word of mouth from satisfied customers and from respected people in your community is the most effective promotional tool you can use. The sport marketer can also pay for advertising in the print or electronic media or for brochures or billboards. Publicity is essentially free advertising, usually generated by giving press releases to the media. Incentives are methods for encouraging people to use or to increase their use of your program or product. Incentives include discount or "two-for-one" ticket offers, merchandise giveaways such as free bats or hats at the ball game, raffles of major products such as a car to a lucky ticket holder, or special events such as fireworks after the game.

Don't be surprised if you accept a job in marketing and promotion or marketing and sales and find that you aren't involved with all of the four marketing activities. The term *marketing* is often misused in business and the sport industry.

Meeting Client Needs

The programs, products, or services must satisfy client needs and accomplish organizational objectives. Remember that one of the major marketing activities is conducting research to determine customer needs and interests. After you accomplish that objective, you must determine which customer needs and interests your organization is most capable of satisfying. You should base this decision on whether you have the trained personnel, the proper facilities and equipment, and the financing necessary to develop a suitable program. Along with the decision about satisfying customer needs, you must determine if the proposed project will enhance your organization's ability to meet its objectives. Organizational objectives might be as altruistic as reducing juvenile crime in your community through sport programming or as basic as increasing revenues by $20,000.

Professional Organizations

North American Society for Sport
  Management (NASSM)
National Association of Collegiate Directors
  of Athletics (NACDA)
National Association of Athletic, Marketing,
  and Development Directors (NAAMDD)
American Marketing Association (AMA)

Professional Publications

Journal of Sport Management
Journal of Marketing Research
The Sport Marketing Institute Manual
Sports Market Place

Products, Programs, and Services

The marketing process must provide products, programs, and services. Products usually are tangible items you can manufacture and store, such as bicycles or baseball bats. Programs and services generally are intangible, inconsistent,

and/or perishable (i.e., tickets for yesterday's game are worthless). One of the several unique aspects of sport marketing is that virtually all sporting events or sport occasions include all three components: products, programs, and services. If you go bowling, you use a bowling ball (product) to bowl a line (program), and you probably buy a drink from the bar or machine (service). As a spectator at a game (program), you watch the players while you sit in the bleachers (product), and you probably take advantage of the concessions and washrooms (services).

In marketing terms, the game or activity (the *core product*) is generally only a small portion of the total package of products and services that make up a sporting event.

Product marketing may be found in many facets of a sport event.

⊖ Sport Marketing Quiz Question 2: What is Sport Marketing?

_____ A. The use of sport or sport figures to promote consumer products

_____ B. The marketing of sport products

_____ C. The marketing of sport as a product

_____ D. All of the above

Most people guess *A* for Question 2. *Advertising Age* magazine is generally credited with coining the term *sport marketing* in 1978 to describe the use of sport as a promotional vehicle for consumer and industrial products. Most people probably still perceive sport marketing in this context, and excellent job opportunities do exist in this area.

If you answered *B*—sport marketing is the marketing of sport products—you are also correct; every sport requires some sort of equipment or apparel. Some less obvious sport products include tickets, bleachers, the stadium, the computer program that schedules our league games, and chlorine for the pool. The sport and leisure industry sells billions of dollars worth of sport products annually. Successful sport product marketers meet the needs of sport participants by arranging the manufacture and delivery of appropriate products for the participants who need them.

If you said that sport marketing was *C*—the marketing of sport as a product—you are correct and very astute, because many overlook this aspect of sport marketing. Sporting events are products, even though they are quite unique from traditional consumer products. For example, successful consumer products thrive on consistency and reliability. If a product does not perform as advertised, the manufacturer generally guarantees a refund of the purchase price or replacement or repair of the product. In contrast to consumer products, sports events and games are notoriously inconsistent and unreliable. Few owners of sports teams guarantee their team will win on any given day, and regardless of how the team performs, the performances of individual players inherently vary from game to game. The consistency of the sport product is further complicated by the very real possibility that at all levels of sport, the roster of players on the team may change from game to game.

Another unique characteristic of sport as a product has significant implications for sport marketers: The sporting event itself has no value after it has occurred. You cannot sell tickets to yesterday's game, nor can you ever recover the revenue lost from an empty racquetball court or open tee-off time. Sport as a product, therefore, must be sold in advance.

The sport marketer must put together a product and convince people to buy that product with no guarantee of outcome or quality of performance. Therein lies the unique challenge to sport marketers.

MARKET RESEARCH

Sport marketing research may assist management in making decisions regarding critical items. Marketing research can help identify the portion of the population that is most likely to use your facilities or products; these segments of the population are *target markets*. For example, some major league baseball franchises have discovered through marketing research that young, childless adults are better prospects for attending games than are families with young children, even though the latter group has usually been associated with the game of baseball.

Based on that kind of research information, management can also determine which kinds of promotional campaigns are most effective in influencing those target groups. Special events such as rock concerts after the game might be more appealing to the young adult crowd, whereas bat days and hat days might be better for drawing families with young children.

Market research can also help identify the needs and interests of the target groups. Cross-country skiing, for example, was not very popular with young adults until the form-fitting Lycra® ski outfits were introduced. Prior to the introduction of those outfits, cross-country skiers typically wore bulky wool sweaters and baggy knickers. The Lycra® outfits permitted the skiers to ski comfortably and, more importantly, stylishly—a very important criterion for the fashion-conscious young population.

Marketing research can also assist management in making key financial decisions. You can determine optimum ticket price levels by conducting studies to determine at what dollar level customers indicate a resistance to buying tickets.

Very few sport organizations conduct all of their own marketing research. Some rely on industry publications such as *Amusement Business*, *Sponsors Report*, *Sporting Goods News*, and Simmons Market Research Bureau's *Study of Media and Markets* for research information. Others hire marketing research consultants to conduct research investigations. One such organization is Joyce Julius & Associates, which through its subsidiary *Sponsors Report* conducts research and analyzes sporting events for clients.

Anheuser-Busch, the well-known brewing company, has been heavily involved in sport marketing for many years and has utilized the services of the *Sponsors Report*. The value of having race cars or hydroplanes decorated in a product's colors is difficult to measure. *Sponsors Report* analyzes each event that Anheuser-Busch sponsors; the consultant reviews a videotape of the event and measures the exact amount of "clear in-focus camera exposure" for the client's name and logo as well as the number of times that the announcers mention the product or company name. *Sponsors Report* then calculates a dollar value for this exposure based on the rate charged to commercial advertisers during the television program. This is an extremely important service, because corporations like Anheuser-Busch spend millions of dollars each year on sport-related marketing, and they need specific price value relationship information.

Careers in this area are likely to expand as more companies enter the sport marketing field and as corporations demand to know the return for their investments. Because many colleges and universities recruit corporate sponsors for their programs, sport marketing research may be a service that universities would provide to their sponsors. Therefore, the path to sport marketing careers may be through advertising agencies or through the corporations themselves. Or, as in many areas of sport marketing, the enterprising young professional can start his or her own company to provide these services on a consultation basis.

As more and more sport organizations and departments are held accountable for revenues and attendance, the need for sport market researchers will grow. If you have appropriate training in research methods and statistics, you may find a number of entry-level positions available in sport organizations. Experienced market researchers have increasing opportunities to serve as consultants to sport organizations or as the directors of newly formed internal marketing research departments.

Specialized Market Researchers

Data collection specialists and *interviewers* spend most of their time conducting personal or telephone interviews. Generally these are entry-level positions that require minimal formal educational training. Usually, organizations conducting data collection for marketing purposes provide on-the-job training. Although these jobs are not difficult in terms of their complexity, they do require a special type of person. Some of the attributes of a good data collection specialist or interviewer are a pleasant personality, a good speaking voice, a willingness to talk with total strangers, patience, attention to detail, ability to record data accurately, and ability to follow instructions explicitly.

Market research analysts are responsible for designing surveys and opinion polls and for supervising the conduct of surveys. These individuals must then collect the data from all the surveys, enter the data into a computer, analyze the results, and perhaps draft a report of their findings and recommendations.

The *senior market analyst* or *director of marketing research* generally is responsible for advising top management about the way that the sport product is packaged. Market analysts should have experience or formal training in statistics, computer operations, research methods, and survey design. Obviously, if you want to work in this type of job, you should enjoy working with numbers and computers. These jobs require much dedication and long hours of work with computer programs and printouts that detect trends in consumer preferences and interests. Sport marketing researchers must be analytical and objective. They must possess verbal and written skills that enable them to communicate clearly, concisely, and convincingly with clients and managers.

You may have an image of the university researcher spending months and months working on laboratory projects and writing dull research reports. That generally is not the case in marketing research; the researcher is usually expected to collect, analyze, and report on research information very quickly. The emphasis in marketing research is on making the best judgments based on the best information that can be obtained in the shortest possible period of time.

Target Markets

Market researchers provide clients with a lot of information about *target markets*, those people or groups of people whom we most want to use our facilities, see our events, or buy our products. This information includes demographic data such as dominant age groups of the population, gender distribution, income categories, and marital or family status. The information should also include some psychographic data such as the attitudes of the people toward the sport and their present leisure interests and activities.

One of the areas in which you can most frequently witness market segmentation and the identification of target markets is in the media and entertainment industry. Every magazine, radio station, and television station compiles data about its readers, listeners, or viewers and uses that information to attract advertisers. For example, NBC Sports ran an advertisement in *Sports Marketing News* (1987) to recruit potential advertisers for the network's sport programming. The ad included data indicating that the network's telecast of the 1987 World Championships of Track & Field attracted a much greater percentage of households with four or more family members and more upper-income, college-educated professionals than the typical summertime sport program.

Target market information and other data (including past experience and trend data from trade publications) tell sport managers that in today's market simply bringing together a couple of teams won't necessarily draw crowds. To be successful today, marketers must put together a product package consisting of the main event; safe, clean, and comfortable facilities; and amenities such as convenient parking, food and concessions, and perhaps additional entertainment.

MANAGERS

The person who is responsible for the program (or product) package might have one of any number of job titles ranging from marketing director to event coordinator to marketing manager; to simplify things we will use the latter title. The process of putting together the product package is often called event management or special event marketing and represents the essence of sport marketing. It is probably the fastest growing and most dynamic segment of the sport and entertainment market.

Sport facility and auditorium managers may do their own event marketing, or they may have a staff member with the title of director of marketing and promotions, special event programmer or coordinator, or marketing specialist. This individual's main task is to contact agents representing teams, players, or entertainers to schedule bookings. If the sport facility or auditorium is a prime venue, the agents may make the initial contact.

Sports Market Place is a trade publication containing comprehensive lists of companies, agencies, teams, and associations connected with sports. The 1987 edition of *Sports Market Place* (Lipsey, 1987) lists nearly 300 agencies offering event management or promotional services. The rapid growth in demand for this type of service is indicated by the fact that most of those agencies were founded during the 1980s. The following is a list of the services offered by some of those agencies.

- Managing sporting events including promotion, facility scheduling, press coverage, recruiting services, and on-site management
- Developing and executing promotional aspects of events such as press releases, celebrity appearances, and media tours
- Creating sports events to reach specific publics and specific product exposure
- Handling on-site press relations and results servicing; building special promotions to maximize exposure for event and sponsor
- Designing, constructing, and merchandising mascot characters for major professional teams
- Marketing companies interested in achieving specific marketing, sales, or public relations objectives through the use of sport and leisure time activities
- Creating events or concepts; handling on-site management, sponsorship, sales support material production, and corporate event usage consulting
- Conducting feasibility studies, public relations, and media buying
- Establishing liaison and contact with sport governing bodies; developing recommendations for on-site signage and advertising; negotiating for sale of national television rights
- Publicizing and promoting programs to achieve maximum target market participation, sponsor identification, and exposure

The International Management Group has been one of the major corporations in the sport marketing and management field for almost 2 decades. Founder Mark McCormack has expanded the company into a worldwide corporation that has produced television programming for Wimbledon, the NFL, the U.S. Tennis Association, the U.S. Golf Association, and the NCAA. The company has advised summer and winter Olympic Games organizers and has represented some of the world's top professional athletes, including Arnold Palmer, Muhammed Ali, Billie Jean King, Martina Navratilova, and Bjorn Borg. The company's annual revenues approach $1 billion (McCormack, 1987). The other major corporations in the sport marketing and representation business, ProServe and Advantage International, also have very impressive lists of clients and services.

According to *Sports inc.* (Pendleton, 1988), sport marketing may be entering a new era in which the major international advertising agencies will dominate the industry. This has been evidenced by the recruitment of the Marlboro Group and Event Programming International Consultants (respective subsidiaries of the Saatchi & Saatchi and Interpublic advertising firms) to serve as consultants for the Barcelona Olympic Organizing Committee. The main reasons that traditional sport marketing firms and advertising agencies are becoming competitors are that more clients are entering the sport arena as sponsors and advertisers, and the ad companies are losing business to sport-specific marketing organizations.

If you consider the diversity of services that sport marketers offer, you'll see that few young graduates are going to enter the job market with all of the skills necessary to head up a special event marketing team. That should not discourage you from entering this field, because you'll learn or hone many skills on the job.

If special event marketing sounds interesting, you should be aware of some of the skills that are indispensable. Sport marketing is the ultimate personal contact type job, involving direct contact with clients, players, performers, vendors, agents, public officials, media representatives, employees, and consumers. You must be able to inform, educate, negotiate, placate, delegate, mandate, and persuade. The event marketer is fair but firm, friendly and honest. The days have passed for the fly-by-night event promoters who relied on promises, promotional gimmicks, and media hype but didn't honor agreements with clients, performers, or customers.

The special event marketer should have a keen understanding of contract negotiation and budgeting. You may put together one of the greatest events ever held in your community, but if it is a financial disaster for your company or your client, you won't be in business very long.

In spite of the glamour of associating with big names and media exposure, the special event marketer spends the majority of time taking care of the details that ultimately will mark the success or failure of the event.

PROMOTERS

Promotion is one of the four Ps of the marketing mix; therefore, it is one part of the marketing process. Frequently, however, job descriptions indicate that the position requires responsibility for "marketing and promotion," implying that promotions are not part of the marketing mix but are a separate entity. This is another example of misuse of terminology.

You will also find numerous instances in which people engage in sport promotions but are not classified as sport promoters. In collegiate settings, for example, many assistant athletic directors handle promotions as their primary responsibilities. Other titles with which responsibilities for promotional activities may not be obvious are public affairs director, public relations officer, media relations specialist, and possibly sports information director.

Promotional Tools

Promotion is the use of communications to persuade a client or customer to buy, consume, or otherwise participate in your sport product or event. Four primary promotional tools are available to the sport marketer: advertising, publicity, incentives, and personal contact.

Advertising

Advertising is any paid form of persuasive communication, but it usually involves either print or electronic media. It may be as simple as distributing a flyer—prepared and printed in your office—to all the dorms on campus, or it may be as sophisticated as a 1-minute, $1-billion advertisement on prime-time television. Most sport agencies utilize professional advertising agencies or printing firms to produce finished ads. Regardless of the process, sport marketers should have a basic understanding of the terms and concepts utilized by the various advertising media. With the advent of microcomputers and easy-to-use graphic arts software programs, sport promoters can produce in-house brochures and other information materials that are quite sophisticated.

Publicity

Publicity is nonpaid advertising that usually comes in the form of articles or news items in the media that are based on information provided by a spokesperson for your agency or client. Generally, the spokesperson is the director of sports information or public relations.

Incentives

Incentives are intended to encourage first-time users and to retain present users or increase their levels of use of your product or facility. The opportunities for incentives seem limitless, but they can be categorized into at least three major themes: price reduction incentives, product give-aways, and special events.

The most common variety of price reduction incentive is the two-for-one coupon, which entitles one person to get in free if accompanied by one paying customer. In the trade, these incentives are known as ''two-fers.'' Other price-related incentives that involve the products of sponsors are pre- or post-event purchases. For example, the local hardware store gives out coupons worth $1 off the price of a ticket to your sports event. Using another approach, you can take your ticket stub to a fast food restaurant after the game and receive a free order of fries with the purchase of a hamburger.

Product giveaway incentives are typified by ''Bat Day'' at the ball park, when bats are given to the first 5,000 youngsters to enter the ball park. Special events such as fireworks displays or rock concerts after the game continue to gain popularity as incentives.

Incentive promotion ideas are perhaps the most challenging and creative job opportunities for sport marketers; these jobs obviously require considerable imagination, creativity, and persuasiveness. The promoter needs to convince the organization that the promotion will have a positive effect on attendance and revenues, and the promoter probably will need to find sponsors for financing and endorsing the promotional events.

Personal Contact

Regardless of the sophistication and magnitude of an agency's advertising, publicity, and incentive campaigns, personal contact and word of mouth generally are the most critical elements of promotion. The sport marketer (or the sports information director) can obtain favorable publicity by aggressively seeking positive personal contacts with representatives of the media. The promoter can arrange for managers, coaches, and players to speak to community groups or appear at major community or public relations events. Ironically, the sport marketer has the least amount of control over word of mouth or indirect personal contact. Those persons who actually use your product or facility will tell their friends and associates about their experiences. If the experience was a good one, the user will probably return and bring some friends along. If the experience was a bad one, the user probably will not return and will discourage others from doing so as well.

Because of the effect that personal contact with users and potential users has on the long-term success of any business, the job of sport marketing ultimately falls on everyone connected with a sport agency. The owner, the players, the director of marketing, and even parking lot attendants must realize that they are in business to satisfy the needs and interests of the customers.

SPECIAL EVENT MARKETING—CORPORATE SPONSORSHIP

We have discussed ways to market sport as a product; another form of sport marketing is the use of sport to promote industrial and consumer products. This form of sport marketing is very prominent today in special sport and entertainment events.

The popularity and positive image of sport and entertainment events prompt many corporations to affiliate with those events as corporate sponsors. Citing corporate special-events marketing as one of "The 25 Hottest Careers of 1987," *Working Woman* magazine claimed that "in 1987 more than 3,000 companies will put up more than a billion dollars to pin their names on dozens of sporting and cultural events" (Konrad & Tedeschi, 1987, p. 58). One of the major functions of many sport-marketing agencies is obtaining sponsors for sporting events, or vice versa. In turn, many major companies hire their own special event marketers to analyze proposals for sponsorship received from event promoters, or companies may even seek out their own events.

Corporate special event marketers today are quite concerned with the appropriate match of their corporate name and products with a sporting event. These marketers devote considerable effort to conduct marketing research that will help define the types of people who watch or participate in various events. Insurance companies and banks are the major sponsors of marathon running events, because marketing research indicates that both the runners and spectators of marathons tend to be upper-income professionals who are prime potential consumers of banking and insurance services. This is one example of the level of sophistication and thoroughness of good marketing research—and of how successful companies are utilizing that research.

FUND RAISING

Fund raising is generally conducted by not-for-profit organizations to raise money for special projects and programs. Fund raising may involve finding one or several corporate sponsors, as discussed in the previous section of this chapter. However, fund raising is usually geared toward solicitation from either the general public or from target groups of people such as graduates or parents of students. Because corporate sponsorship has already been mentioned, the following discussion concentrates on solicitation.

Solicitation projects are of two types: direct and indirect. Direct solicitation involves contacting people by telephone, by mail, or in person with a request for contributions. University athletic departments often engage in direct solicitation of graduates and friends to raise funds for athletic scholarships or new athletic facilities and equipment that cannot be obtained through the schools' budgets.

Indirect solicitation generally involves raising money through ticket and merchandise sales at special events planned specifically for that purpose. The events might range from candy sales to extravagant cocktail parties and dinners.

The need for skilled and creative people to handle fund-raising efforts is becoming more acute in all areas of amateur sport. Successful fund raisers will quickly pay for their salaries and generate far more revenues for the organization.

Fund raisers should have strong communication and human relation skills. They must be persuasive, well organized, and capable of organizing others. Most important is the ability to utilize marketing skills to measure the types of programs and events that will encourage target populations to donate generously to the cause.

SALES

If you do a good job of marketing, no selling should be necessary because the product will sell itself. If you put together the right program package at the right time, place, and price—a package that meets the needs and interests of the target market—then all you should have to do is let people know about it and be prepared to take orders and collect money for tickets.

Of course, things do not always work out that well. But, when you interview with the marketing and sales department of an organization, find out how much time is spent on marketing compared to the time spent on sales. A company with an effective marketing program will spend far more time marketing than trying to sell.

Selling is important to any organization, but it should be utilized as only one component of a powerful set of marketing tools. Selling, as with all the other components of the marketing process, is easier and more successful if the product package is designed to satisfy the identified needs and interests of the customer.

Contrary to popular belief, the successful salesperson is a better listener than talker. After listening to the customers express their needs, the good salesperson will sell a package of benefits designed to satisfy those needs, rather than selling products or services. For example,

the salesperson offers potential customers the opportunity to look better and feel good about themselves, rather than simply offering an aerobics program. Few senior citizens go to baseball games alone, but groups of senior citizens could enjoy an outing to the ball park if refreshments and souvenirs are part of the package.

PUBLIC RELATIONS

A growing trend in the sport marketing field is for individual states and municipalities to form sport authorities or sport commissions. The purpose of these organizations is to attract major sporting events to their area. These range from professional boxing matches to events such as the Olympic Festival. The ultimate rationale is the attraction of the tourist dollar, but the public relations that a city or state receives from these events can have positive effects that last for years. In the 1980s, Indianapolis made major

This team was one of many that participated in major sporting events in Indianapolis during the 1980's.

strides in persuading several national sport organizations to move their headquarters to the city and was also successful in hosting the Pan American Games in 1986. In the future, many more cities and regions of the country will form such enterprises, and this should increase your job possibilities.

⊖ Sport Marketing Quiz Question 3: Which of the Following is the Primary Objective of a Marketing-Oriented Organization?

_____ A. Numbers through the door and dollars in the drawer

_____ B. Customer satisfaction

If you answered *A*, go back and read the chapter again. If you answered *B*, you now realize the exciting challenges and growing opportunities in sport marketing. A knowledge of sport marketing is a powerful management tool that can greatly enhance your career opportunities in sport management.

LEARNING ACTIVITIES

1. Look through magazines and newspapers (such as *USA Today*) and collect examples of ads or articles dealing with or depicting various aspects of sport marketing. Include with each item an explanation of the message the ad was trying to convey or how the article relates to sport marketing.

2. You are the director of marketing at a university sports arena, and you have just booked the Harlem Globe Trotters and the noted rock band, Mogen David and the Grapes of Wrath, for a special event. The Trotters will be flying into the nearest airport, whereas the Grapes have their own bus. Both groups will stay overnight and will leave the following morning. Make a list of the details you must handle.

REFERENCES

Careers in marketing. (1983). Chicago: American Marketing Association.

Konrad, W., & Tedeschi, J. (1987, July). The 25 hottest careers of 1987. *Working Woman*, pp. 57-64, 90-91.

Lipsey, R.A. (Ed.), *Sports market place 1987*. Princeton, NJ: Sportguide.

McCormack, M.H. (1987). *The terrible truth about lawyers*. New York: Beech Tree Books.

Pendleton, J. (1988, October 10). Marketing's added status. *Sports inc.*, pp. 40-41, **1**(38).

Sports Marketing News. (1987, March 30). [Advertisement], p. 24.

CHAPTER 8

Sports Journalism

Catherine A. Pratt

The Ohio State University

Most of us realize at an early age that our interests in sports are not going to lead us to careers in professional athletics, because most of us do not have the talents that a pro sport career demands. But a love of athletics has led many amateur athletes to a career associated with athletics: sports journalism. Sports journalists may write for newspapers or magazines or may cover and package reports on sports-related topics for radio or television stations. Sports journalism can also mean a career in the visual aspects of journalism—as a photographer for print publications or a videographer/editor for television.

Success in the field may lead to a similar position on a bigger publication or in a larger market, but it can also result in a position of greater authority at the same media outlet (e.g., an editor's job) or a promotion to a higher level of print or broadcast management. Some sports journalists cross over from the journalistic side of covering athletics to public relations jobs with professional or collegiate athletic organizations. Practitioners in the field range from your local newspaper's sports reporter to the head of ABC Sports, plus everything in between. Because the field's most prominent jobs are those connected with network television and professional athletics, sports journalism tends to have an aura of glamour. Many people head into the field without giving enough thought to the demands of a career in this area, and many people fail in the field because they don't secure the proper

academic and extracurricular preparation necessary to land and succeed in that critical first job.

WHAT SPORTS JOURNALISTS DO

It has been said that journalists write the first draft of history. Sports journalists are no different from other journalists in that respect. Some recent articles written about sports have included events more likely to be found on the front page of the news section than on the sports page. The involvement of professional and college athletes with drugs, the controversy over whether college athletes are getting a real education, and other not-so-positive stories are not necessarily what some die-hard sports fans really want to read about; but these stories are news, and a journalist's job is to investigate the news and get the facts to the public.

These kinds of investigations, however, are not usually a part of the daily routine of the sports journalists. A sports journalist working in a small city might be most involved in high school and amateur athletics, whereas a sports reporter in a city with one or more professional sport franchises might be assigned exclusively to cover a professional team. Day-to-day work includes both news (e.g., game stories, unusual events from player trades, or a change in ownership) and feature stories (e.g., player profiles, background pieces on the competition, or a history of the team name or mascot). A sports reporter is also frequently called on to offer analyses or commentaries about the prospects of teams or the strengths and weaknesses of some aspect of the team or game. News reporters don't routinely write these kinds of stories, because commentary is usually reserved for the editorial page, but sports reporters are frequently involved in this sort of analysis.

Of course, the biggest coverage is always reserved for special events in sports: the Olympics, the World Series, or the Superbowl. During these major events—and in the weeks (sometimes months) preceding them—a plethora of stories appears from all levels of sports reporting. National publications cover the upcoming events in great detail, and local publications frequently send sports reporters to cover the event itself or pre-event activities. If the national event involves participation by a local athlete or team, even the small town sports reporter can become involved in the continuous coverage that includes pre-event predictions, event coverage, and post-event analysis.

Whatever their specific jobs, sport journalists work in one of two general categories: print or broadcast journalism. Print journalism includes newspapers—from your local paper to the *New York Times*—and magazines like *Newsweek* and *Esquire* that may do occasional stories on athletics, and *Sports Illustrated* or *Sporting News*, publications that concentrate exclusively on covering athletics. Broadcast journalism includes local radio and television stations as well as networks like ABC and CNN. Although print and broadcast journalists share many common tasks, there are definite differences, both in the prerequisites for getting into the field and in the daily routine.

REQUIREMENTS FOR A CAREER IN PRINT JOURNALISM

Working for a newspaper or magazine as a sport journalist requires a talent for writing with speed, clarity, and accuracy. On a daily newspaper, the deadlines come every 24 hours or even more frequently. On a weekly newspaper, the deadlines are a bit less pressured but they are not leisurely. Magazines have a number of different deadlines, depending on the kind of material involved. For a journalist, deadlines are part of the career package. A person who cannot adhere to established deadlines should steer clear of a career in journalism.

The clarity and accuracy aspects of journalism are just as important for sports journalists as for journalists covering any other kind of story. Journalists write in a style that may vary a bit with the individual paper or magazine involved, but in general, a career in journalism involves communicating through writing in a clear, crisp style that is as objective as possible.

The field also requires a healthy curiosity. Being a reporter means spending a lot of time figuring out the right questions to ask as well as figuring out how to get the answers. There is a lot of "homework" involved in sports

The post event interview is but one of the activities of a sports journalist.

journalism—a lot of background research you must do before the interview or story begins.

THE WORLD OF PRINT JOURNALISM

More than 1,600 daily and 4,000 weekly newspapers are published in the United States. Nearly all of these cover sports to some extent, although the number of staff members exclusively handling sport journalism assignments is quite limited on smaller papers. In the world of magazine publishing, more than 100 magazines are devoted entirely to sports. Some of these, like *Sports Illustrated*, cover a variety of sports, whereas others are devoted to a single sport.

Sports journalists working for newspapers usually start as reporters and may eventually work into an editor's slot. Reporters are usually assigned a specific area of coverage or *beat*. On a very small newspaper, this may mean covering all area high school sports. On a larger newspaper the total sport coverage is likely to be greater and the staff is likely to be larger, so the beats may be more narrowly defined. A reporter working in a market with one or more major college or professional teams may end up covering a single college or team during the season, writing game stories and news about the team as well as generating feature stories.

Reporters for very small papers sometimes take photographs in addition to writing about sports, but most papers have full-time photographers. Magazines like *Sports Illustrated* have an entire staff of photographers. A photographer interested in sports is likely to start out as a general assignment photographer and, with luck and talent, eventually work into full-time sport photography for a large paper or magazine.

Novice journalists generally have difficulty landing a full-time job on a magazine. Many magazines keep their full-time writing staff relatively small and rely on freelance writers. Editors at magazines are rarely entry-level personnel, and photographers usually have significant experience prior to joining the staff.

YOUR CAREER PATH AS A PRINT SPORTS JOURNALIST

If you are contemplating a job as a sports reporter or photographer for a newspaper or magazine, get as much experience as possible while still in college. The first step is usually to volunteer for your college paper. Sometimes that is not as easy as it sounds, because the sports section is usually a popular place for volunteers. You may have to be persistent and write a few stories *on spec*, that is, write the story as if the paper had assigned it to you and turn it in to the sports editor to demonstrate your writing skills. In addition to good writing skills, college

The sports section is a major feature of almost every newspaper.

newspapers also hold dependability in high regard. Because most staffers are not paid, editors know that the sports writer has some other reason to keep on grinding out the copy. If you see your college paper as a stepping-stone in your career path and can convince your editor that you are willing to work hard and are dependable, you have a good shot at climbing the first step on the proverbial ladder of success.

A good second step is to approach the sports editor of your local newspaper with several of your best *clips*, your stories that have appeared in print. Some local newspapers will hire college students during the school year or in the summer either as interns or as *stringers*, part-time writers who get paid only when they are given a specific assignment or when something they write is accepted by the paper. Small newspapers with limited staff resources are especially interested in good stringers during high school tournament time, when the regular staff may be stretched in a number of different directions.

The professional experience you gain while still in school should help minimize the most frequent problem college graduates encounter when they look for their first job: no experience. Although your full-time experience will be limited, your job search will be easier if you have clips to show a prospective employer. These clips are proof that you can produce good copy. If the stories carry your name, or *by-line*, all the better. You should neatly collect your clips (use the actual newspaper copies, not your original copy) in a portfolio and present this during your job interview, or in some cases, send it to the prospective employer prior to the interview. The portfolio can be as simple as several stories neatly placed in a manila folder or as formal as a collection presented in a three-ring binder. The important thing is to collect clips that best showcase your ability to cover a variety of assignments well. Your first full-time sports reporting job is likely to be with a small newspaper, but this may lead to a job at a larger paper and perhaps a position as sports editor.

REQUIREMENTS FOR A CAREER IN BROADCAST JOURNALISM

All of the concerns about writing well and quickly apply even more strongly to broadcast journalism, where deadlines may be hourly, not daily, and where stories usually have to be told in 30-second or 1-minute packages. Broadcast writing style differs a bit from the style that print journalists use, however. Broadcasters tend to use the present and present perfect tenses in their reports, whereas print journalists almost always write in the past tense. Thus, a print journalist might write the following: "The coach *said* his team is ready for the playoff game" (past tense of *to say*). But a broadcast journalist would phrase the copy one of these two ways: "The coach *says* his team is ready for the playoff game" (present tense of *to say*), or "The coach *has said* his team is ready for the playoff game" (present perfect tense of *to say*). This differing style has developed, in part, because of the distinction traditionally cited between print and broadcast journalism: Print journalism provides a relatively permanent record of news events and offers the opportunity for in-depth analysis; broadcast offers more immediacy and brings us the latest-breaking news events but is frequently limited to the highlights of an individual story because of time constraints. Broadcast journalists also use more contractions and less formal construction than print journalists. The reason for this, of course, is that print journalists write to be read; broadcast journalists write to be heard. Writing for the ear rather than the eye requires straightforward sentence structure and the ability to condense complex ideas into a clear, concise style.

The healthy curiosity required of print journalists is just as important in broadcast journalism. However, in addition to worrying about the questions to ask and the background information to research, the broadcast journalist must also be aware of the aural and visual requirements of broadcast media. Radio reporters, including sports reporters, always look for a good *actuality*, a quote from the news maker that is sandwiched into the middle of a news story to allow the listener to hear the actual words of the person being interviewed. Television reporters have to be aware of possible *pictures* to go along with their stories: the video that shows a terrific reception in the waning minutes of a Superbowl game or a close-up look at a local high school basketball player explaining how she developed her unstoppable hook shot.

Broadcast journalism also has some requirements that do not pertain to print journalism. These center around the performance aspect of broadcasting and include voice and appearance concerns. Although broadcast journalism is frequently criticized as a place where "pretty people" make "happy talk," jobs in this field are not limited to attractive, deep-voiced males and pretty, perky women; however, the abilities to speak well, think quickly, and maintain composure on the air are critical.

In television journalism, you have to get both the picture and the story.

THE WORLD OF BROADCAST JOURNALISM

The United States has no shortage of radio and television stations. *Broadcasting Yearbook* lists almost 1,600 television stations and nearly 11,000 radio stations. Some television stations are noncommercial or educational, and others are smaller independent stations with no network affiliation and no local news or sports programs. But most network affiliates do have local news and, thus, sports programming. Radio stations are less likely to have full-time sports journalists on staff, but in bigger markets the top stations may have someone who handles sports reporting.

Sports journalists who are interested in broadcast work usually want to be on-air sports reporters. Major radio stations in very large markets and television stations in the smaller markets have at least one full-time sports reporter who also serves as the sports anchor on newscasts. These reporters frequently carry the title of sports director or sports editor. Many stations also have one or more assistants in the sports department who handle stories assigned by the sports director and perhaps handle on-air anchor assignments during weekends. At smaller stations these assistants may spend only part of their time covering sports and the rest of their time as general assignment reporters. In a market that occasionally broadcasts the games of local sports teams, the local radio or television sports reporter may have the opportunity to do play-by-play or color commentary. If a specific station broadcasts all of the team's games, a contractual agreement between the station and the team may determine who anchors the broadcast. If the broadcasts are sporadic, however, the station generally assigns the task to a member of its sports staff.

Radio sports reporters usually work alone, sometimes using a portable cassette player to record quotes for on-air use. This is called a *sound bite* or, if recorded over the telephone, a *voicer*. Television sports reporters have to be concerned with getting the *pictures* for the story as well as the sound, and at smaller stations the reporter may use a video camera and recorder, acting as reporter and videographer for routine assignments. In larger stations and at most stations with union labor contracts, the reporter is assigned a videographer who operates the camera while the reporter directs the story and conducts the interview. At most television stations, the reporter must know how to edit videotape, usually in 3/4-inch or Betacam formats.

Although the entire text of a typical half-hour local or network news program would not even fill the front page of a typical newspaper, deadlines are a real concern. A story finished at 6:30 p.m. cannot be used on the 6:00 p.m. news. Radio stories frequently require audio production time, and television stories often include video that must be shot, selected, and edited with the journalist's *voice-over*. These additional requirements mean that preparation time in broadcast sports journalism is sometimes very tight.

Behind-the-camera jobs in sports broadcasting are not always technically considered journalism careers, but they are certainly related to the business of sports journalism. These jobs include the directors, producers, videographers, and other technical personnel necessary to air a sports event or a news program. Many broadcast journalists get valuable experience or make important industry contacts early in their careers by working as freelance production assistants on sport productions.

YOUR CAREER PATH AS A BROADCAST SPORTS JOURNALIST

The career path for a successful sports journalist in broadcasting would probably involve a number of moves from smaller to larger markets (i.e., bigger cities with larger news and sport operations) and in many cases might lead to a job with one of the networks—either with the sports department of one of the major networks, like CBS Sports, or with an all-sports network like ESPN. Many people view television as the more prestigious broadcast medium, but many sports reporters prefer to remain in radio where the time constraints are not as restrictive.

If you are interested in a career in broadcasting as a sports journalist, you should look for experience while still in college. Many colleges have campus radio stations, and some have campus television stations; if these stations broadcast news programs or cover sporting events, you have a great opportunity to establish yourself in the field while still a full-time student. Opportunities can include reporting on sports, giving play-by-play or color commentary, and hosting a sports talk show. At this level, your knowledge of sports and your dependability will be key assets. Once you get the opportunity to try your hand at on-air coverage, you will begin building the kind of experience that will help open doors to an internship or part-time work at a local radio or television station.

Some local stations have internship programs available for college students, but many more would probably be willing to set up some supervised work experience if you can convince the sports editor or director that you have something to offer—even if it's just your services as a "gofer" (go-fer this, go-fer that) during a live telecast of your university's basketball team. Getting your foot in the door and showing that you are able and willing to help out is the first hurdle. Once you are there, you can start working your way up to actually reporting or writing, perhaps eventually getting on the air with your stories. This sort of initiative will pay off when you begin looking for your first full-time job.

In addition to these more obvious places to hone your skills, you can find other places to get started. Because voice considerations are important in broadcasting, your college debate club can provide you with some excellent experience in public speaking and thinking on your feet. Theater productions are also a source of good experience. The performance nature of these activities can help reduce the initial nervousness that invariably results from knowing that an audience is listening to you. The best kind of broadcast voice is strong, confident, and free from pronounced regional accent.

Your career path in broadcast sports reporting is likely to be much less predefined than one in print journalism. The big names in broadcast sports journalism today have a great diversity in backgrounds and experiences. Many of the commentators, like Joe Namath or Billie Jean King, came from the ranks of professional players. Others worked their way up from local radio and television stations to the network level. A few, like Howard Cosell, do not appear to have any sort of background for their type of sports coverage but instead seem to have been in the right place at the right time for their talent to be noticed.

Some sports journalists go from covering a university sports team to covering a major professional team in just a few years, but that is the exception rather than the rule. In the broadcast business—whether you are covering sports or hard news—you generally have to "pay your dues" in smaller markets for a number of years before you can work your way up to major markets. Of course, superstar professional athletes who become overnight sport journalist successes pay their dues in different ways and are hired as broadcast journalists because of their fame and their knowledge of the game. These former athletes must frequently undergo extensive training before they can competently handle their new assignment.

THE JOB MARKET

Journalism is a highly competitive profession, and sports journalism is one of the most competitive areas within the field. Beginning salaries are quite low for the most part, but that does not seem to dampen the enthusiasm of the hundreds of print and broadcast journalism graduates who seek careers in sports journalism. Those most likely to find jobs are the students who take enough journalism courses to understand and execute good writing style under deadline pressure and those who use their undergraduate years as an opportunity to gain relevant internship and extracurricular experience. A knowledge of sports is, of course, critical for success in the field, as are good interpersonal communication skills.

Professional Organizations

Associated Press state and national
  organizations
Baseball Writers Association

Professional Publications

Sports Illustrated
Sporting News
USA Today
Broadcasting

A WORD ABOUT ETHICS

No discussion of sport journalism should end without some attention to the ethics of the profession. Sports reporters should remember that they are members of the journalism profession, not fans who just happen to be covering the game. Journalists are obligated to provide objective, fair coverage of events. Journalism is not the place for airing personal vendettas disguised as commentary, although it can be a place for opinion that is labeled as such and is presented in a professional manner. Journalists do not accept "freebies," because that compromises both the appearance of and the adherence to standards of objectivity. Seats in the press box and access to the athletes are a part of the job, not freebies.

A sports reporter is likely to have access to a great deal of information, but not all of it can be appropriately labeled *news*. Good reporters, whether they are covering sports or any other beat, are interested in facts, not rumors. Good reporters follow up on lots of leads that never become news stories. Sport journalists must remember that they are not press agents, publicity staffers, or gossip columnists, and they must maintain the profession's ethical standards.

SPORTS JOURNALISM AS A PROFESSION

Sports journalism has its superstars, professionals who become so famous that their names evoke the same sort of awe as those of the athletes they cover. These journalists, however, are in the minority. The path to success in a sports journalism career is usually a long one that necessitates hard work and is built on a talent for writing and reporting news as well as a genuine interest in sports. Those who achieve success approach the field understanding the professional standards involved in reporting the news, and they work hard for their opportunities. Most sports journalists understand and appreciate the accomplishments of athletes and the world of athletic competition and are, for the most part, talented individuals who have managed to combine an interest in sports with a career in journalism.

Like much of the professional world, most of these sport journalism superstars are white males. Black athletes who have made the transition from the playing field to the broadcast booth have helped make entry into the field easier for minorities in general. Women, however, have not experienced the same opportunity. The prospect of a career in sports journalism is, at present, more difficult for women than for men. In addition to the fact that

a women journalist covering a sports team may present logistics problems (e.g., locker room availability or travel arrangements), a fact of the business is that much of the information exchanged between sources and reporters and among journalists themselves is conveyed through interpersonal contacts that tend to be ''old boy'' networks. And because women's sports are not as visible as men's sports, fewer women athletes are pursued as sports commentators. Until an NBC football telecast on December 27, 1987, no woman had done professional football play-by-play commentary on network television. Gayle Sierens was the first female sports reporter to achieve the distinction, and her appearance on the telecast received much more media attention than either the teams playing or the eventual outcome of the game.

A woman intending to go into sports journalism has to prove herself to an extent that most men do not. Many editors and publishers presume that a woman cannot possibly know as much about sports as a man. A great many people still think of athletics in traditional male terms, and some think that because women usually do not participate in organized athletics to the same extent as men, women may not be able to understand the physical and mental realities of athletics, especially at the professional level. Sexism, like racism, is an unfortunate reality of our society and cannot be legislated away. This should not discourage an aspiring female sports reporter from pursuing a career in the field, but an individual entering a profession ought to know the pitfalls as well as the rewards. Men's and women's professional sports will not likely gain any sort of parity in the near future, and although many men's sports at the college level are not revenue producing, the traditional concept of collegiate athletics is that only men's basketball, football, and perhaps hockey draw money into a program. Even a mediocre men's basketball program can draw an audience, but a women's program usually has to be outstanding (and winning) to do the same.

This disparity in the marketplace means that the opportunities for women are not as obvious or as easy as for many men. But talented, assertive female sports writers and broadcasters are making headway in the field and providing role models for others to emulate. For a bright young woman willing to put in the long hours and hard work that this career demands, sport journalism can be a challenge worth the extra effort.

LEARNING ACTIVITIES

1. Carefully watch and take notes during a network-televised sports event. Pay attention to how much information the various sportscasters relate to the audience during the course of the game. Pay particular attention to events that have a great many pauses in the action (for example, between plays during a football telecast or between batters and innings of a baseball telecast). Select a favorite sport or team and try to research the kind of information necessary for a color commentary for the team's next match. If you have access to a video recorder and a tape recorder, tape both television and radio coverage of the same sporting event. Listen to the similarities and differences in how the announcers handle the play-by-play and the color commentary.

2. Collect one week's worth of sports pages from your local newspaper, and analyze the kind of stories included in the sports section. Try to determine which stories are *hard news* and which are feature stories. Look at the stories that have by-lines and those that don't; notice which are written by local reporters and which are from the wire services. Compare several of the stories with stories from the front page of the paper. Do their styles differ? Does the sports story contain more reporter opinion? If you live in a community that does not have a professional or major college team, find at your library a copy of a daily newspaper from a large city like New York or Chicago and compare the sports section of that paper with your local paper.

SUGGESTED READINGS

Anderson, D.A. (1985). *Contemporary sports reporting*. Chicago: Nelson-Hall.

Cosell, H. (1985). *I never played the game*. New York: Morrow Publishing.

Cosell, H. (1973). *Cosell*. Chicago: Playboy Press.

Ford, R. (1986). *The Sportswriter*. New York: Vintage Books.

Garrison, B. (1985). *Sports reporting*. Ames, IA: Iowa State University Press.

Gelfand, L.I. (1969). *Modern sportswriting*. Ames, IA: Iowa State University Press.

Koppett, L. (1981). *Sports illusion, sports reality: A reporter's view of sports, journalism and society*. Boston: Houghton Mifflin.

Woodward, S. (1967). *Sportswriter*. Garden City, NY: Doubleday.

CHAPTER 9

Sports Club Management

John McCarthy
International Racquet Sports Association

The athletic and fitness club business is a large and growing industry that can be broken down into three major segments. First is the large segment of old-line, member-owned country clubs, urban athletic clubs, yacht clubs, and tennis and swim clubs; at least 6,000 of these clubs operate in the United States. Second is the new breed of investor-owned, for-profit racquet, athletic, and fitness clubs; between 8,000 and 10,000 of these clubs operate in the United States. Third is the large number of "quasi-clubs" such as YWCAs, YMCAs, JCCs, and semipublic facilities such as community tennis clubs and swimming clubs. Approximately 5,000 of these centers operate in the United States.

In addition, a growing number of new, club-type businesses are sprouting up everywhere. Examples of such businesses are hotel clubs, corporate fitness centers, resort spas, wellness centers, university recreation centers, and hospital centers.

This wellness center for mature adults typifies a current trend in the sports and fitness club industry.

CHARACTERISTICS OF THE CLUB INDUSTRY

Each athletic or fitness club is unique in some ways. However, there are several characteristics that most share.

The Athletic and Fitness Club Industry Is Highly Fragmented

This means that the industry is composed of a large number of independent companies that have little or no relationship to one another. Less than 20 percent of this industry is integrated to any significant degree. Two companies (Club Corporation of America and Health & Tennis Corporation of America) control 200 to 300 clubs, and the YMCA operates more than 2,000 franchise units. Approximately 70 percent of all clubs are small businesses that are independently owned and managed.

This implies that few clear career paths exist for advancement within the industry. Going to work for a club is not like going to work for Proctor & Gamble, where one can, within a single company, track a long career. The fitness club industry is expected to experience considerable integration over the next 10 years; presently, however, the industry is primarily composed of independently owned and operated small businesses.

Most Clubs Are Small Businesses

The Small Business Administration (SBA) defines a business as *small* until its sales reach $3.5 million. No more than 1 percent of clubs today gross more than $3.5 million. Of course, a wide range of gross sales figures exist for the club industry, but at least 70 percent of the industry is composed of clubs whose total sales are under $1 million. Probably 30 percent of all clubs have total sales under $500,000.

Why is this important in assessing a career in the club industry? The term *career* implies long-term employment; it also implies compensation that is sufficient to support a family. Small businesses generally can compensate only a few people (between one and three) who will earn enough to provide a reasonable standard of living for a family. Sports clubs are no exception to this rule.

Professional Organizations

International Racquet Sports Association
Association for Fitness in Business
American College of Sports Medicine
International Dance-Exercise Association
Aerobics and Fitness Association of America
Club Managers Association
National Club Association
National Strength and Conditioning
  Association

Professional Publications

Club Business International
Club Industry
Athletic Business
Club Management
Perspective
Peak Performance
Club Marketing and Management Newsletter
Fitness Management
The Physician and Sportsmedicine
Fitness Industry
IDEA Today
National Strength and Conditioning Journal
Running and Fitness News

Pay Scales Are Rising in This Industry

The typical club general manager at an investor-owned club or at a YMCA-type club earns between $30,000 and $40,000. Normally, becoming a club general manager requires at least 3 to 5 years of club experience. This fact means that most available managerial jobs in the club industry are at the assistant manager or department manager level. These positions pay between $14,000 and $20,000. As a result, these jobs are generally held by relatively young women and men.

The Club Business Is a "Trade-Off" Industry

The people who choose this industry do so not primarily because of its inherent financial rewards but rather because it is what they want to do. They enjoy working in this arena, and money is not the only or primary factor in their choices of career. An important by-product of this fact is that the industry is composed of men and women who enjoy their work and enjoy each other; it is a positive environment in which to work.

The Sports Club Industry Is Not Yet a Major Industry or Profession

Many outsiders do not consider working for a club a legitimate profession, like being a lawyer, accountant, or securities analyst. Rather, people often perceive such a job as a continuation of a summer job. Status is not a standard "perk" that comes with a position in this industry.

Most People in the Sports Club Industry Begin "On the Floor"

They work for an hourly wage that often is not much above minimum wage. Typically these are young people who begin working at a club part-time during their college years or during their summer vacations; they might be front desk assistants, part-time assistants in the fitness or sales departments, or racquetball, squash, tennis, swimming, or golf instructors. Usually this first work experience leads people to pursue full-time positions in this industry. Upon graduation from college, these people frequently take positions such as front-desk manager, sales director, or member services director, positions that normally pay between $14,000 and $18,000 a year. Although pay is relatively low, hours are long, and weekend and evening work is an integral part of the job, young men or women who enter this industry get valuable business and managerial experience at an early stage in their careers.

The Club Industry Is a "Thin" Industry

A "thick" industry, such as banking or insurance, is one in which employees do not get much real responsibility until they have worked in the industry for 2 to 4 years. In a "thin" industry, motivated people can attain substantial responsibility in 1 or 2 years.

Because this industry is young, is growing rapidly, and still has relatively few trained and skilled managers, plenty of room exists for talented people. A proactive employee will often move relatively quickly from a $17,000 sales assistant's position to a $35,000 general manager's position. The industry has no glut of experienced management talent; in fact, demand greatly exceeds supply. This fact has important long-term implications for salary levels and career paths.

Club Management May Be Incompatible With Family Life

Club people work when everyone else is playing—nights and weekends. Furthermore, most clubs are open 17 hours a day, 7 days a week, 12 months a year; therefore, the club needs to be staffed and managed for three full 40-hour shifts per week. Management-level employees usually work at least 50 hours per week. Moreover, on weekdays, clubs are busiest between 4:00 p.m. and 8:30 p.m. Thus, even under ideal conditions, club managers often do not get home until 9:00 p.m. or later. Most club managers get no more than 1-1/2 days off per week, rather than the normal 2 days per week. If you aspire to a career in a sports club, be prepared to reconcile the demands of the industry with your personal life. Without understanding, support, and shared interests, relationships can suffer because of the unique factors involved.

EDUCATIONAL PREPARATION

Before deciding to pursue a career in the club industry, you should be aware of the realities of the profession. Most jobs in the club industry are not salaried but are hourly jobs, and no one in this industry works a normal 40-hour week. Although you will have more responsibility than your classmates who enter more mature industries, you will often make substantially less money. It is unrealistic to believe that upon graduation a full-time, salaried position paying at least $25,000 a year awaits you; this simply is not the case.

If after understanding and accepting the realities you still wish to work in the club industry, you should make every attempt to acquire the education and training that will help you succeed in this venue.

Undergraduate Education

Does it make a difference whether a prospective club manager has college preparation in sport and fitness management? Yes, because you learn fundamental business skills in such curricula. A college education affords opportunities to acquire the all-important analytic skills in areas such as accounting, market planning, sales, and advertising. But these courses do not and cannot teach the ultimate essential of club work—attitude. Club people need to be welcoming and hospitable, integrated and encouraging, enthusiastic and communicative. They need to enjoy serving others. Most of all, they need to be proactive, and this is primarily a function of personality, not education.

Graduate Education

People sometimes ask whether a master's degree in business administration (MBA) or other academic equivalents are essential for long-term growth in the club industry. Sooner or later, the skills taught in an MBA program will be essential to advancement in club management. Club managers must know how to read an income statement and balance sheet, segment a market, develop a marketing plan, budget funds, and orchestrate an organization so that it is both efficient and effective. Managers can learn much of this on the job, but without formal training and continued professional development, personal and professional growth in this industry is limited.

SKILLS

What skills are required for employment and advancement in the club industry?

Sport or Fitness Expertise

Expertise in specific sport or fitness activities is essential for anyone who wants to be an instructor or director in a specialized department. If you excel in golf, tennis, swimming, aerobics, or squash, you can probably parlay these skills into an attractive club position; you should seek to be certified or accredited by the professional association that governs your activity. Examples of such associations are the Professional Golf Association (PGA), the United States Professional Tennis Association (USPTA), the International Dance-Exercise Association (IDEA), and the American College of Sports Medicine (ACSM). Compensation for coaching and directing athletic and fitness activities at the club level is already attractive for tennis and golf specialists and is becoming more attractive for fitness specialists.

Sales Ability

The skill most dear to the heart of every club owner and general manager is sales. Every club needs someone who can develop an integrated membership plan that draws prospects into a club and facilitates their membership decisions. Today, the average full-service racquet, athletic, and fitness club has approximately 1,600 to 2,000 members. In many of these clubs, membership turnover (the *attrition rate*) runs between 30 and 40 percent. That means that for a club simply to hold its own, it needs to sell 500 to 600 new memberships per year. Growth, which most clubs want, means adding members as well as replacing them. Thus, every club has a clearly perceived need for sales specialists. Without question, achievement in this area is fundamental to advancement in the industry.

Versatility

Many people who work in the club industry must wear two or three hats. The employee who

Most racquet clubs are independently owned small businesses.

teaches an aerobics class in the morning may work at the front desk in the afternoon and assist with club sales in the evening. This is an economic necessity both for clubs and for the people who work in them.

HOW FAR CAN YOU GO IN THIS INDUSTRY?

The answer to this question becomes more encouraging every year. The market for club services is growing rapidly, and signs show that this is a trend rather than a fad. Today, and surely for the next 5 to 10 years, the industry has a relative dearth of experienced management talent. Hence, this is an ideal time to enter the industry. Further, the industry is rapidly changing from being what could be called a "mom and pop" industry to an increasingly integrated and professionally managed industry. Therefore, the career potential for those now entering the industry is rapidly expanding; many club managers now earn more than $40,000 a year.

THE FUTURE OF SPORTS CLUB MANAGEMENT

Can we see positive signs regarding the future of this industry? Yes, we can. For example, a growing number of well-established companies, such as the Hyatt Hotels and Bally Manufacturing, have recently decided to become players in this industry. This is an indicator that the industry is beginning to attract larger, more sophisticated corporations. Another positive sign is that the fitness-oriented lifestyle is becoming a basic rather than a discretionary part of life for an ever-growing number of Americans. As this trend continues to unfold, we can expect that clubs of all types will play greater roles in people's leisure choices. Yet another sign is that the leadership within the club industry is now dominated by people who believe that quality is the key to long-term profitability. Hence, a pervasive effort exists within the industry to upgrade both the quality of the facilities and the quality of club services.

LEARNING ACTIVITIES

1. Interview a manager or staff member at a local sports club. Ask about his or her job role and work hours per day. Also ask about the age range of the club's clients and what they pay for services.
2. Conduct a panel presentation to compare and contrast the for-profit, nonprofit, and not-for-profit approaches toward the following components of the sports club industry: methods of publicity, types of services, accessibility and design, and staffing.
3. Investigate a publication that addresses sports club management: *Club Business International*, *Club Industry*, *Club Management*, *Perspective*, *Fitness Management*, or *Peak Performance*. Determine which items are unique, such as feature articles, the cover, advertisements, graphics, coverage of disabled or aging populations, readability, cost, and publication frequency.
4. Invite professionals to address questions designed by the class.
5. Prepare a sales approach for an imaginary sports club.

SUGGESTED READINGS

Abbott, C., & Starker, J. (1987, May). Great places to live: The ten best places for active women. *Women's Sports and Fitness*, 9, 42-46.

Bannon, J., & Busser, J. (1987). *Sports club management*. Champaign, IL: Management Learning Laboratories.

Clayton, K. (1986, December). Hotels fight for fitness market. *Marketing*, **27**, 46-47.

Feldinger, F. (1986, November). A $260-a-share bargain stock (Los Angeles Athletic Club Co.). *Fortune*, **114**, 77-79.

Freeman, D. (1985, April). Marketing takes the game. *Oregon Business Magazine*, 33-37.

Neff, C., & Sullivan, R. (1986, April). Nearest ocean, 620 miles: Beach volleyball club in

Toledo constructed with truckloads of sand. *Sports Illustrated*, **64**, 13.

Sullivan, R. (1986, November). One barrier stands, another falls (Maryland country club bars female Secret Service Agent, New Orleans Athletic Club admits first blacks). *Sports Illustrated*, **65**, 14.

You don't need a great body at L.A.'s cushiest health club, but a big name and a fat wallet help. (1987, November). *People Weekly*, p. 113.

CHAPTER 10

The Physical Fitness Industry

Michael D. Wolf
International Fitness Exchange

Several years have passed since the last "Is Fitness a Fad or a Trend?" article appeared in one of our nation's newspapers and magazines. A staggering number of polls (some more scientifically conducted than others) show that fitness is here to stay and is still growing.

Job opportunities abound in the physical fitness industry, although those of us in the field often have a difficult time explaining to family and friends that professionally and emotionally satisfying and often financially lucrative careers exist in fitness. Thirty years ago, who would have thought such a thing possible?

WHAT IS THE PHYSICAL FITNESS INDUSTRY?

Careers that involve management, planning, or supervision of fitness-related activities exist in a wide variety of settings. You can find positions ranging from entry-level floor instructors to program directors, facility managers, or consultants, with salaries ranging from $12,000 to more than $100,000 per year, in the following settings.

- Commercial fitness centers and athletic clubs
- Tenant- or guest-only fitness centers in hotels, apartment buildings, and office parks
- Private athletic clubs

- YMCAs, YWCAs, YW/YMHAs, JCCs, and community centers
- Corporate fitness centers
- Cardiac rehabilitation centers
- Sports medicine centers
- Amateur or professional sports team conditioning programs
- Consulting companies
- Facility management companies

The physical fitness industry encompasses all these settings and more, and a bountiful diversity of career options and an expanding number of employment opportunities are available.

Physical fitness professionals work in a variety of settings.

CAREERS IN THE FITNESS INDUSTRY

At least six career paths exist in the fitness industry, and each career possibility has a distinctive set of answers to the following questions.

- What are the professional requirements for being hired?
- What are the duties and responsibilities of the position?
- What are the growth opportunities in such a position?
- What are the financial rewards of the position?

Fitness Instructor

For many people, the first step in a fitness career is as an instructor or trainer in a fitness center or program. Although the financial rewards of employment in such a setting are limited, the exposure to day-to-day operations and to the range of positions requiring additional experience or academic preparation can be invaluable. These positions may also involve greater rewards, both personal and financial.

Regardless of the type of fitness center an instructor may choose (e.g., for-profit, not-for-profit, corporate, or residential), the answers to the four key questions remain consistent.

Professional Requirements

An interest in the field, as well as evidence of a personal commitment to fitness, are frequently all you need to obtain an instructor-level position in most commercial fitness centers. In contrast, instructor positions in higher priced commercial operations and in corporate fitness settings are most frequently filled by people with undergraduate degrees. College graduates with backgrounds in physiology, sport/fitness management, physical education, or athletic training generally have advantages.

With the liability insurance crisis facing most fitness operations, managers pay increasing attention to the question of professional certification. Though salaries for full- and part-time instructors are usually anything but generous, many facilities now require aerobic dance certification from either of the two most highly respected certifying agencies in the field, the International Dance Exercise Association (IDEA) or the Aerobics and Fitness Association of America (AFAA).

The American College of Sports Medicine (ACSM), the Institute for Aerobics Research (IAR, part of the renowned Cooper Clinic in Dallas), and the National Strength and Conditioning Association (NSCA) offer certifications that, although not yet widely required for employment, can be decisive in winning a job— even at the instructor level. Requiring a greater degree of hands-on experience than any of these certificates is the Athletic Trainers Certification (ATC) granted by the National Athletic Trainers' Association (NATA). Certified athletic trainers are being found in high frequency outside of the training room and in the fitness center.

What is the value of certification from an organization other than the six identified above? At the least, certification will show a potential employer that you have made a commitment to professional growth. Not every undergraduate student can, after all, financially afford certification from any of those six. Many employers will take the time to look over the syllabus and materials of a lesser known certifying group to determine its level of sophistication. Others, unfortunately, may condemn a nonmainstream certifying group without assessing its integrity and educational value. The prudent course is for you to make all reasonable sacrifices to be certified by one of the better known agencies. Like your diploma, it may be expensive but it is an investment in your future.

Duties and Responsibilities

Depending on the level of technical sophistication instructors bring to their position, they may be given duties and responsibilities that range from minimal to extensive. Although the instructor position rarely requires management skills, the first-hand experience acquired by the instructor will enable him or her to more efficiently manage other instructors at a later date.

Instruction.   As a general rule, instructors supervise and instruct clients in safe and effective exercise programs. In higher quality commercial fitness centers and athletic clubs and in corporate fitness settings, instructors guide clients through one or more initial workouts according to a physiologist-designed *exercise prescription*, for which the instructor receives in-service training in the principles of proper warm-ups, cool-downs, stretching, and equipment use. In commercial fitness centers with lower membership fees and admittedly less intensive service, clients are by no means assured that instructors are sufficiently trained to supervise such programs.

Program Supervision.   Supervision of ongoing programs, although generally not regarded in the past as the most noble or important of tasks, has become the focus of so many fitness center lawsuits that it is becoming a key job component, one that is rewarded if performed properly and enthusiastically. Fitness facilities that once only professed to offer quality care now have to employ qualified professionals to substantiate these claims.

Instructors with more advanced levels of preparation may also be responsible for fitness testing and counseling, exercise prescription, the teaching of classes (aerobics, calisthenics, aquatics, and more), and one-on-one training.

Sales.   In the typical health spa, instructors are responsible for sales as well as for fitness instruction. Such positions offer exposure to an additional side of the business and can double or triple annual income through sometimes-generous sales commissions.

Private Training

Personal or private trainer is a new career option. Though such services are more common in major metropolitan areas or affluent suburbs where personal income allows such a luxury, private trainers across the country can collect fees of $20 to $60 per hour (and more in New York and Los Angeles) for serving as one-on-one coaches and program designers. As usual, individuals with more advanced training, skills, and abilities garner higher fees.

Growth Opportunities

Former instructors who learn the business over several years and augment their fitness training with some academic preparation in business fill many management-level positions in commercial fitness centers. Those with aspirations toward a management-level position almost always benefit from making this clear to their supervisors. More often than not, supervisors are glad to expand your job description and show you the ropes.

Financial Rewards

As in any business, salaries are commensurate with responsibilities. Instructors who are limited to instructing and supervising can expect part-time work to pay $5 to $8 per hour. Dance instructors may earn $15 or more per class. Those who test and counsel may earn as much as $18,000 per year on a full-time basis. As expected, the instructor who sells memberships earns the greatest income. In the New York metropolitan area, for example, instructor-level positions with sales responsibilities currently show annual salary-plus-commission totals of

$35,000 and up. A top salesperson in a high-traffic fitness location can earn over $50,000 per year.

Strength and Conditioning Coach

Although today's coaches place tremendous emphasis on high-tech conditioning for athletic performance, as recently as 10 years ago most coaches feared that strength training and skill training were incompatible. This fear persists somewhat even today in sports such as golf, for example. The National Strength and Conditioning Association (NSCA), begun in the early part of this decade (as the National Strength Coaches Association) to promote the viability of strength coaching as a profession, is a potent force in certification and the setting of quality standards.

Strength training is a requirement for top performance in almost every sport.

Professional Requirements

Most strength coaches possess a minimum of an undergraduate degree in physical education, exercise physiology, or sport-fitness management. Many possess an NATA athletic training certificate, and growing numbers are earning certified strength and conditioning specialist (CSCS) credentials from the NSCA. The requirements for the CSCS certificate include at least a bachelor's degree.

Duties and Responsibilities

Strength coaches and their assistants design sport-specific conditioning programs, administer the programs and necessary evaluative tests, and make modifications where indicated. Except at some major universities and in the professional sport ranks, most conditioning coaches are responsible for several sports, which increases the level of technical sophistication required for effectiveness in the job. A thorough knowledge of physiology, conditioning, anatomy, and sport biomechanics is essential to success in a career as a strength and conditioning coach.

In a small program, the strength coach position does not require extensive personnel or budget management skills. As the number of teams under care and the number of assistants grow, the strength coach's need for management skills becomes more important.

Growth Opportunities

Conditioning coaches usually start at smaller schools and colleges, then progress to larger universities and to the professional sport world. Because this career track is so new, we can't easily judge where today's successful conditioning coaches will be in 10 years.

Financial Rewards

Salaries are small to modest for assistant coaches in schools and colleges and are more sizable in the professional arena. Conditioning coaches at major universities can earn $30,000 per year and more, and salaries of professional football conditioning coaches frequently exceed that figure.

Professional Organizations

American College of Sports Medicine
American Alliance for Health, Physical Education, Recreation and Dance
Association for Fitness in Business
National Strength and Conditioning Association
National Athletic Trainers Association

Professional Publications

Club Business International
Club Industry
Athletic Business
Fitness Management

Exercise Physiologist

A wide range of job titles may be grouped under the heading *exercise physiologist*. Advanced undergraduate training or graduate degree work in exercise physiology or exercise science can open up more challenging and generally more rewarding career paths for those investing the time and effort. Fitness program directors, fitness specialists, fitness technicians, and many consultants have begun their careers with training in the exercise sciences.

Professional Requirements

The majority of those in senior positions, such as exercise physiologists, hold master's degrees in a related field such as physiology, physical education, exercise science, or fitness management. In addition, the ACSM, a heterogeneous group of professionals and students interested in sports medicine and fitness, offers the most widely respected certification programs. Though many exercise physiologists begin with the Exercise Test Technologist certificate, the new Health/Fitness Instructor certificate is popular and appropriate for those who plan to work in the nonrehabilitation areas of fitness. Employers seeking to expand the skills of their exercise physiologists or fitness technicians or specialists frequently fund week-long trips to the Cooper Clinic in Dallas, Texas for the IAR certificate program.

Fitness technicians or specialists rarely need academic work beyond the bachelor's degree, but employment possibilities are enhanced by professional certifications such as the ACSM Health/Fitness Instructor.

Duties and Responsibilities

Exercise physiologists and fitness specialists or technicians generally are responsible for fitness testing and programming or prescription. This includes the design and administration of fitness test batteries, the design of exercise prescriptions, client counseling, and occasionally exercise instruction and supervision. Exercise physiologists may be responsible for the activities and conduct of floor fitness personnel and, as such, may need personnel management skills. Many physiologists have budgetary authority in setting up the facility's equipment complement as well as in acquiring equipment as the program develops.

As the use of computers spreads through the fitness industry, physiologists, specialists, and technicians more and more frequently customize and use fitness software in the testing and prescription process. One widely used program allows the user to create a test battery from a wide menu of choices in anthropometry, flexibility, muscular strength and endurance, aerobic endurance, and pulmonary function and then to write and store 250 detailed exercise prescriptions that are directly keyed to results on the test battery. With responsibilities that will include computer use in the near future, physiologists and technicians should be familiar with computer hardware and the nature of computer operating systems.

Growth Opportunities

Many exercise physiologists progress professionally to earn the ACSM Program Director or Health/Fitness Director certificates and then to secure such positions on university campuses, in hospitals, or in clinics. Whether exercise physiology can be a career in itself is difficult to say, given the fact that the job category is so new outside the university setting. A 40-year-old fitness professional with 15 years in the field might be professionally quite satisfied as a program director, but would probably not remain in the field long enough to attain this position if he or she were limited to conducting fitness tests and writing exercise prescriptions. Frequently, growth opportunities depend upon the degree of challenge desired.

Many physiologists and technicians venture into private training, either on their own or with others. The most successful and well-known private trainers (who hold graduate degrees and professional certifications) now manage their own teams of trainers and work with only a select clientele.

Financial Rewards

A step above most instructors in professional preparation and job responsibilities, physiologists and fitness specialists or technicians enjoy significantly greater financial rewards.

Specialists or technicians can expect full-time salaries of up to perhaps $25,000 in large metropolitan areas. A surprising number of exercise physiologists with broad experience now collect annual salaries in excess of $50,000 for positions that are below top management. Such positions are found almost exclusively in consulting companies, where physiologists can use their talent on a number of projects each year. Some private trainers, similarly entrepreneurial, also enjoy annual incomes between $40,000 and $60,000 in certain geographic areas, though most earn far less.

Facility Director/Manager

Many instructors and exercise physiologists who aspire to lifelong careers in fitness, with financial rewards sufficient to allow home ownership, travel, and the other trappings of success, will track toward facility management. With various estimates of the number of fitness facilities in the United States alone exceeding 10,000, there are indeed many management-level positions to be filled. As the fitness trend spreads to Europe and Asia, the need for good managers will grow even more rapidly.

Professional Requirements

With their incredibly diverse ranges of tasks and responsibilities, managers need not be degreed and professionally certified in management, although these accomplishments can hasten advancement and success. In fact, the growing number of academic programs in fitness or sport management will likely provide a large percentage of successful fitness managers in the years ahead. Most fitness management professionals in the field today won their positions through years of working in the "trenches" of instructor and sales positions.

Though certainly not a professional requirement, attendance at management seminars and national meetings such as those sponsored by the International Racquet Sports Association (IRSA), the Association of Physical Fitness Centers (APFC), and *Club Industry* and *Athletic Business* magazines boosts one's knowledge and chances of employment.

Duties and Responsibilities

Managers plan, organize, lead, and evaluate. Their day-to-day tasks may include all of the following and more: coordinating and supervising sales, administrative, and floor staff; designing and implementing staff training programs; recruiting, hiring, firing, and promoting; designing and implementing marketing strategies; planning and administering business plans and budgets; handling public relations and public speaking; purchasing equipment; scheduling the facility; and planning or designing facility additions or renovations. However, most facility directors or managers in commercial centers are clearly charged with one priority task: maximizing revenue while minimizing costs.

Growth Opportunities

Nowhere in the fitness industry is career potential equal to that in the management path. As professionals develop management skills, they can move into larger, more challenging facilities that offer commensurate fiscal rewards. Because several major fitness center or spa chains have become publicly traded companies in the past few years (e.g., U.S. Health, Spa Lady), good managers are needed in even greater numbers. Undoubtedly, you can create a lifelong career in management.

Financial Rewards

With salaries and bonus structures that reflect success of the business, career managers may achieve compensation equal to that in most older, more established industries. Depending on the size of the facility and its for-profit or not-for-profit status, salaries may range from $20,000 up to and beyond $50,000 per year, plus bonuses. The compensation structure of positions in publicly traded companies often includes stock options as well as cash or stock bonuses.

Program Director

In fitness industry settings that are less commercially oriented and more directed toward results, such as corporate and hospital-based fitness centers, command usually goes to the program director. Certainly a management-level position, but distinct in its requirements, duties, and responsibilities, the program director career path is but a few years old and still evolving. To an increasing degree, fitness and health promotion go hand in hand in program director positions, challenging job aspirants to develop extremely broad competencies.

Professional Requirements

Golaszewski, Miller, Sol, and Pfeiffer (1986) developed a detailed and comprehensive functional description of the requirements for directors of fitness/health promotion programs. The authors emphasized that the successful program director must be multitalented, with training and skills in fitness, health promotion, and business.

> It became apparent that the fitness director of the future would function as a business manager having a health product rather than a health professional operating in a business environment. . . . Today's fitness director has evolved from a quasi-specialist in an undefined discipline to a recognized professional at the cutting edge of major national health trends. (p. 83)

What does this need for such expansive skills imply? At the least, program director aspirants must ensure that their academic preparation includes work in business and management theory, fitness and exercise science, and health promotion.

In addition to requiring academic work, many positions of note in this aspect of the fitness business require professional certification. The ACSM offers two director-level certification programs, the Preventive and Rehabilitative Exercise Program Director certificate and the Health/Fitness Director certificate. The applicant requirements for the latter are as follows (ACSM, 1989).

1. A postgraduate degree in an allied health field or the equivalent.
2. Be certified as an ASCM Health/Fitness Instructor (Fitness Instructor), an ACSM Exercise Specialist or an ACSM Preventive and Rehabilitative Exercise Program Director.
3. Documentation of hours of experience in program supervision:

ASCM Certification/ Hours Required

Health/Fitness Instructor/800
Exercise Specialist/800
P&R Exercise Program Director/0

4. Recognized ability to organize and administer preventive exercise programs for a wide range of persons with no known disease or with controlled disease.
5. Minimum of three (3) years experience in an administrative management capacity of a health-fitness program.
6. Current certification in cardiopulmonary resuscitation (CPR).
7. Two (2) completed recommendations supporting academic qualifications and experience. Forms must be completed by someone with knowledge of candidate's administrative experience. (Recommendations must be made on official ACSM recommendation forms.)[1]

The Health/Fitness Director certificate requires only successful performance on a written examination; the Preventive and Rehabilitative Exercise Program Director certificate requires completion of both written and practical examinations.

Duties and Responsibilities

Golaszewski, Miller, Sol, and Pfeiffer (1986) identified the following functions of the fitness director in the corporate or hospital setting.

- Develop and promote health and fitness among employees
- Conduct and analyze a needs assessment within the organization and develop appropriate program objectives
- Plan and implement the health/fitness program and manage and give direction to the staff
- Evaluate the progress of the health/fitness program toward its stated objectives
- Articulate and publicize the fitness program within the organization, to the outside community, and to other professional groups
- Understand the workings of the corporate structure and demonstrate personal conduct consistent with the norms of that culture (p. 84)

Even with the sometimes-unique constraints of corporations and hospitals, however, the day-to-day tasks of these program directors overlap to a great degree with those of facility managers.

Growth Opportunities

Program directors are at the top of the career path and, as such, may move laterally but probably not vertically. As more and more companies and hospitals move into fitness and wellness, however, the number of director positions will grow.

Financial Rewards

Program directors command compensation packages that reflect the weighty nature of their

[1]Reprinted with permission of the American College of Sports Medicine. *Health/Fitness Director*, 1989.

tasks. Top people in this position today earn in excess of $50,000 per year.

Consultant and Entrepreneurial Ventures

For many fitness professionals who have worked in the field 5 to 10 years, consulting and entrepreneurship provide the greatest challenges and rewards.

As the fitness industry grows more complex and business success thereby becomes less easily attained, more and more facility owners and operators turn to consultants. With expertise in the very problem areas many owners and operators are least knowledgeable about, consultants in design, marketing, and programming often play key roles—and usually are paid well for their work.

Entrepreneurial ventures can include fitness facility ownership, creation of a personal training service, or formation of a consulting company. An entrepreneur with appropriate skills and background can attain business success and financial rewards rather early in a career.

Professional Requirements

Successful consultants and entrepreneurs possess few or no common threads in academic preparation. Unquestionably, consultants offering design services must be knowledgeable in areas critical to design efficacy. But, as in other jobs, this knowledge is attained not through academic courses of study but by hundreds or thousands of hours of work in actual facilities, both well and poorly designed. Similarly, entrepreneurs whose business plans call for service in multiple roles must be able to carry these roles out to the degree required. If you contemplate—even slightly—a consulting or entrepreneurial career, you should not leave campus without the widest selection of auxiliary course work possible in the business and marketing spheres. But remember that the professional requirements for

success in this career path are more related to experience than to academics.

Duties and Responsibilities

Consulting is like fire fighting: Sometimes facility owners or operators are smart enough to call consultants to help prevent the "fire"— but more often than not, the consultants arrive to find the problem "in full flame"!

Consultants frequently team up to create firms that can offer a wide or complete range of services to the fitness industry. The duties and responsibilities of these consultants are identical to those of the facility director. Indeed, the inability of in-house staff to successfully manage their duties and responsibilities often brings the consultant on board. Of course, many start-up projects—a new multimillion dollar YMCA or community center, for example—come with no in-place management teams to create the facility and its professional complement. Consultants in such cases are hired simply for otherwise-unavailable talents.

In the course of day-to-day operations, fitness consultants design facilities, create marketing strategies, run sales programs, select and order exercise and other equipment, hire and train staff, develop testing and fitness programs, and on occasion manage an entire facility.

The entrepreneur, being the risk taker in a business venture, has the duties and responsibilities of the owner and operator. These include planning, budgeting, managing personnel, and conducting daily business.

Growth Opportunities and Financial Rewards

The consulting and entrepreneurship path offers unlimited growth potential. Successful small businesses may expand to multiple locations, and consulting groups may grow to include a large team of professionals with a national clientele. One well-known entrepreneur began his company nearly 20 years ago with about $3,000 of savings and has since guided his company to management of over 30 fitness centers and annual revenues of over $2 million, with significant personal wealth for himself. Truly, being in business for oneself offers unparalleled risks but equally unparalleled rewards.

LEARNING ACTIVITIES

1. Visit a local university, community, or corporate physical fitness center, and interview the sport management or fitness professionals concerning their primary job duties. Then ask yourself the following questions. Can I picture myself in this job environment? What type of preparation do I need to obtain this job? Would the salary be satisfactory? Is this something I would be happy doing? Do I need professional certification for this job?

2. Attend a local health fair or sports medicine seminar. Interview the participating sport management professionals.

3. If your university has a copy of the *Directory of Professional Fitness Certifications*, published by the National Association for Sport and Physical Education (NASPE), investigate the various certifications available and evaluate each in terms of its compatibility with your intended career.

REFERENCES

American College of Sports Medicine. (1989). 1989 ACSM certification workbooks. *Sports Medicine Bulletin*.

Golaszewski, T.J., Miller, R.E., Sol, N., & Pfeiffer, G. (1986). A functional description of directors of fitness/health promotion programs in occupational settings. *Fitness in Business*, **1**, 82-86.

National Association for Sport and Physical Education. (1988). *Directory of professional fitness certifications*. Reston, VA: Author. (Available from the National Association for Sport and Physical Education, 1900 Association Drive, Reston, VA 22091)

CHAPTER 11

Athletic Training and Sports Medicine

Crayton L. Moss
Bowling Green State University

Throughout the history of competitive sport, a wide assortment of individuals including coaches, teachers, students, and interested lay-people have served the health-related needs of athletes. In recent years, however, public demand has increased for highly trained professionals who demonstrate appropriate degrees of skill in evaluation, management, and care of sport-related injuries.

Although most attention is currently focused on the preparation of athletic trainers who can provide quality care for varsity athletes at the high school and college levels, there is a measurable trend toward preparing athletic trainers who will work in nontraditional settings such as hospitals, sports medicine clinics, and industrial sites. A survey conducted by Johnson & Johnson (National Athletic Trainers' Association, 1988) revealed that in 1987, 22 percent of certified trainers were employed in private or hospital-based clinics. According to projections made by Grace (cited in National Athletic Trainers' Association, 1988), "Independent and hospital-based clinics, which employ about 1200 athletic trainers today, are expected to provide twice as many positions for athletic trainers in 1994" (p. 4). In addition, Grace predicted that "American industry, which has fewer than 50 certified trainers on the payrolls today, is expected to

provide career opportunities for 1,000 athletic trainers in 1994" (National Athletic Trainers' Association, 1988, p. 4). Grace predicted that of the approximately 4,000 new athletic trainers expected to be NATA-certified by 1994, 2,150 will be employed in the private sector, but only 1,200 will work in high schools and colleges.

If these predictions are valid, the athletic trainers of the future will be expected not only to provide care to injured athletes but also to function as managers of health care teams, groups of individuals working in concert to manage the entire health care setting. The professional preparation of athletic trainers, therefore, must include not only the traditional health- and injury-related courses but also course work identical to that needed by prospective sport and fitness managers in other settings. As part of the "new breed" of athletic trainers, you will be a provider of services and, as such, will manage people as well as injuries. In addition, you will be required to manage the environment in which sport- and fitness-related activities occur. This expectation mandates that you be thoroughly prepared in the tenets of risk management and legal liability and that you be capable of developing risk management plans that will withstand the legal challenges of our litigious culture.

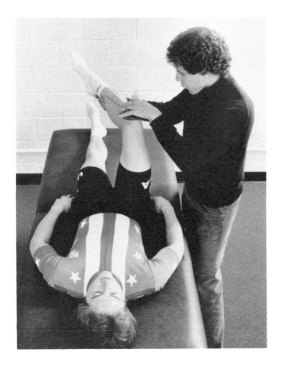

Athletic trainers work in nontraditional settings such as the sports medicine clinic.

CAREER AREAS

Confusion over terminology has accompanied the growth in visibility and popularity of sport and fitness activities. Many people consider the terms *sports medicine* and *athletic training* to be synonymous and frequently use them interchangeably. This use is technically incorrect and can be very misleading.

Sports Medicine

The American College of Sports Medicine (ACSM) is the professional association that establishes guidelines for the practice of sports medicine. According to the ACSM (Lamb, 1981), sports medicine is

the study of the physiological, biomechanical, psychosocial, and pathological phenomena associated with exercise and athletics and the clinical application of the knowledge gained from this study to the improvement and maintenance of functional capacities for physical labor, exercise, and athletics and to the prevention and treatment of disease and injuries related to exercise and athletics. (p. 2)

Specifically, the ACSM considers sports medicine to be concerned with

- basic physiological, biomechanical, and behavioral mechanisms associated with exercise;
- improvement and maintenance of functional capabilities for daily living;
- prevention and rehabilitation of chronic and degenerative diseases;
- evaluation and conditioning of athletes; and
- prevention and treatment of injuries related to sport and exercise.

McCloy (1958) provided evidence of the complexity of sports medicine when he identified 17 major areas of study within the field: physiology, anatomy, anthropology, hygiene, pathology, clinical setting, rehabilitation, surgery, exercise, psychology, sport participants, conditioning, pedagogy, athletic training, research, publications, and tests and measurements. Clearly, sports medicine is a multidisciplinary endeavor requiring knowledge that extends into the medical field.

In recognition of the incredibly wide scope of sports medicine and the fact that an academic specialization in sports medicine is a practical impossibility, the concept of sports medicine teams has developed. These teams include not only medical doctors but also personnel who specialize in one or more of the areas indicated in Table 11.1.

Table 11.1 reveals that sports medicine personnel include physicians, exercise physiologists, researchers, nutritionists, coaches, trainers, therapists, and athletic trainers. Many of these professions require advanced academic

Table 11.1 Disciplines/Fields in Sports Medicine

| I. Training and conditioning for sports activity | | | | II. Clinical/injury aspects of sports medicine | | | |
| Exercise physiologists, coaches, athletic trainers | | | | Physicians | | | |
Physiological aspects of training	Diet/nutrition for sports	Youth, aged, and gender considerations	Miscellaneous; environments, drugs	Preseason evaluations	Diagnosis	Treatment	Rehabilitation
Exercise physiologists, researchers	Nutritionists, dieticians	Coaches, trainers	Physiologists, physicians	Physicians	Physicians	Physicians, therapists	Therapists, athletes

Other allied health professionals may help out here—physical therapists, athletic trainers preparation and experience. Athletic training, however, is a field you can enter with an undergraduate education and one that offers diverse career opportunities.

Athletic Training

The NATA defines athletic training as "the art and science of prevention and management of injuries at all levels of athletic activity" (Booher, 1989, p. 4). The provider of athletic training services is an athletic trainer, a qualified health professional and a vital member of the sports medicine team.

In a study conducted by the NATA, Grace and Ledderman (1982) divided the responsibilities of athletic trainers into six major categories: prevention; recognition and evaluation; management and treatment; rehabilitation; organization and administration; and education and counseling. Each of these areas is extremely important, and all are interrelated. Athletic trainers must develop knowledge and competencies in each category in order to provide athletes with optimal care and to manage the health care setting effectively. Athletic trainers must integrate and apply a wide array of complex practical skills with medical and scientific information in the areas of anatomy, physiology, kinesiology, psychology, physiology of exercise, health, physics, nutrition, and first aid. In addition, athletic trainers must have a sincere interest in athletics and in working with athletes.

Primary Functions of Athletic Trainers

Athletic trainers have a wide variety of responsibilities; primary duties come from each of the six categories identified by Grace and Ledderman (1982).

Prevention of Injuries.   Prevention of injuries requires knowledge of common risk factors and variables affecting the causes of athletic injuries.

Prevention is the best method of managing and caring for athletic injuries; therefore, the athletic trainer devotes much time and effort to preventing injuries.

Athletic trainers should insist that sport enthusiasts receive a thorough physical examination prior to participation. The preparticipation evaluation cannot guarantee that a person will not be injured, but it can affirm that no discernible clinical reason precludes participation.

The most important concept in preventing injuries is physical conditioning. Proper conditioning is the preventive medicine of sport participation, and athletic trainers often work in conjunction with other individuals to establish preseason, in-season, and postseason physical conditioning programs.

Another facet of athletic injury prevention is the selection, fitting, and maintenance of protective equipment. Most sport enthusiasts are familiar with protective tape, pads, bandages, braces, and other devices applied by trainers.

Observation of sport participants plays a critical role in the prevention of injuries. If recognized early, minor problems can often be treated with minimal inconvenience to the individual and with little to no significant effect on performance. Early recognition and effective treatment prevent most minor injuries from becoming more severe and disabling.

Recognition and Evaluation of Injuries.   Recognition and evaluation require a familiarity with signs and symptoms of a variety of sport injuries. Athletic trainers are usually at the scene of the injury and are expected to provide emergency care, recognizing and treating conditions such as severe head or spine injuries, hemorrhaging, shock, heat illness, and choking. In these situations, athletic trainers must be prepared to administer cardiopulmonary resuscitation, apply emergency splinting, or supervise the transportation of an injured participant.

An athletic trainer's initial assessment creates the foundation or data base for the ensuing procedures. The assessment begins with the collection of data related to the injury. From this information, the athletic trainer must determine and initiate the appropriate course of action. This action may include emergency medical care, follow-up treatment recommendations, transportation, medical referral, rehabilitation strategies, or return to the sport activity. Once the trainer has taken action, he or she must continually evaluate the results; assessment and reassessment are ongoing procedures in athletic training.

Management and Treatment of Injuries. Management and treatment involve the provision of appropriate care for sport injuries and illnesses according to accepted standards (e.g., American National Red Cross, American Heart Association, and NATA). Treatment procedures in which athletic trainers must be skilled include administering immediate first aid, providing therapy to promote healing and recovery, applying protective devices to support and protect an injured area, and referring an injured individual for medical assistance when necessary.

Rehabilitation of Injuries. Rehabilitation involves efforts toward the restoration of normal form and function after an injury. Rehabilitation of a sport injury is a three-step process involving examination of the signs and symptoms, application of reconditioning routines, and assessment of the effects of these techniques on the signs and symptoms. During rehabilitation, the trainer should repeat assessment techniques to evaluate progress and indicate appropriate follow-up care.

Organization and Administration of Programs. Organization and administration refer to the management of the athletic training room or sports medicine clinic. As managers, athletic trainers must plan, organize, lead, and evaluate in the same way that managers in other settings function. Trainers must develop and implement procedures and policies necessary to provide the sport participant with effective health care and

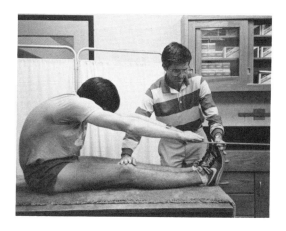

Assessment of readiness to play after rehabilitation is an important role of the athletic trainer.

risk management, and they must maintain accurate and detailed records to document injuries and treatments as well as services rendered to the client. Selecting, purchasing, and maintaining equipment and supplies necessary for operation of a training room and instructing others how to use these items are also among the athletic trainer's management responsibilities. Effective leadership skills are imperative for success in organization and administration of athletic training programs.

Education and Counseling. Education and counseling responsibilities require athletic trainers to stay current in their knowledge of sports medicine issues and to share this information with others. In addition, athletic trainers must be able to recognize situations that call for consultation with other health care professionals and must ensure referral of the injured person to the appropriate professional.

To be effective in education and counseling, athletic trainers must possess communication skills that enable them to interact with sport enthusiasts, parents, coaches, administrators, physicians, and other professionals.

Certification of Athletic Trainers

The NATA administers a certification examination designed to assess specific athletic training competencies. Most authorities consider certification by the NATA as the standard qualification for the practice of athletic training. Indeed, most professional positions in athletic training require Athletic Trainer Certification (ATC), the official designation granted to individuals who successfully complete the written, oral, and computer-simulation portions of the NATA Certification Examination.

Academic preparation for the certification examination and, hence, for a career in athletic training requires extensive course work in the following areas of study: first aid and emergency care, therapeutic modalities, therapeutic exercises, athletic training program administration, human anatomy, human physiology, kinesiology, biomechanics, nutrition, psychology, personal and community health, instructional methods, and prevention, care, and evaluation of injury and illness. In addition to having proper academic preparation, the applicant must spend a specific number of hours in clinical settings.

The NATA strives constantly to improve both the quality and the status of athletic training. Increasing legal complexities and the significant degree of overlap among various health-related professions prompted the NATA in 1976 to launch a nationwide effort to encourage state credentials in the form of licensing, registration, or state-regulated certification. Several states have implemented such legislation, although other states are still in the planning stages. This trend should continue, and eventually most states will have rules and regulations regarding the practice of athletic training.

Employment Opportunities for Athletic Trainers

The employment picture for athletic trainers is changing rapidly. Traditionally, trainers have worked in high schools, teaching one or more curricular subjects in addition to performing duties in the training room and on the field or court. Sport management students, however, are less likely to seek employment in the secondary school setting but may work in other settings such as sports medicine clinics, hospitals, corporations, university athletics, or professional sport.

Clinic or Corporate Trainer.   During the past decade, the number of people participating in both organized and recreational sport has multiplied exponentially. This explosion of interest in physical activity has been accompanied by a marked increase in the number of sports medicine clinics devoted to serving the needs of both high-profile athletes and "weekend warriors." Services provided by these clinics vary considerably. Some specialize in therapy and rehabilitation, whereas others include physiological and biomechanical testing and analysis. Some of these programs are managed by physicians, others by registered or licensed physical therapists. In sports medicine clinics, physical therapists or physical therapy aides usually administer therapy. The number of athletic trainers employed by sports medicine clinics should increase significantly by 1994. With an eye toward the future, Don Wilson of the Rehabilitation Clinic of Houston is currently conducting a role-delineation survey to ascertain the responsibilities of these clinic or corporate trainers. According to Wilson (cited in National Athletic Trainers' Association, 1988), the survey is "intended to determine where they are, what they do, who they work for, and what their income is" (p. 5). A goal of this research is to alter the athletic training curriculum "to include more specific education to prepare students who will graduate into clinic/corporate positions" (p. 5).

University Athletics.   At the university level, the status of athletic trainers varies considerably from one institution to another, depending on the size and philosophy of each institution. Many smaller colleges employ trainers in the dual capacities of instructor and athletic trainer. This type of situation commonly prevails when athletic programs are part of an academic unit such as sport management or physical education.

In many universities and colleges, athletics and academics function as separate entities. Athletic trainers in this situation generally have little, if any, connection with the teaching faculty. In such cases, trainers are members of the athletic staff and function on a full-time basis with no other duties, unless an academic department offers them part-time teaching positions. Pay scales and job security vary with each institution. Regardless of the organizational structure of the athletic and academic programs, trainers who wish to teach in the classroom on either an assigned or adjunct basis usually must possess at least a master's degree. The Johnson & Johnson survey revealed that 70 percent of the NATA-certified trainers in 1987 held graduate degrees (National Athletics Trainers' Association, 1988, p. 4), which indicates that advanced degrees are the rule rather than the exception among athletic trainers.

Professional Sport. Relatively few opportunities exist in professional sport for novice athletic trainers. Those employed in professional sport generally have a great deal of prior experience working with athletes in the specific sport and frequently possess a degree in physical therapy. In either event, the athletic trainer in professional sport is usually a seasonal employee. As with the higher education setting, salary and job security vary markedly.

Salaries

Starting salaries in athletic training range from approximately $14,000 per year to $25,000 per year. The lower salaries are found in schools with scarce financial resources, which may issue contracts for a 9-month period. The 12-month sports medicine clinic salaries are higher. As with other careers associated with sport, financial reward may not be a primary factor in your decision to become a certified athletic trainer.

LEARNING ACTIVITIES

1. How many athletic trainers are hired by your institution? List their names, job titles, and responsibilities.
2. What benefits does an athletic trainer offer a sport participant?
3. At what age group or level of competition do you believe an athletic trainer is most needed? Why?
4. Interview one of the sports medicine professionals listed in Table 11.1 and consider whether you would enjoy this person's job.

REFERENCES

Booher, J.M., & Thibodeau, G.A. (1989). *Athletic injury assessment*. St. Louis: Times Mirror/Mosby.

Grace, P., & Ledderman, L. (1982). Role delineation study for the certification examination for entry level athletic trainers. *Athletic Training*, **17**(4), 264.

Lamb, D.R. (1981). Sports medicine—What is it? ACSM president's report. *Sports Medicine Bulletin*, **16**(2), 2-3.

McCloy, C.H. (1958). What is sports medicine? *Journal of Health, Physical Education and Recreation*, **29**(1), 45-48.

National Athletic Trainers' Association. (1988). The future of athletic training. *NATA News*, **1**(1), 4.

National Athletic Trainers' Association (1988). Update on new NATA committees. *NATA News*, **1**(1), 5.

Professional Organizations

American Academy of Pediatrics, Sports Committee

American Board of Physical Therapy Specialists, American Physical Therapy Association

American College of Sports Medicine

American Orthopaedic Society for Sports Medicine

National Athletic Trainers' Association, Inc.

National Collegiate Athletic Association, Competitive Safeguards and Medical Aspects of Sports Committee

The National Federation of State High School Athletic Associations

Professional Publications

Athletic Training: The Journal of the National Athletic Trainers' Association

The Journal of Orthopaedic and Sports Physical Therapy

Medicine and Science in Sports

The Physician and Sportsmedicine

CHAPTER 12

Aquatics Management

E. Louise Priest
Council for National Cooperation in Aquatics

The aquatics field offers a variety of opportunities in agency, commercial, and educational careers. Although most professionals who are in the aquatics field today received little prior career counseling or preparation, these professionals recognize the value of the carefully planned academic and work experiences now available to students (Quain & Parks, 1986). Intrinsic to aquatics careers are opportunities and responsibilities that many people value, such as motivating and teaching, helping people achieve, working in a relaxed environment, and excelling personally.

TYPES OF CAREERS

Aquatics careers fall into three broad categories: public and private agencies; commercial settings, which offer both career and entrepreneurial opportunities; and the educational sector. Most settings offer both managerial and program opportunities; those who work in programs have more client contact, whereas managers and administrators are involved in activities such as marketing, accounting, budgeting, public speaking, personnel supervision, and designing, directing, and coordinating programs.

Aquatics management specialists need the knowledge to oversee projects such as this pool repair work.

CAREERS WITH PUBLIC AND PRIVATE AGENCIES

Some of the public and private agencies that offer careers in aquatics are the YMCA, YWCA, JCC, youth clubs, ARC, and city park departments. These agencies employ aquatics specialists for program positions that offer potential for career advancement. For example, many chapters of the American Red Cross employ aquatics specialists who can eventually advance to director positions. Red Cross directors of health and safety often carry both program and administrative responsibilities. Most agencies use similar job titles and position descriptions and require similar competencies. Aquatics specialist/program coordinator, aquatics director/water safety director, and aquatics program manager are three titles frequently used in association with aquatic positions.

Aquatics Specialist/Program Coordinator

An aquatics specialist has maximum client contact. This person must have current certification, a strong base in aquatics content, an effective teaching style, strong interpersonal communication skills, and good physical and personal safety skills. Table 12.1 identifies the characteristics essential for aquatics specialists.

Certifications

In addition to basic competencies, agencies often require certain specialty certifications.

Table 12.1   Characteristics of Aquatics Specialists

1. Knowledge of aquatics, including abilities to
   a. demonstrate or describe correct performance of numerous aquatic skills and
   b. analyze and correct errors
2. Knowledge of sound teaching styles, including abilities to
   a. use biomechanical principles in demonstrations or explanations,
   b. use teaching strategies appropriate to the group,
   c. minimize students' fears, and
   d. employ flotation devices as needed
3. Knowledge of factors that affect instruction, including
   a. age of students,
   b. frequency, location, and quality of practice,
   c. learning plateaus, and
   d. skill progression
4. Knowledge of procedures and techniques, including abilities to
   a. ensure safety of students,
   b. classify students according to skill levels,
   c. prepare appropriate objectives,
   d. construct sound lesson plans,
   e. select effective drills and formations, and
   f. evaluate skills
5. Patience

Note. From *Teaching Aquatics* (p. 6) by J. Torney and R. Clayton, 1981, Minneapolis: Burgess. Copyright 1981 by Robert Clayton. Adapted by permission.

Table 12.2, adapted from Torney and Clayton (1981), lists specialty areas and those agencies or organizations that offer instructor training and certification.

The following duties are usually performed by aquatics specialist/program coordinator: teaching at all levels, lifeguarding and safety education, handling emergency situations on both individual and group levels, coaching in any specialty area, conducting special events (e.g., water shows), assisting in development of promotional materials, scheduling classes and meets, training volunteers and aides in various capacities, and overseeing equipment and facility maintenance.

Aquatics Director/ Water Safety Director

Aquatics directors and directors of water safety generally have the qualifications and competencies of aquatics specialists plus the bonus of practical experience. The ability to supervise incorporates organizational skills that may be gained through experience and additional study. Responsibilities of this position are program evaluation and planning, staff evaluation, record keeping, budget planning, equipment evaluation and recommendations, in-service training of staff, development of promotional materials, public relations, and crowd control.

Table 12.2   Certification Specialties and Sponsoring Agencies

Specialty certification	Beginning instructors
Swimming	Universities throughout U.S. and Canada, American Red Cross, Boy Scouts, Canadian Red Cross Society
Swimming for preschoolers	YMCA, American Red Cross
Lifeguarding	YMCA, United States Life Saving Association, Royal Life Saving Society—Canada, American Red Cross
Competitive swimming	Colleges throughout U.S. and Canada, YMCA, Canadian Amateur Swimming Association
Springboard diving	Colleges throughout U.S. and Canada, YMCA, Canadian Amateur Diving Association, U.S. Professional Diving Coaches Association
Swimming for disabled persons	YMCA, American Red Cross
Scuba	YMCA, National Association of Underwater Instructors, Professional Association of Diving Instructors, National Association of Underwater Instructors—Canada, Association of Canadian Underwater Councils
Boating	YMCA, American Red Cross
Synchronized swimming	YMCA, Canadian Amateur Synchronized Swimming Association, U.S. Synchronized Swimming
Water polo	Colleges throughout U.S. and Canada, YMCA, Canadian Amateur Water Polo Association
Pool chemistry	Colleges throughout U.S. and Canada, local health departments, National Spa and Pool Institute
Aquatic facilities manager	Colleges throughout U.S. and Canada

Note. From *Teaching Aquatics* (p. 3) by J. Torney and R. Clayton, 1981, Minneapolis: Burgess. Copyright 1981 by Robert Clayton. Adapted by permission.

Aquatics Program Manager

Many agencies do not differentiate between a director and a manager, and many aquatics directors are indeed the managers and supervisors of all aquatics programs and staff. Where there is a differentiation, aquatics program managers assume additional tasks such as financial accounting and management; budgetary control; staff counseling and evaluation; public relations and public speaking; recruiting and management of staff; and promotion and marketing.

Competencies for Management Positions

Many organizations and agencies follow a "logical" progression of promotions—from aquatics instructor or specialist to aquatics director and finally to aquatics manager or supervisor. Thus, the aquatics manager is sometimes a program specialist promoted to a managerial position. Many program-oriented people learn good managerial skills and are quite successful managers, because they acquire basic competencies necessary for advancement; these competencies are as follows.

- Understanding of personnel and administration policies, including the professional counseling of staff, the ability to interview effectively, and the ability to deal with confrontation
- Familiarity with state and federal legislation affecting the agency or organization
- Familiarity with local (city or county) needs and trends
- Perspective on the role of the agency within the total community
- Ability to manage information that is pertinent to aquatics and to implement its inclusion in staff education

Advancement Within Agencies

Most agencies employing aquatics staff offer advancement opportunities to qualified personnel, especially advancement within a program (e.g., from specialist to program manager). In addition, many opportunities exist in other areas, including agency management. The person who enjoys aquatics may not want to leave the field to go into agency management, though others perceive these positions as advancement. Direct program involvement provides many people sufficient challenges and rewards, and they prefer to stay in that area rather than moving to agency management. Intrinsic rewards combined with satisfactory pay scales make program management positions the choices of many fine professionals.

COMMERCIAL AND ENTREPRENEURIAL CAREERS IN AQUATICS

Opportunities for commercial careers in aquatics and for entrepreneurial experiences are almost unlimited. In Table 12.3, Johnson (1984) identifies commercial, health and fitness, and "aquapreneur" opportunities.

Additional administrative and managerial positions are found with aquatics theme parks, water flumes, amusement parks, marine facilities, government facilities, military pools and beaches, small lakes, and private swim clubs.

Generally, commercial and entrepreneurial careers require the basic competencies defined earlier in this chapter, with the possible addition of special training and experience. To be a successful entrepreneur, you must have finance and marketing skills. In addition, personal fitness is required for employment in this area (Quain & Parks, 1986). Active practitioners prioritized the following competencies neces-

Table 12.3 Commercial and Entrepreneur Careers in Aquatics

Commercial careers in aquatics	Health and fitness careers
Aquatic retail—selling swimming, water skiing, scuba, surfing, boating, and fishing equipment	Health spas—working for private clubs or hotels
Swimming pool sales	Health centers—working in rehabilitation or therapy
Swimming pool contracting	Hospitals—working in rehabilitation or therapy
Swimming pool services—providing staff, equipment, and maintenance	**Aquapreneur* Opportunities**
Resort/hotel services—managing lessons, rentals, and equipment	Private swim schools—e.g., Jack Nelson
Swim schools—teaching competitive, tiny tots, and synchronized swimming	Private clubs—swim and tennis
	Consulting—design, water safety, sanitation, and scuba
Small craft school—teaching sailing, canoeing, and wind surfing	Special programs—e.g., Macmillan Offshore Survival Training (MOST)
Scuba diving—teaching, resort/hotel photography, salvage, treasure hunting, law enforcement	Expert witness—aquatic liability cases
Marina operation	Writing and editing—agencies, publishers, magazines, and journals

Note. From "Preparation for a Career in Aquatics" by Ralph Johnson, 1986, *National Aquatics Journal*, **2**(2), p. 2. Reprinted by permission.

*One who organizes, manages, and assumes the risk of an aquatics-related business.

sary for success in management: (1) human relations and personnel management, (2) time management, (3) money management, (4) personal fitness, (5) public speaking, (6) writing, and (7) knowledge of sports (Quain & Parks, 1986).

CAREERS IN THE EDUCATIONAL SECTOR

Aquatics careers in the educational sector primarily involve teaching and coaching positions. Teaching in public schools requires a 4-year college degree and a state teaching certificate; most colleges and universities require graduate degrees. In addition, educators—particularly in higher education—are involved in curriculum design and research and need extensive knowledge of related technical literature. Coaching in high schools, colleges, and universities may or may not require a state teaching certificate, depending on the hiring practices of the institutions. Instructing aquatics in schools for disabled children requires a specific program of study. Directing aquatics facilities in colleges or universities requires a business management background.

In a survey of 140 colleges and universities, Thomas (1986) indicated 16 types of aquatics courses taught in universities, with more than 90 percent of the institutions having the basic courses of swimming, lifesaving, and water safety instructor training. Sixty-three of the institutions surveyed offered aquatics fitness, 56 listed springboard diving, and 84 listed scuba instruction. These institutions offer a diversified teaching experience by qualified faculty members and provide basic aquatics training to future professionals.

In addition, the International Swimming Hall of Fame in Ft. Lauderdale, FL, houses a library of aquatics publications.

THE JOB MARKET

Professional associations provide the best information regarding the job market. NRPA and AAHPERD both offer position referral services and regularly list many vacancies in their publications. The American Red Cross, Boys Clubs of America, and YMCA national offices list positions throughout the United States on a regular basis. Most university campuses offer placement services to students, and many professional organizations include placement services and interview opportunities as a part of their national conventions.

A career in aquatics looks promising, especially if you have carefully prepared. The diversity of the field, the expansion of commercial ventures, and the ever-increasing participation in aquatics sport and recreation by millions of Americans will only increase professional opportunities for those who are interested and well prepared.

LEARNING ACTIVITIES

1. Form a team of three persons and evaluate an aquatics facility, the programs offered, and the management of the facility. Each person should review an area, focusing on the following considerations.

   a. Facility—pool design, filtration system, disinfection system, equipment, safety standards, and security considerations

   b. Programs—planning, schedule, equipment needs, staffing needs, and program standards

   c. Management—philosophy, chain of command, operations budget, rules and regulations, records and reports, and emergency action plan

2. Interview several aquatics professionals, focusing on their educational and professional backgrounds, management philosophies, administrative duties, professional involvements, and opinions on national trends. Also ask them what preparation young professionals need for success in the field.

REFERENCES

Johnson, R. (1986). Preparation for a career in aquatics. *National Aquatics Journal*, **2**(1), 2-3.

Quain, R.J., & Parks, J.B. (1986). Sport management survey: Employment perspectives. *Journal of Physical Education, Recreation and Dance*, **57**(4), 18-21.

Thomas, D. (1986). Survey of aquatic education in 140 colleges and universities in the United States. *National Aquatics Journal*, **2**(2), 10-14.

Torney, J., & Clayton, R. (1981). *Aquatic organization and management*. New York: Macmillan.

Professional Organizations

American Alliance for Health, Physical
  Education, Recreation and Dance
American Camping Association
American Canoe Association
American Red Cross
American Water Ski Association
Council for National Cooperation in Aquatics
Handicapped Boaters Association
Handicapped Scuba Association
National Association of Underwater
  Instructors
National Recreation & Park Association
Professional Association of Diving
  Instructors
United States Coast Guard Office of Boating
  Safety
U.S. Rowing
United States Synchronized Swimming
YMCA Scuba Program

Professional Publications

*Journal of Physical Education, Recreation
  and Dance*
National Aquatics Journal
Conference Reports
Parks & Recreation
Therapeutic Recreation Journal
Splash
Palaestra
Swimming World
Diving Journal
The Olympian

CHAPTER 13

Consulting and Entrepreneurship

David L. Groves
Bowling Green State University

Two professional opportunities within sport management are consulting and entrepreneurship, which both require an understanding of business principles. Positive incorporation of the appropriate principles helps increase profits and ensures success during economic stress. Changing an ineffective operation or developing a new one is more difficult than managing a business to show a profit. The difference lies in knowing which principles to apply.

It is common for a consultant to use simple trial and error to solve the problems of an ailing sport enterprise. Or an entrepreneur who has been successful in some industry will invest heavily in a sport enterprise and try to apply the same management principles that made the other industry a success, with the result usually being failure. The common denominator to these situations is a lack of understanding of the business theories that apply to sport management and an inability to apply these principles in a scientific manner to solve problems.

SUCCESS

Sport enterprises do not respond well to the traditional supply and demand processes or to the traditional sport concept of winning and losing. Success requires a thorough understanding of sport as a content area as well as of the particular sport. For example, arena management techniques differ for hockey games and basketball games. The audiences are different and expect different outcomes; a good manager must be sensitive to these needs and provide differing conditions accordingly.

Application of Information

Beyond understanding existing sporting circumstances, successful sport consultants or entrepreneurs must be able to actually create or become a part of the process to change those circumstances. They understand a sport as well as its business principles and conditions, and they have the know-how to change conditions to bring success, whether as advisers or investors. For example, some universities manage football games as if all spectators were football enthusiasts. Other universities emphasize the tailgate party aspect, thus reaching more people with a different type of experience. Their emphasis is not upon winning but the conditions surrounding the game.

129

Self-Assurance

Self-assurance is another prerequisite for success. Most business ventures can be successful if time and energy are put into implementation, with enough flexibility to fit changing needs. A good idea must be field-tested and developed through an evolutionary cycle, with the barriers that cause failure removed during the implementation phases. It takes confidence in an idea to work through such barriers. For example, managers of professional football franchises that have been successful throughout the years (such as the Dallas Cowboys, the Los Angeles Raiders, and the Miami Dolphins) have had enough confidence in their systems to stay with them through both good and bad years. The system itself did not make the difference as much as the confidence in implementing the system and making needed changes.

Patience

Patience and time are primary ingredients for success. Frequently, however, consultants and entrepreneurs do not allow for these two dimensions in their time frames. Investors typically have very short time frames for judging success. The United States Football League, for example, did not have the financial resources to compete with the National Football League. They had a very short time frame and did not use their resources well, and consequently failed.

Plans or recommendations for investments must allow enough time for an idea to work, and the idea must be continuously revised to fit the system. Failure is an important part of implementation, especially in the short run, because it is through mistakes that one learns to modify and refine a system. Most business successes could not have occurred without some failures. Successful consultants and entre-

preneurs learn from mistakes and effectively use this knowledge to change.

RISK

A critical aspect of consulting and entrepreneurship is risk. Consulting represents passive risk (advice) and entrepreneurship active risk (investment). If consultants' recommendations are not successful, their reputations suffer. Reputation is a primary risk because it is the very basis for attracting new business. For an entrepreneur who invests money in a particular enterprise, the risk is not only no return on the investment but a loss of the entire investment and maybe more if other assets must be encumbered to cover losses. The key to reducing risk is an understanding of why certain systems work under certain circumstances and how conditions may be created for change to occur.

CONSULTING

Consulting services encompass a wide range, from conducting market studies to working on facility design. Consultants usually have specialties and focus on areas in which advice is needed but cannot be provided by expertise within an organization. Sometimes internal expertise does exist, but an objective outsider's view is necessary to formulate a different perspective. Most consultants develop procedures over a number of years that enable them to generalize principles, see the bigger picture, and provide appropriate perspective. An initial investigation is needed for the consultant to understand the client's circumstance in comparison with other operations to determine what solutions might be effective.

Consultants are typically hired on the basis of established records of success. Sometimes an established firm that has built its reputation on creativity and ingenuity becomes conservative to avoid risking failure and, as a result, its reputation. Such consultants often cease to provide effective advice. Frequently, the failure of a business can be traced to a poor study by a consultant.

Years of experience do not automatically translate to success as a consultant. The primary ingredient, rather, is an understanding of the principles underlying a particular sport and what makes it successful. This understanding may be the result of education, experience, or intuition. Success requires a mix of these elements as well as a mechanism for establishing a reputation. The reputation is the most critical element because it is the entree to a successful career. Another avenue is a junior position in an established consulting firm.

Client relationships are important, especially understanding a client's information needs. Quality of services can range from ineffective to effective to efficient. Dollars spent by clients do not directly correlate with the quality of advice or expertise that is applied to a problem. Selecting the right consultant is extremely important for the client. There are few guidelines for the process, but a number of consultants should be interviewed and a rigorous questioning process used to determine that the chosen consultant can deliver the types of services needed.

Recommendations of consultants must be scrutinized. Complete operations are built around a consultant's report, and an operation is only as good as the accuracy of the information provided. Millions of dollars may hinge upon the advice of these individuals. Ideas must be field- or pilot-tested (by an independent party to avoid bias) to help predict the probability of success.

It is unfortunate that advice given by consultants has been responsible for the failure of many businesses, resulting in a new dimension in the consulting arena: liability. The question of whether consultants can be held accountable for financial losses incurred by clients will be decided by the judicial system and may require legislation.

The primary reason for many failures is that consultants frequently base decisions on a single circumstance or success pattern that is not generalizable. It can be difficult to get objective information about a consultant's success rate. If more than one consultant is commissioned, the opinions presented may be quite divergent—consulting is more of an art than a science because intuitive, practical processes must be applied. A more scientific, empirical approach is needed and is taken by many successful consulting firms. A contingency approach must be developed, that is, giving advice that is appropriate to the specific situation.

Experience and education are necessary if a consultant's advice is to be sound.

Another important question is whether consultants' fees should be contingent upon the success of the operation. The best answer is no, but those who want to get into the consulting arena may use this technique as an avenue into the profession. Anyone interested in becoming a consultant in sport management must have expertise in a specialty, such as service marketing, feasibility studies, or business plans, to fill clients' needs for information in a particular area. A consultant needs both education and experience to be able to give advice for various contingencies. The individual must have confidence to make recommendations and to see them through with tenacity, ingenuity, and creativity.

ENTREPRENEURSHIP

Entrepreneurship involves active risk of money, time, and effort in an idea or endeavor. Entrepreneurship is often wrongly considered possible only for those with great financial resources. It is true that individuals without the necessary resources must have the know-how to obtain them or the ingenuity to create them. The important factor is independence, meaning that entrepreneurs must have sufficient resources to sustain them if a venture fails. Those without such resources should not undertake the investment.

Objectivity

Entrepreneurship involves great risk, and the risk takers may lose objectivity by becoming obsessed with an idea and committed to seeing it to fruition. Objectivity is critical to entrepreneurship, to the ability to assess one's chances of success. Most entrepreneurial efforts in sport are undertaken by individuals outside of sport. Their purposes may include a desire to be associated with a sport, an avid interest in a particular sport, or a desire to control individuals

who have athletic talent. All of these are laden with emotional and subjective overtones, and ventures started for such reasons typically have little stability over time. An owner-operator who lacks the required expertise and understanding of sport and business principles may face catastrophic losses and damage beyond the initial operation. As more individuals with formal education and practical experience in sport management become instrumentally involved with entrepreneurship, they will bring scientific elements of management to their endeavors and consequently reduce risks, increase stability, and enhance the chances of success.

Innovation

Another key to successful entrepreneurship is the ability to be an innovator, not merely a follower of trends. "Papa Bear" Hallas of the Chicago Bears and Art Rooney of the Pittsburgh Steelers, team owners who have had a significant impact on professional football, are examples of innovators. They recognized the value of football to American society and helped popularize the game. Although innovation has the greatest potential for profit and satisfaction, it also involves the greatest risk. As an innovative venture develops and grows and others invest in the same product or service, an oversupply may develop and result in failure. It is important, therefore, to be involved in the upswing of a business venture, not the leveling off or downswing.

Innovative entrepreneurial efforts are not restricted to new products or services. Innovation and creativity are just as important to ongoing ventures because it is the competitive edge in delivering sport services that will bring success.

Critical Dimensions of Entrepreneurship

There are four critical dimensions to entrepreneurship: creating new demand; controlling costs; generating diversified revenue; and procuring adequate investment capital.

Creating Demand

Creating new demand is achieved through understanding business principles that relate to providing quality products or services and applying those concepts to the marketing function. Consumer satisfaction determines the success of an operation and brings consistent growth. Entrepreneurs must be able to deliver quality products and services to bring high customer satisfaction and retention. Word-of-mouth advertising by satisfied customers is the least expensive and most effective form of promotion. Minor league baseball's Louisville Cardinals are a good example of a consumer-oriented enterprise, and their success is ample proof of the validity of the concept; they have developed a sound foundation based on client satisfaction.

Novice entrepreneurs frequently overlook the facts that only a specific population will support a particular type of sport enterprise and that a minimum number of people must demand a product or service to ensure success. A basic idea will not sell just as a result of its natural potential or attraction. Experienced entrepreneurs know that demand *may* occur as a natural outgrowth of an activity itself but that more often demand is the direct result of a conscious effort to create it.

Controlling Costs

An understanding of cost control within an operation is critical. In many facility-oriented parts of the sport industry, such as fitness clubs, the danger of excessive expenditures is inherent. Many sport facilities have failed because the owners did not know how to control costs. The key to cost reduction is efficient operation. Higher costs are not necessarily associated with higher quality services. Many entrepreneurs, however, do not understand this concept: The relationship between efficient operation and

maximum profit is critical. Revenue centers must be well understood and diversified so that if one part of an operation fails, another may be able to pick up the balance. Examples of revenue centers include gate receipts and auxiliary services such as concessions, sponsorship, merchandising, and licensing. A financial plan must be developed to maximize the revenue centers; it must be detailed and directly tied into the initial planning stages of the business.

Professional Organizations

Enterprise Development Association
International Association of African
 and American Black Business People
International Council for Small Business
International Franchise Association
Society for Business Information
World Association of Women Entrepreneurs
International Association of Consulting
 Actuaries
International Marketing, Public Relations,
 and Advertising Consultants
International Association of Economic
 Consultants
International Consultants Foundation
European Federation of Management
 Consultants' Association

Diversifying Revenue

Crucial to a financial plan is developing a process for extracting dollars from consumers. Sport is an intangible service, and money must be elicited from the patron in an effective and efficient manner to create satisfaction. Low gate fees are essential for maximum demand. Some events are natural attractions and a capacity crowd is the result of the event itself. But if demand does not exist, a high entrance fee is a deterrent to attendance.

Understanding motivation behind participation or attendance is important. The event itself is often seen as the primary reason that people participate or attend, but often an event represents something else to the individual. Marketers must understand this concept to know how to promote an event. Sport is not an end in itself but a means to something else for the participant or spectator.

Procuring Capital

Investment capital may be a stumbling block to entrepreneurial effort. Someone without adequate resources has a number of options to consider, including these:

- exchange personal and professional expertise for investment dollars;
- find "creative financing," either public or private;
- form a corporation and sell stock to the public; or
- take over a facility in need of management expertise and put it on a sound financial basis for a percentage of the profits.

It is important to explore many investment avenues and to understand various investment structures. An individual who does not have a large capital investment or expertise, can also enter into a smaller part of an operation. This usually occurs in auxiliary services and involves some type of independent operation. This involves minimal investment but can reap maximum profits and rewards.

A FINAL WORD

Consulting and entrepreneurial efforts can bring monetary rewards and intangible satisfactions but do involve great risk. Keys to success are expertise and confidence applied in practical settings. Consulting or entrepreneurship should be undertaken only after thorough consideration of the impact on the individual and the intended organization, based on both written material and contact with other consultants and entrepreneurs. Although caution is important, many opportunities exist in sport management. There will be new and potentially profitable challenges for those who understand the profession well.

LEARNING ACTIVITIES

Use the case study method common to business and law (in which an initial question is followed with "why" questions to determine cause and effect of operations) to collect information from at least three consultants or entrepreneurs. Analyze the responses you get to help develop a perspective on opportunities in sport consulting and entrepreneurship.

Your interview might include questions like the following:

- How did you get started in your business?
- Where does one obtain financing to start such a business?
- How do you take an idea from initiation to implementation?
- Are any elements in the start-up of a new business in the sport industry especially important to increasing one's success?
- What does it mean to be successful in the sport industry?
- What are the monetary rewards for a consultant or an entrepreneur in the sport industry?
- What are the satisfactions of your association with the sport industry?

- What elements have made you successful in the sport industry?
- What elements will be important to future success in the sport industry?
- What skills or competencies are needed to succeed in the sport industry?
- How do you keep from failing?
- How does the sport industry differ from other industries?
- What business principles apply to the sport industry?
- How do these principles work and why?
- Why do these particular principles work in your segment of the sport industry?

SUGGESTED READINGS

Bermont, H. (1978). *How to become a successful consultant in your own field.* Washington, DC: Bermont Books.

Block, P. (1978). *Flawless consulting: A guide to getting your expertise used.* Austin, TX: Learning Concepts.

Bracus, S.U., III, & Wilkinson, J.W. (1986). *Handbook of management consulting services.* New York: McGraw-Hill.

Brandt, S.C. (1982). *Entrepreneuring.* Reading MA: Addison-Wesley.

Cole, A.H. (1959). *Business enterprise in its social setting.* Cambridge, MA: Harvard University Press.

Costanza, J.L. (1977). *Building and maintaining your own outside consulting practice.* Woodland Hill, CA: Eckman Center.

Czanda, W.M. (1986). *The application of social systems thinking to organizational consulting.* Lanham, MD: University Press of America.

Drucker, P.E. (1985). *Innovation and entrepreneurship: Practices and principles.* New York: Harper and Row.

Gilder, G. (1984). *The spirit of enterprise.* New York: Simon and Schuster.

Golightly, H.C. (1980). *Consults: Selecting, using and evaluating business consultants.* New York: Franklin Watts.

Greenfield, W.M. (1987). *Successful management consulting.* Englewood Cliffs, NJ: Prentice-Hall.

Greiner, L.E., & Metzger, R.O. (1983). *Consulting to management.* Englewood Cliffs, NJ: Prentice-Hall.

Kelley, R.E. (1986). *Consulting: The complete guide to a profitable career.* New York: Scribner.

McLean, J. (1987). *Consultants and consulting organizations directory.* Detroit: Gale Research.

More, G.L. (1984). *The politics of management consulting.* New York: Praeger.

Silver, A.D. (1983). *The entrepreneurial life: How to go for it and get it.* New York: Wiley.

Silver, A.D. (1985). *Entrepreneurial megabucks: The 100 greatest entrepreneurs of the last twenty-five years.* New York: Wiley.

Stryker, S.C. (1984). *Guide to successful consulting.* Englewood Cliffs, NJ: Prentice-Hall.

Taffi, D.J. (1981). *The entrepreneur: A corporate strategy for the '80s.* New York: American Management Association.

Tepper, R. (1985). *Become a top consultant.* New York: Wiley.

Tepper, R. (1987). *The consultant's problem-solving workbook.* New York: Wiley.

Tisdall, P. (1982). *Agents of change.* London: Heinemann.

Weinberg, G.M. (1980). *Secrets of consulting.* New York: Dorset House.

Welsh, J.A., & White, J.F. (1983). *The entrepreneur's master planning guide: How to launch a successful business*. Englewood Cliffs, NJ: Prentice-Hall.

Wilken, P.H. (1979). *Entrepreneurship: A comparative and historical study*. Norwood, NJ: ABLEX.

William, W.B. (1978). *Management and consulting*. Ithaca, NY: Cornell University.

PART II

DEVELOPING PROFESSIONAL SKILLS

CHAPTER 14

Career Planning

JoAnn Kroll and Robert Moomaw
Bowling Green State University

Career development is a comparatively new concept in its application to the world of work. As career development experts who have been involved in career consulting for many years, we have concluded that work choices are more than single exercises in one's life. Rather, they are based upon the total development of an individual as a growing entity who possesses past life experiences and anticipates the future. Fundamental to the process is the concept of career development as a lifelong activity requiring thoughtful analysis, dissection of information, and reconstruction of ideas in the quest for a happy and productive life. In the words of Mark Twain, ''The happiest and most successful person works all year long at what he would otherwise choose to do on his summer vacation.'' Thus, the significance of career development is eminently clear.

This chapter should assist you in making reasoned, well-informed choices about your career and your life. Holland (1973) concluded that individuals with accurate self-knowledge make realistic career choices more frequently than do individuals with less accurate self-appraisals. Likewise, individuals with more information about occupational environments make more congruent and consistent choices than individuals with less information. As Campbell (1974) stated, ''If you don't know where you're going, you'll probably end up someplace else'' (p. 138).

The more information you have, the more sound your career choice will be.

WHAT IS A CAREER?

A career is your total life in the world of work. According to Bolles (1978), ''Careers are often, in everyday conversation, spoken of as though they were synonymous with 'FIELDS of knowledge' or 'majors' so that when we mean to say 'field change' we often content ourselves instead with the less precise phrase 'career change' '' (p. 68). At many stages in your life and career, you will select between two or more roads or paths. Planning for a career and for the changes inherent in a lifetime of work is an active, continual process and requires countless hours of self-evaluation, career exploration, assessment, and reassessment.

You may think about career planning during your freshman year in college or just before your sophomore year. After that time, however, your career thinking begins to take a back seat to the necessary emphases upon courses, study hours, grades, and activities—the gist of being a college student. Careers become less important as you immerse yourself in several more years of being a student. Later, as a junior or senior in college, your thoughts again focus upon career goals rather than upon course work. Work, occupation, and career begin to loom as newly important considerations.

You may ask, Why think about this now? The answer is that an understanding of career planning is essential at this point in your education because most students between the first and fourth years of college typically think of a college education as a "ticket of admission" to the world of work. During these years, many institutions give little assistance to you in your quest for a career. The notable exception to this unfortunate circumstance is usually found at the academic departmental advising level, provided you take advantage of this service.

MYTHS ABOUT CHOOSING A CAREER

Many students choose to avoid career planning because they are influenced by some of the most common myths about career decision making.

Myth 1:

Your academic major predicts your career choice. In reality, careers follow from skills, and even students in vocationally specific majors take jobs outside their major fields of study.

Myth 2:

You begin your career at age 21 and progress in a straight line to your ultimate career objective. Research shows that as you develop new abilities and interests, your career patterns may change. It is not unusual to change career fields 3 to 7 times in your lifetime (Michellozzi, 1984).

Myth 3:

Career planning is an irreversible process (*Ginsberg, 1972*). Your talents and abilities are in a continual state of change, being shaped and reshaped by new experiences. Skills that you acquire through your course work, leisure activities, volunteer experiences, and summer and part-time jobs may affect or alter your long-range career plans (Bolles, 1987).

Myth 4:

Upon graduation from college, you will have few talents that are valuable in the working world (*Madler, 1985*). Most graduates, when assisted in defining and labeling their talents, can claim numerous identifiable skills at graduation (Powell, 1981).

Myth 5:

Career counselors provide instant solutions. Career counselors do not provide instant solutions but can help you manage your career development (Crites, 1981; Tolbert, 1980).

VALUES, INTERESTS, AND SKILLS

Much of what we are and who we become may be attributed to our value structure. This part of our existence helps us to move toward or away from that which we like or dislike and that with which we are comfortable or uncomfortable. According to Rokeach (1973), "A value is an evolving belief that a specific mode of conduct or end-state of existence is personally or socially preferable to an opposite or converse mode of conduct or end-state of existence" (p. 5).

Value Clarification

Rokeach (1973) also states that the total number of values that a person possesses is relatively small; that everyone possesses the same values but to different degrees; that values are organized into value systems; that the antecedents of human values can be traced to culture, to our personalities, and to society and its entities; and that the consequences of human values will be found in virtually all phenomena that social scientists might consider worth investigating and understanding. Because our values and value systems seem to be so pervasive, we can understand why our values play important roles in the hows, whens, whys, whos, and whats of choosing our careers.

Within the context of the world of work, we can define values as the "emotional salary" of work. Values relate to the importance one places on work; they encompass how individuals perceive their work and its contribution to others. During the next 30 to 50 years, you probably will spend 50 to 80 percent of your waking hours involved in a career. If your basic values are in conflict with your career, you may become frustrated, unhappy, and discontented with what you are doing. Your career then becomes something to get away from rather than an integral part of your leisure, work, and educational life.

A career is not merely a way to make a living; it is a way to live, encompassing work, education, and leisure time (Bolles, 1978). Your career represents a major part of your personal identity; your identity influences what you bring into your career and what you feel about your career. As you proceed with your career plan-

ning, you must assess your personal and work values and add them to the other factors you will consider when researching careers. Ultimately you will seek a career position that will enhance and strengthen those values most important to you.

WHAT IS IMPORTANT TO ME IN CHOOSING A CAREER?

Completing the rating scale in Figure 14.1 will help you decide which factors are most important to you in selecting a career. Later you will use these factors to explore possible career alternatives for yourself.

Interests

Interests are integral aspects of our personality structures and are related to values as determinants of where we want to go with our careers. Interests are not entities in themselves but are derived from value systems. Holland (1973) states, "If vocational interests are construed as an expression of personality, then they represent the expression of personality in work, school subjects, hobbies, recreational activities, and preferences. In short, what we have called 'vocational interests' are simply another aspect of personality" (p. 7). Thus, we can consider vocational interests as expressions of total personality. Holland (1973) further states that the theory that interests are expressions of personality is mainly an elaborate engineering of this key idea: "Interest inventories are personality inventories. If vocational interests are an expression of personality, then it follows that interest inventories are personality inventories" (pp. 7-8).

Interests are best described as activities you enthusiastically engage in and find most attractive (Strong, 1943; Super & Crites, 1962).

Check one of the three columns to the right of each statement to show how important you feel that factor is.

	Very important or essential	*Desirable but not essential*	*Not important or necessary*
Example			
A career that permits me to			
16. Travel	X		

The check in Column 1 shows that the opportunity to travel is a very important or essential factor for this person.

	Very important or essential	*Desirable but not essential*	*Not important or necessary*
A career that permits me to			
1. Use my education and training			
2. Have a feeling of accomplishment and achievement about my work			
3. Work at something that is helpful to others			
4. Learn new things and take new responsibilities			
5. Feel important and respected			
6. See the results of my work			
7. Use my initiative			
8. Be challenged			
9. Achieve professional status and prestige			
10. Feel personally satisfied			
11. Express myself			
12. Adhere to a definite time schedule			
13. Work during the day rather than at night			
14. Have my weekends free			
15. Work close to home			
16. Travel			
17. Remain in one area			
18. Work in a comfortable climate			
19. Work with people with whom I could socialize and make friends			
20. Feel a part of a team			
21. Supervise other people			

(Cont.)

Figure 14.1 Important factors in career selection. *Note.* From *Junior/Senior Employment Seminar Workbook* [unpublished manuscript] by S.E. Shumate and J. Kroll, 1983, Kent State University, Kent, OH. Adapted by permission.

	Very important or essential	*Desirable but not essential*	*Not important or necessary*
22. Work independently without constant supervision or pressure from others			
23. Meet many different kinds of people			
24. Meet members of the opposite sex			
25. Work with efficient and good co-workers			
26. Work for a just, fair, and competent supervisor			
27. Compete with others			
28. Have a variety of work responsibilities			
29. Have a highly structured work enviornment			
30. Be on my feet and moving			
31. Organize my own work routines			
32. Work at my own speed, as quickly or as slowly as I like			
33. Work at a fast pace and keep busy all the time			
34. Be creative			
35. Execute the work from start to finish			
36. Work in a pleasant physical environment			
37. Work in an office			
38. Work indoors			
39. Work in a job that is not too demanding physically			
40. Do work that involves little chance of physical injury			
41. Be physically active			
42. Work in a relaxed atmosphere that is free of stress and tension			
43. Work in a small, personal environment where people know each other well			
44. Work in a large, well-organized environment			
45. Work with equipment, machines, and tools			
46. Work with printed materials, ideas, and data			
47. Have a sense of security			

(Cont.)

Figure 14.1   (Continued)

	Very important or essential	Desirable but not essential	Not important or necessary

48. Belong to a union that will look after my rights

49. Be paid well

50. Have work benefits such as health insurance, sick leave, and paid vacation

51. Participate in a retirement plan

52. Earn extra money by working overtime or earning commission or bonus

53. Use my expertise as a consultant

54. Obtain on-the-job training or release time for training

55. Be promoted if I get extra training outside of regular working hours

56. Be promoted based on a seniority system

57. Receive promotions based on my own performance

58. Transfer between departments

59. Advance to new kinds of jobs that may develop in the future

Figure 14.1 (Continued)

Students who are undecided about their career choices are frequently asked, ''What are your interests?'' Although we seem to know what our interests are, we sometimes have difficulty articulating them to ourselves and to others— we frequently cannot put them into words or give them labels. Thus, the interests that we perceive in ourselves lack expression in our oral communications.

We do, however, communicate our interests through our play and our work. Interests that we perceive in ourselves are called *expressed interests*. Those that we exhibit in our work and play are *manifested interests*. To better understand yourself and to be able to identify your interests, you can use interest inventories. These instruments may help you assess your interests and compare them with interest patterns of professionals working in a variety of occupations. A measured assessment of your career interests, coupled with a measure of your abilities and aptitudes (high school and college grades and scores on college entrance exams) can help predict your potential satisfaction with career choices (Crites, 1981). Most counseling and career development centers will administer and interpret interest inventories.

Personality

Holland (1973) maintained that individuals in our culture can be characterized by their resemblances to six personality types and their proclivities for six corresponding types of environments. "Because different types have different interests, competencies, and dispositions, they tend to surround themselves with special people and materials and seek out problems that are congruent with their interests, competencies and outlook on the world" (Holland, 1973, p. 3).

Realistic

Individuals with this orientation enjoy physical activities, aggressive action, and motor coordination. They prefer concrete, well-defined problems as opposed to abstract, intangible ones. They prefer to "act out" rather than "think through" problems. Usually they avoid situations requiring verbal and interpersonal skills. These individuals are often typified by their physical strength and skills, their concrete, practical ways of dealing with problems, and their lack of emphasis on social skills and sensitivities.

Investigative

These people are task oriented and generally prefer to "think through" rather than to "act out" problems. They have marked needs to organize and understand the world. They enjoy ambiguous work tasks and "thinking" activities and may possess somewhat unconventional values and attitudes. They usually avoid problems that require close, interpersonal relationships with others. They cope with the social and physical environments predominantly through the use of intelligence. Characterized by adjectives such as analytical, rational, independent, abstract, cognitive, and perceptive, they typically solve problems primarily through the use of ideas, words, and symbols rather than through physical and social skills.

Artistic

Artistic individuals prefer dealing with problems through self-expression in artistic media. They usually avoid problems requiring intense interpersonal interaction or a high degree of structure or physical skills. The artistic type achieves in the environment by using feelings, emotions, and imagination to create art forms or products. These people use their imaginations through the conception and execution of art to solve problems. They rely principally on subjective impressions and fantasies for interpretations of and solutions to problems. They are characterized further by complexity of outlook, independence of judgment, and originality.

Social

The social types prefer teaching or therapeutic jobs, which may reflect a desire for socializing in a structured setting. Characterized as socially oriented people, they possess verbal and interpersonal skills. Their chief values are humanistic or religious. They usually avoid situations requiring intense intellectual problem solving, physical skills, or highly ordered activities, because they prefer to deal with problems through feelings and interpersonal relationships with others. They are concerned with the welfare of the disadvantaged, poor, uneducated, sick, unstable, young, and aged. They rely on emotions and feelings rather than on intellectual resources to solve problems.

Enterprising

Individuals with this orientation prefer to use their verbal skills in situations that involve influencing, selling, or leading others; they consider themselves leaders. They avoid well-defined language or work situations requiring long periods of intellectual effort. They enjoy power, status, and material possessions.

Conventional

Individuals in this cluster prefer structured verbal and numerical activities. They achieve many of their goals by avoiding ambiguous situations or problems involving interpersonal relationships and physical skills. They fit well into large organizations with a structured chain of command. They select goals, tasks, and values that are usually sanctioned by custom and society. Their approach to problems is practical, consistent, and at times lacking in spontaneity. They are well-controlled, neat, sociable, somewhat inflexible, and persevering.

The explanation of the personal and environmental codes may assist you in discovering your dominant interest/value theme. Although one dominant theme always emerges, it is usually accompanied by at least one or more others, which will give you a more comprehensive understanding of your dominant interest patterns. This information can give you general knowledge of what you like and dislike in comparison with individuals in certain occupational fields.

Skills

Central to the self-exploration process is skill assessment—determining what you have to offer. Unfortunately for some students, the mere mention of the word *skills* triggers a panic response, such as, "I've been attending school the past 4 years and I haven't had the opportunity to acquire any real job skills." The confusion and fright many students feel when asked to list important relevant skills often stem from a misunderstanding of their own abilities.

A method to consider skills involves dividing them into three categories: *work content skills, functional skills*, and *adaptive skills* (Michellozzi, 1984). Work content skills relate to a specific occupational and subject area, which limits their transferability to other occupations. For example, a coach's understanding and knowledge of softball rules are work content skills. Functional skills relate to personal experience and preference. They are more generally classified than work content skills, and they are transferable across many careers and

occupations. A coach's abilities to teach skills, solve problems, and motivate players are excellent examples of functional skills. Adaptive skills reflect personality traits and are characteristics that you bring into a situation because of your disposition, attitudes, and personal qualities. In the sport setting, team loyalty, dependability, competitiveness, and flexibility are typical adaptive skills.

You may have difficulty deciding what abilities you possess. You unconsciously demonstrate many skills every day, and yet you hesitate when someone asks, "What are your strengths?" or "What do you do well?" To determine your skills, follow a four-step process. (1) Become aware of what you do every day. Identify all past accomplishments, whether they are related to academics, extracurricular activities, work, or leisure time. (2) From your list of accomplishments, label the skills involved in those

Assess what you have to offer to particular occupations.

accomplishments. (3) Rearrange the skills, clustering them according to any patterns that may emerge from your list. (4) Prioritize your skills in an order that appeals to you. You may want to order them starting with your greatest strengths, or you may begin with the skills that you most enjoy performing. When assessing your skills, apply the following guidelines offered by Figler (1979): "(1) Do not compare yourself with other reference groups, (2) look for evidence, (3) consider functions, not position titles, (4) be certain you enjoy the skills, (5) label your skills using your own descriptions, (6) focus on seemingly irrelevant as well as relevant experiences" (pp. 72-73).

OCCUPATIONAL INFORMATION

Making realistic career decisions requires that you gather extensive, accurate information about the occupations you consider. Your goal is to identify careers that are congruent with your values, interests, skills, needs, lifestyle, environmental preferences, and other personal planning concerns. Using a systematic approach to collect information is most efficient and will enable you to compare occupations. For each occupation you are considering gather the following information: nature of the work; work setting and conditions; personal qualifications required; education, training, and other qualifications required; earnings; employment outlook and competition; methods of entering the occupation; opportunities for advancement; opportunities for exploring the occupation; related occupations; and sources of additional information.

Sources of Occupational Information

You can obtain occupational information through the resources of print media, computer software, and informational interviewing. Test the usefulness of the resources for career information by considering gender bias, clarity, objectivity, and date of publication. Carefully consider all of the factors mentioned to ensure that the information is accurate and realistic.

Print Media

Three excellent sources published by the U.S. Department of Labor are the *Occupational Outlook Handbook*, the *Dictionary of Occupational Titles* (4th ed., 1977) and the *Guide for Occupational Exploration* (1979). Published every 2 years, the *Occupational Outlook Handbook* contains occupational projections and relevant information on more than 850 occupations in 30 industries. The *Dictionary of Occupational Titles* contains about 35,000 occupational titles and definitions for approximately 22,000 occupations. The *Guide for Occupational Exploration* lists 12 broad job interest areas, which are organized into 60 work groups and 348 subgroups with titles and a list of jobs within each subgroup (Lock, 1988). These publications are standard references in any career resource center, university library, or large public library.

Other useful sources of printed occupational information include the *Encyclopedia of Careers and Vocational Guidance* (1981), *Occupational Outlook Quarterly*, *Emerging Careers: New Occupations for the Year 2000 and Beyond* (Feingold & Miller, 1983), *Jobs of the Future* (Cetron & Appel, 1985) and *Career Paths* (Adams, 1984). You can also find occupational information in recruitment literature published by private companies, professional associations, and labor unions and in national magazines.

As a consumer of occupational information, you must evaluate all material to ensure that it is accurate, objective, up-to-date, comprehensive, and understandable (Fredrickson, 1982). Material over 5 years old could be erroneous given the rapid changes in the world of work. Unbiased occupational information will neither encourage nor discourage you from entering the occupation (Lock, 1988).

Software

Another way of collecting data regarding occupations, educational institutions, and programs is through your friendly computerized career information system. Advantages of these systems are that information gathering is usually instantaneous and relatively uncomplicated, up-to-date, and enjoyable for you, because you become a part of the exchange of information. Most career planning and placement offices have one of the following computer-based career programs: *Discover* (Rayman & Bowlsbey, 1977), *Guidance Information System* (Timeshare Corporation, 1978), or *System for Interactive Guidance and Information (SIGI)* (Educational Testing Service, 1975). A new program, *Ex-Sport 1* (Parks, Quain, Chopra, & Alguindigue, 1988), was developed exclusively for exploring careers in sport management. You should seek out the nearest computerized career information system on campus or in the community and use one of these systems to gather information that will assist you in making a personal career decision.

Informational Interviewing

After the library and computer research, you may still want additional information about the careers you are investigating. An excellent way to gain firsthand, detailed information about jobs and work environments is to interview and observe workers on the job. By conducting *informational interviews*, you will learn how people feel about their work, and you can relate this to your own interests and values. You will also discover the skills and personal qualities needed for the work.

Although such an interview may initially cause you some anxiety, you will be pleasantly surprised by how receptive and interested most professionals are in helping students learn about careers. Professionals are usually most willing to share their knowledge and experiences if they understand what you want and how they can help. The six-step procedure found in the Learning Activities at the end of this chapter will help you set up and conduct an informational interview.

Networking

An important source of information in choosing an occupation involves personal contacts (Bolles, 1987). You may not be able to discern the extent to which contacts affect your life. The contacts, who by themselves may assist you in varying degrees, become even more important when you perceive them as part of a vast network of relationships and interrelationships that can help you in your career search.

Reality Testing

What do you do after you have explored all the aforementioned factors? Super (1957) extensively discussed reality testing as the next step in the career decision-making process. In this context reality testing involves testing tentative career decisions.

Newspaper want ads, prospective employer vacancies, and word-of-mouth job leads all seem to beg for related job experience. Your question becomes, How do I gain the experience necessary to qualify?

As a college student you have many avenues for obtaining at least the minimum experiences. Examples of such opportunities are volunteer experiences, internships, cooperative education, practicums, summer jobs, part-time jobs, and specific (in this case, sport) experiences. These may help you decide if your identified career path is what you really want to pursue.

A practicum, for example, might help you define and refine your values, interests, and skills. The reality experience can help you gain new information and knowledge about yourself and your relationships with others. You'll also experience the duties, skills, and the organization's culture of the job environment, and you'll learn that dealing with employers and coworkers is a reality of the workaday world. Your experiences will point out your personal uniqueness as well as your interpersonal relationship skills.

Other skills you may learn are evaluating talent and recruitment; getting diverse groups to work together; charting and organizing; speaking (and thus gaining in self-confidence); demonstrating initiative (which is of utmost importance because you will need to initiate your own training activities at times in order to get as much experience as possible); participating; identifying and solving problems; developing and demonstrating courage; leading yet benefiting from advice and criticism; planning; developing creative and innovative projects; coaching and encouraging; training and facilitating; developing sensitivity; writing; being alert and listening; anticipating problems; reviewing; evaluating; and finally developing confidence in your decision-making skills.

If reality testing shows that your chosen field is right for you, then go for it. If you still are not certain, talk to advisers, mentors, or counselors. Only careful sequencing and interrelating of values, interests, skills, information, and reality testing will give you the answer.

Try to keep yourself and your chosen field in perspective throughout your collegiate career. Participate in activities that will help you gain valuable insight by testing your reality throughout your college life. Only then may you claim organized and learning-based career decision making.

DECISION MAKING

All of your life, you have made decisions about yourself and others, including what you want to do and be, and you will continue this pattern. You make many decisions daily and so quickly that you do not even know that you are making

choices (e.g., when to get up, what to wear, where to go, or what to eat).

Many times you will intuitively or "by the seat of your pants" make decisions that are important to you. At other times you will make important decisions in a more organized manner. The latter process is called *scientific decision making*, a process that is more orderly and is executed with more care.

The situation and its relative enormity seem to dictate which process you will use. Some decisions don't require scientific decision making. The first step, therefore, is to evaluate the problem and decide the importance of the decision. At this stage, you could ask yourself questions such as, How quickly must I make the decision? What people are affected by this decision? What are the consequences of a poor decision? Is the choice easily reversible? If the responses to these questions indicate that it is a very important decision, a scientific decision-making process is appropriate. Obviously, decisions concerning career plans fall into the *very important* category.

The Partin Model for Decision Making

Partin (1981) provides a comparatively simple model of the scientific decision-making process (see Figure 14.2). Before examining the various steps in the model, be aware that at each step, you put information into the system. Gathering information from a wide variety of sources is critical to making the model work and cannot be overemphasized.

Step 1 in Partin's model is to identify the problem or situation and determine why you need to reach a decision. What effect will your decision have on your long-range goals? What difference will it make?

Step 2 involves a process known as *brainstorming*. When you brainstorm, you generate numerous solutions without regard to their value. Once you develop a list of possible

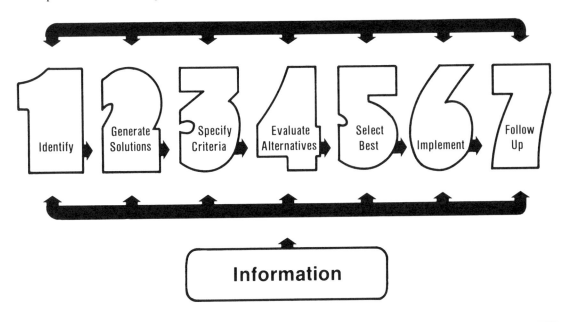

Figure 14.2   Partin's model of decision making. *Note.* From *Participatory Decision Making Training Manual* by R.L. Partin, 1981, Toledo: Toledo Board of Education. Copyright 1981 by R.L. Partin. Reprinted by permission.

choices, move to Step 3, in which you examine your basic beliefs about life—your needs, wants, values, and goals. You will judge your final choice against these criteria, and they must be clear to you. "Know thyself" is particularly sound advice when it comes to making decisions about careers!

In Step 4, you evaluate each alternative and attempt to match the various choices with the needs, wants, values, and goals identified in Step 3. Only those choices that are compatible with your criteria will ultimately be acceptable.

In Step 5 you select the best choice based upon its compatibility with your value system and your intuitive senses. Several choices may seem appropriate, and a good question to ask is, Which alternative offers the greatest advantages and the fewest disadvantages?

Step 6 involves developing a plan of implementation. "Good decisions succeed because effort is put into making them work" (Partin, 1979, p. 17). You must make a commitment to

approach the action called for by your decision with energy and dedication, and you must be willing to see the decision through to fruition. Decisions do not stand alone; they must be implemented.

In Step 7, you follow up on your decision, periodically reviewing your needs, wants, values, and goals and determining whether the original decision is still compatible with your criteria. Remember that needs, wants, values, and goals change over time, frequently dramatically. Decisions you make in college may be appropriate at the time, but you must review those decisions as you grow personally and professionally, because you become a different person as time passes and your decisions must keep pace with your development.

There is no perfect career, just as nothing in life is perfect. The scientific decision-making process is not guaranteed to help you make the perfect decision, but it will help you approach decisions in a purposeful manner by applying sound principles to the situation. This process can be time consuming, but choosing your career is among the most important decisions of your life and justifies the time and energy you expend.

LEARNING ACTIVITIES

1. Choose a professional from an area of sport management in which you are considering a career. Conduct an informational interview following these six steps.

Step 1: Identify and investigate an organization that employs professionals in your target career. Ask professors, career planning and placement officials, family members, friends, professionals, and trade association executives or consult the reference section of the university library for appropriate employer directories to identify such organizations.

Step 2: Identify individuals within the organization who work in your targeted career. Utilize membership directories published by professional associations, which contain names, titles, addresses, and telephone numbers, or ask receptionists and secretaries, who usually will gladly furnish names and titles of employees.

Step 3: Write or telephone for an appointment. Explain that your purposes for the meeting are to (a) get advice on how to prepare for and gain entry into your field of interest, (b) obtain useful information about the job and its work environment, (c) check the accuracy of information you have previously gathered from print and other sources, (d) discover leads to internships and practicums, and (e) identify other contacts in the field. Emphasize that you are only seeking information for personal development or for a class career project and are not looking for a job. If possible, arrange to meet at the individual's work setting so you can experience the environment. This will help you understand how organizational settings affect job satisfaction.

Step 4: Prepare questions for the informational interview. In advance, develop scientific questions regarding qualifications, position responsibilities, training programs, career paths, and methods for entering the field. Shumate and Kroll (1983) developed the following list as a guide. Add other questions you might have and write all questions in the order you plan to ask them.

1. What are the most interesting aspects of the job?
2. Is it an entry-level job or above? Explain.
3. What are your basic duties?
4. What is a typical day in this position?
5. What hours are you expected to work?
6. Does the job offer security? Is it seasonal or irregular? How vulnerable is the job to recessions, government contracts, and so on? When people leave this job or career area, what are their usual or most prevalent reasons?
7. What is the work environment like? Are there hazards, heat, noise, or pollution?
8. Are elements of the job unpleasant to you?
9. What are the maximum, average, and minimum wages for this job?

10. What are the normal promotional steps for this job? How long do the steps take on the average? How does the pay change with advancement to each step?

11. Do you work primarily alone or with other people?

12. Do colleagues in this job compete, such as for commissions or promotions?

13. Are the relationships between employees usually formal or informal?

14. Given the nature of the job, do you have opportunity to develop close personal relationships?

15. Is previous experience or training required? What is the source, nature, and length of time required for such experience or training?

16. Is any preference given on the basis of age, sex, or race?

17. Are there any visual (including color vision), hearing, height, strength, stamina, speech, or general physical appearance requirements?

18. Does entry into this job or career area require a formal high school diploma, associate degree, bachelor's degree, master's degree, doctorate, or postgraduate work?

19. Does advancement on the job require formal education, degrees, special classes or training, or training at technical institutes?

20. Are any specific courses particularly beneficial in this field?

21. What aptitudes, abilities, and personality characteristics are needed to secure and master this job?

22. Are any types of screening exams or psychology tests given? What is the nature of such exams?

23. What experience, if any, is required for entry-level and higher level jobs?

24. What special skills must one possess to qualify for this job?

25. Are any skill tests given to screen applicants? What is the nature of such tests? What do they attempt to measure?

26. What licenses or certificates are required, if any?

27. How are such licenses or certificates acquired? What are the steps and qualifications required to get the license or certificate?

28. Are any examinations required? What is the nature of the exam? What, where, and under what conditions is it given?

29. Is citizenship required?

30. Is preference given to veterans or minorities?

31. To what extent are workers in demand today?

32. Where is the greatest demand geographically?

33. Is employment likely to increase, decrease, or stay the same?

34. Are there other areas of this field to which workers may be transferred?

35. How do you see jobs in the field changing over the next 2 years?[1]

Step 5: Conduct the informational interview. One of the greatest benefits of informational interviewing is the opportunity to meet with professionals in a nonstressful, casual atmosphere. You will make a positive impression by dressing appropriately, being punctual, knowing about the organization, using your prepared, written questions when conducting the inter-

[1]*Note*. From *Junior/Senior Employment Seminar Workbook* [unpublished manuscript] by S.E. Shumate and J. Kroll, 1983, Kent State University, Kent, OH. Reprinted by permission.

view, and listening carefully. You can usually take notes or tape-record the session; be sure to ask permission first. You may also give a copy of your résumé to the professional for his or her critique. If time permits, ask for a tour of the office or department. Conclude the interview by thanking the professional and asking for the names of others in the field who may be helpful.

Step 6: Write a thank-you letter after every informational interview and send the letter within 3 days. This letter may be brief, but it should express your appreciation for the interview and mention some key points that you found helpful in considering the career. If you incorporated any of her or his suggested improvements in your résumé, enclose a copy with your thanks for the ideas.

2. Create a list of people in your personal network. Be sure to include relatives, former employers or fellow employees, people you've met throughout the educational process, and professional contacts such as doctors and clergy members.

REFERENCES

Adams, B. (Ed.) (1984). *Career paths*. Boston: Adams.

Bolles, R.N. (1978). *The three boxes of life: And how to get out of them*. San Francisco: Ten Speed Press.

Bolles, R.N. (1987). *What color is your parachute? A practical manual for job hunters and career-changers*. San Francisco: Ten Speed Press.

Campbell, D. (1974). *If you don't know where you're going you'll probably end up somewhere else*. Niles, IL: Argus Communications.

Cetron, M., & Appel, M. (1985). *Jobs of the future: The 500 best jobs—Where they'll be and how to get them*. New York: McGraw-Hill.

Crites, J.G. (1981). *Career counseling: Models, methods and materials*. New York: McGraw-Hill.

Educational Testing Service. (1975). *A Computer based system of interactive guidance and information* [Computer Program]. Princeton, NJ: Educational Testing Service.

Encyclopedia of careers and vocational guidance (5th ed.). (1981). Chicago: J.G. Ferguson.

Feingold, N.W., & Miller, N.R. (1983). *Emerging careers: New occupations for the year two thousand and beyond*. Garrett Park, MD: Garrett Park Press.

Figler, H. (1979). *The complete job-search handbook*. New York: Holt, Rinehart and Winston.

Fredrickson, R.H. (1982). *Career information*. Englewood Cliffs, NJ: Prentice-Hall.

Ginsberg, E. (1972). Toward a theory of occupational choice: A restatement. *Vocational Guidance Quarterly*, **20**(3), 169-176.

Holland, J.L. (1973). *Making vocational choices: A theory of careers*. Englewood Cliffs, NJ: Prentice-Hall.

Hopke, W.E. (Ed.) (1987). *Encyclopedia of career & vocational guidance* (7th ed.). Chicago: J.G. Ferguson.

Lock, R.D. (1988). *Taking charge of your career direction: Career planning guide, book I*. Belmont, CA: Brooks/Cole.

Madler, B.J. (1985). *Liberal arts power: How to sell your résumé*. Princeton, NJ: Peterson's Guides.

Michellozzi, B.N. (1984). *Coming alive from nine to five: The career search handbook* (2nd ed.). Palo Alto, CA: Mayfield.

Occupational Outlook Quarterly (most recent). Washington, DC: Government Printing Office.

Parks, J.B., Quain, R.J., Chopra, P.S., & Alguindigue, I.E. (1988). *ExSport 1* [Computer Program]. Chattanooga, TN: TPR International, AI Solutions Division.

Partin, R.L. (1979). A dozen ways to enhance your decision making. *NASSP Bulletin, 63,* 15-18.

Partin, R.L. (1981). *Participatory decision making training manual.* Toledo: Toledo Board of Education.

Powell, R.C. (1981). *Career planning today.* Dubuque, IA: Kendall/Hunt.

Rayman & Bowlsbey. (1977). *Discover* [Computer Program]. Westminster, MD: Discover Foundation, Western Maryland College.

Rokeach, M. (1973). *The nature of human values.* New York: The Free Press.

Shumate, S.E., & Kroll, J. (1983). *Junior/senior employment seminar workbook.* Unpublished manuscript, Kent State University, Kent, OH.

Strong, E.K. (1943). *The vocational interests of men and women.* Stanford, CA: Stanford University Press.

Super, R.E. (1957). *The psychology of careers.* New York: Harper and Brothers.

Super, R.E., & Crites, J.G. (1962). *Appraising vocational fitness* (rev. ed.). New York: Harper and Brothers.

TimeShare Corporation. (1978). *Guidance information system* [Computer Program]. Hanover, NH: Houghton Mifflin.

Tolbert, E.L. (1980). *Counseling for career development* (2nd ed.). Boston: Houghton Mifflin.

United States Department of Labor. (1977). *Dictionary of occupational titles* (4th ed.). Washington, DC: U.S. Government Printing Office.

United States Department of Labor. (1979). *Guide for occupational exploration.* Washington, DC: U.S. Government Printing Office.

United States Department of Labor. (1986-1987). *Occupational outlook handbook.* Washington, DC: U.S. Government Printing Office.

United States Department of Labor. (1988-89). *Occupational outlook handbook.* Washington, DC: The Bureau.

CHAPTER 15

Professional Style

Beverly R.K. Zanger and Janet B. Parks
Bowling Green State University

Style is an individual perception—each of us has our own idea of style. ''Now, that's style'' is a remark that we hear often, and it could refer to clothes, cars, or people. Let's concentrate on people, specifically an individual's performance. How do we determine if the individual has style?

WHAT IS STYLE?

The following concept offers a process for understanding style (Zanger, 1981). The concept is titled Image Path and is defined by a model that involves style and two adjunct elements of skill and technique. Definitions of skill, technique, and style are specific to this concept.

The image-path concept is critical for mobility in professional fields such as sport management. How do you perceive professional style? Describing someone as ''professional'' is a compliment, implying proper business ethics, good service, and quality products. In addition, professionalism involves a neat appearance, pleasant voice, and fluent but succinct speaking and writing abilities.

Skill

Skill is the basic learning, the foundation. For example, speaking, writing, counting, running,

Your professional style is the total professional picture that you present.

dribbling, and pivoting are basic skills. Basic skills are present in all areas of learning, and they are stored in our amazing memory banks. Information appears on an invisible ''disc'' that we automatically ''boot up''—almost like having covert robots operating inside us. Just as you never forget how to ride a bicycle, you have memory bank capabilities for any level of learning.

155

Technique

Technique is the development of basic skills into specific approaches and defined ranges of abilities. For example, people who are interested in dance will study with certain masters or dance schools. You go to certain basketball, hockey, or football camps to study with specific coaches. Writers learn techniques ranging from journalism to fiction, and actors adapt particular methods and have lifetime coaches. Can you give an example in gymnastics or ice skating?

Style

Now the coup de grace, style, makes its entrance. After you have skill and technique, you add your signature to the performance of a skating routine, a football pass, or a reading of an original poem. Style is personal, singular, and one of a kind. We can identify the silhouette of an athlete just by watching the movement. We can identify an author by reading a passage or a speaker just by listening to the voice. So style is what individuals give of themselves to performances. A performance built on basic skill and technique becomes one of a kind when style is present.

The image-path model (see Figure 15.1) shows how skills and techniques identify the critical path of individual style and, as shown by the continuous line, the growth pattern for a lifetime. The model is an open concept representing continuous skill practice, changes in technique, and perfection of style.

PUBLIC SPEAKING

Public speaking is a nightmare for some people and a breeze for others. What makes this ability draw such an individual response? Possibly the

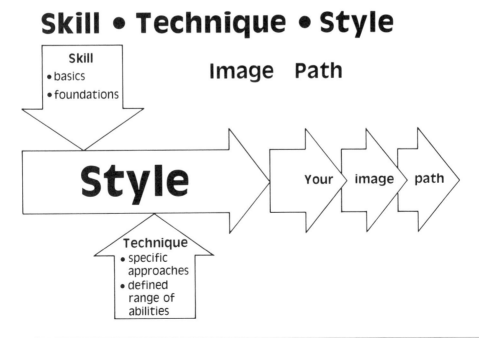

Figure 15.1   Image path.

difference stems from individual differences in skill, technique, and style.

Using the image-path model (Figure 15.1), mentally assess where you are on the continuum of skill, technique, and style in public speaking. This assessment might help you determine how much skill learning, practice, and technique you need to develop in order to improve your speaking ability. Zanger's Oral Presentation Inventory, shown in Table 15.1, may help you identify your specific strengths and weaknesses in public speaking.

Table 15.1 Zanger's Oral Presentation Inventory

	No	Seldom	Some-times	Yes
1. Do you have "nervous jitters" before a speech?	1	2	3	4
2. Do you breathe shallowly before and during your speech?	1	2	3	4
3. Does your voice quiver during your speech?	1	2	3	4
4. Do your hands and legs shake during your speech?	1	2	3	4
5. Do you actually identify (see) individuals in the audience?	1	2	3	4
6. Do you have eye contact with the audience?	1	2	3	4
7. Do you feel comfortable with your appearance?	1	2	3	4
8. Do you overuse "verbal fillers" (e.g., *and*, *uh*, *um*, and *ah*)?	1	2	3	4
9. Do you research and outline your topic when preparing your speech?	1	2	3	4
10. Do you practice your speech aloud several times before delivering the presentation?	1	2	3	4

Note. Results: Scores between 40 and 30 points indicate a need for basic skill courses in oral presentations. Scores between 29 and 20 points indicate a need for technique coaching that will build on established skills. Scores between 19 and 10 indicate a need for continued experimentation with individual style.

More important than scores on the inventory, a look at the list of inventory questions in reverse order will give you clues to better speaking. If you concentrate on Numbers 9 and 10, *preparation* and *practice*, you will lessen problems with 1 through 8 (see Figure 15.2).

Charismatic Speakers

When preparing a speech, think about speakers you have heard in the past. What made the speaker effective? Why did you listen? Review the following list, and then prioritize the listening factors (where, how, what, and who) that might be most important to each type of speaker (see Figure 15.3). For example, decide which listening factor is most important for religious speakers. Then list the second, third, and least important factors.

Religious speakers

Political speakers

Humorists

Figure 15.2   Prepare and practice.

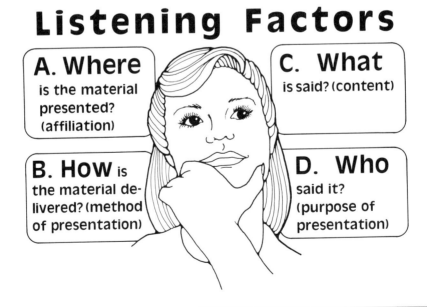

Figure 15.3   Listening factors.

Teachers

Stand-up comedians

Special event speakers (patriotic, school, organization)

Depending on the speaker and the situation, an audience remembers factors about the content of the speech, the personality of the speaker, the emotion of the occasion, or the joy of entertainment. This review of types of speakers and listening factors may help to reinforce your need to prepare, practice, and stylize your speech.

Your Style

A conversational style is one approach to presenting a speech. To persuade and entertain the group are two other possibilities, or a dramatic appeal might be appropriate to your content. Figure 15.4 offers a few of the many approaches toward stylizing the delivery of a speech. Be sure the style is comfortable for you and appropriate for the listeners; your goal is to present content to an actively listening audience.

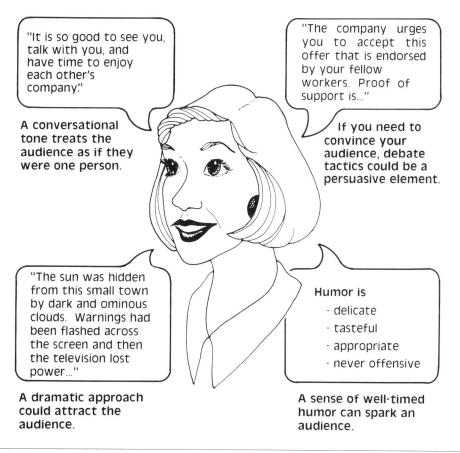

Figure 15.4 Approaches to style.

WRITING STYLE

Sport management practitioners have consistently identified communication coursework as a critical component of the sport management curriculum (Parks & Quain, 1986; Ulrich & Parkhouse, 1982). *Writing* skills are among the most important communication competencies a sport manager should possess, and the development of writing skills is essential to a career in sport management (Quain & Parks, 1986). You must be able to communicate effectively and correctly with the written word.

Among the many types of writing expected of a sport manager are business correspondence, reports, technical instructions, and articles for publication. Brief discussions of each of these forms of communication follow.

Business Correspondence

All business correspondence should be typed and professionally presented on letterhead. You can find explicit directions for composing the various forms of business correspondence in a wide variety of etiquette and business correspondence books. Your campus placement office may also provide information concerning composition and types of business correspondence.

Cover Letters

Usually cover letters are designed to do exactly what the name implies—they "cover" other documents. For college students, cover letters usually accompany résumés submitted in applications for field experiences or professional positions. Cover letters should not repeat everything in the résumé, but should highlight your qualifications for a specific position.

Thank-You Letters

Thank-you letters express gratitude to someone who provided you with information or with his or her time. Thank-you letters may be sent within an organization, as well as to outsiders. Making a habit of thanking individuals who help you will go a long way toward establishing your reputation as a professional with style.

Informational Letters

You will frequently need to organize events, give directions, write instructions, and communicate a variety of information to your patrons, clients, and colleagues. Effectiveness in technical writing that uses a clear, concise style is essential for this type of communication. Many universities offer courses in technical writing, a skill quite different from creative writing.

Letters of Recommendation

Currently, you may be asking teachers, employers, and other individuals to write letters of recommendation for you. When you become a professional, however, others may request you to provide these recommendations. Knowing what not to say as well as what to say are two equally important facets of writing letters of recommendation. You could practice this skill by writing a letter of recommendation for yourself!

Responses to Complaints

When a customer complains, you should consider the complaint valid; defensiveness and arrogance are never acceptable business practices. Plus, you may be able to improve your product or service as a result of the complaint. You must respond to the complaint promptly and politely. Remember, customers have a vast network of friends and acquaintances, and word about dissatisfaction with a particular business spreads quickly.

Letters of Commendation

Everyone likes to be commended for outstanding achievements! Congratulatory letters are appropriate for acknowledging the accomplishments of employees, supervisors, colleagues, or their family members. People enjoy receiving well-deserved accolades, and these acknowledgments can indicate a supportive atmosphere in the work place.

Reports

Reports may be formal or informal and may include documents such as evaluations, feasibility studies, memos, travel reports, occurrence reports, and grant proposals. Reports are an important form of communication, because they alert your supervisors or colleagues to your accomplishments and plans. Many businesses have specific formats that employees use in writing and filing reports.

Technical Instructions

The quality of your instructions can mean the difference between getting the job done well and having to do it again. Writing clear and accurate instructions is well worth the time it takes, because revising unclear instructions and correcting misunderstandings that may occur as the result of miscommunication take even more time.

Articles for Professional Publications

Sport management practitioners are frequently called upon to submit manuscripts to professional or trade journals. A positive response to such a request is one way to make a valuable contribution to your community and to the sport management profession. Others benefit when you share knowledge from experience and research. Disseminating knowledge and expanding the knowledge base are recognized obligations of businesses and universities.

Suggestions on Writing Style

When you write, you should first consider the purpose of the writing and the needs of your intended readers. The purpose and needs will dictate the level of formality you choose, the strategy you take, the degree of development necessary, and the tone of the writing. For example, in an informational memo to your colleagues in the sports information department, the level of formality would be quite different from the formality of an annual report to the Athletic Director. By the same token, a letter of congratulations to a valued customer would be more spontaneous and perhaps more humorous (tone) than would a response to a complaint from a dissatisfied patron. Thank-you letters have no particular strategy, whereas letters of recommendation may be worded in such a way as to highlight the best qualities in the person about whom the letter is being written.

Biased Language

Longstanding habits of using words and phrases that are demeaning to certain cultural groups, such as women and minorities, are so commonplace that they may go somewhat unnoticed in many situations. According to Aldrich (1985), "Language reflects our attitudes. As we change our attitudes, we change our language. But change never comes smoothly either in life or in language" (p. 34). The alert sport manager, therefore, must be sensitive to the vagaries of the language with respect to women and minorities. A conscious awareness of the problem and a sincere willingness to develop inclusive communication skills are essential if bias is to be eliminated in society.

PERSONAL IMAGE

VanderZwaag (1980) underscored the importance of personal image in his discussion of qualifications that employers seek. He said, "To be successful . . . requires the ability to breed confidence through effective total presentation of self" (p. 23).

Appearance

What kind of first impression do you make? Upon meeting you, other people rely on your physical appearance to make judgments about you. Although this may seem unfair, and although first impressions can change later, remember that you can make a first impression only once—so why not make it a good one?

The impression you make through your physical presentation is related less to physical beauty than to other factors within your control. Following are some aspects of personal appearance.

- Hygiene (hair, fingernails, and clothing)—note that the smell of smoke or alcohol on your clothing may give negative impressions.
- Good posture—both sitting and standing.
- Eye contact—to express interest and sincerity.
- Meaningful gestures—appropriate to the content.
- General composure—if you are comfortable with yourself, you will be able to focus on others, both socially and professionally.

Responsibility and Intellect

Do you have a healthy intellectual curiosity? Are you up-to-date on professional, social, and political events? Are you confident in your abilities? Appropriate academic preparation for the sport management profession is conducive to continued intellectual development and increased responsibilities. Consider these tips.

- Study hard and acquire the knowledge for intellectual capacity and understanding that employers expect of a college graduate.
- Commit yourself to lifelong learning, both formal and informal, so you can grow professionally and personally.
- Demonstrate commitment through dependability and responsibility on assignments.
- Do your homework (prepare) before meetings in order to be a contributing member.
- Ask for help if you need it.
- Participate in professional associations; interaction with colleagues can be stimulating and allows you to grow professionally.

Manners

Gracious people who help other people feel comfortable demonstrate professionalism; they have good manners.

Baldrige (1985) emphasized the importance of good manners in the work place:[1]

Manners are the very keystone of good human relationships. They govern how people treat each other, whether in the coal mines or in a mahogany-paneled boardroom. When people who work together in either place adhere to the rules of social behavior, their workplace becomes efficient. There is an absence of confusion and wasted time. When people treat each other with consideration, they do not run into each other; there is a minimum of stumbling about, feeling awkward, groping for words, or wondering what to do next. (pp. 5-6)

Baldrige continues, "Manners should be part of the curriculum of management. . . . It is a new and most important element of human

---

management training'' (p. 7). The education of sport management majors is incomplete without serious attention to this critical element of manners. Consider the following reminders.

- Regardless of your gender, you should rise when others enter the room or office, particularly if they are older than you.
- Use a firm handshake, but do not crush the other person's hand. Grasp the entire hand, not just the fingers, because the latter technique is painful, particularly if the person wears rings or has arthritis. Adjust your grip to the state of health or physical strength of the person you greet.
- Don't use chewing gum, tobacco, or cigarettes at work, especially during an interview or while someone else is eating.
- Although freedom to choose personal style in apparel is important, remember that employers and customers have their own ideas of what is appropriate attire and will expect you to conform to the demands of the situation.
- Avoid gossip.
- Try to look at the positive side of every situation. Problems are opportunities to make changes and make things happen; they are challenges you should meet with creativity. If you try to be optimistic, this will become part of your style.

Style is unique. Style represents you. Take all the suggestions in this chapter and mix and match them to fit you as an individual. Skills and techniques can have positive effects on performance but most important is your signature of style to the performance.

LEARNING ACTIVITIES

1. Conduct mock interviews in which you seek a position as an intern. Your classmates can evaluate the quality of your professional style.

2. Look up articles in professional and popular journals that discuss professional style and etiquette. Report your findings to the class. Your library will have an extensive listing of such publications.

REFERENCES

Aldrich, P.G. (1985, December). Skirting sexism. *Nation's Business*, 34, 36.

Baldrige, L. (1985). *Letitia Baldrige's complete guide to executive manners*. New York: Rawson Associates.

Parks, J.B., & Quain, R.J. (1986). Sport management survey: Curriculum perspectives. *Journal of Physical Education, Recreation and Dance*, 57(4), 22-26.

Quain, R.J., & Parks, J.B. (1986). Sport management survey: Employment perspectives. *Journal of Physical Education, Recreation and Dance*, 57(4), 18-21.

Ulrich, D.O., & Parkhouse, B.L. (1982). An alumni oriented approach to sport management curriculum design using performance ratings and a regression model. *Research Quarterly for Exercise and Sport*, 53(1), 64-72.

VanderZwaag, H.J. (1980). Preparation of the sport manager of the future. *Arena Review*, **4**(3), 22-27.

Zanger, B.K. (1981). *Style in athletics: The triad of techniques, strategy and style with com-parative patterns in education and business*. Paper presented at the annual meeting of the American Society of Cybernetics, George Washington University, Washington, DC.

CHAPTER 16

Avoiding Self-Sabotage

Dorothy V. Harris
The Pennsylvania State University

Most of us prepare for our careers in an organized, purposeful manner. We plan, study, and gain experience in the field in which our ideal job exists. Frequently, however, once we get that job, we proceed to "self-destruct" because we have not learned to take care of ourselves. Without first taking responsibility for ourselves, we are unable to assume other responsibilities that come with the position.

Pressure, which produces stress day in and day out, is the name of the game in today's society. You will face more than just the pressure to get ahead; you will face the cumulative pressure of trying to make it in today's world. Fast-paced days plus the struggles to earn a living, to be recognized for your efforts, and to get ahead—all these activities place heavy demands on your energy, emotions, and mental capabilities.

The average American changes jobs about every 3 years, and each job requires nearly 25 times the information than was required a generation ago. In fact, most management personnel spend only 40 percent of their time actually doing the job and 60 percent learning new information! So, how do you prepare yourself for dealing with this type of pressure?

In both personal and professional pursuits, we frequently prevent ourselves from maximizing our potential. We, not others, are the obstacles between ourselves and success. Because we are the problem, we can be the solution. We can assume responsibility for our own well-being through practicing established guidelines for developing fitness and by learning skills and strategies for coping with pressure and stress. Consequently, we can avoid self-sabotage.

PERSONAL FITNESS

Your own personal fitness should be at a level that guarantees that you can cope with the mental, physical, emotional, and social demands of your job. All of your physical systems should interact smoothly in meeting the demands you place on them at work, during leisure, and at home.

The four elements of physical fitness that give you energy, alertness, and stamina are muscular strength and endurance, cardiorespiratory endurance, flexibility, and body composition. *Muscular endurance* involves the ability of the muscle to perform over an extended period of time. *Cardiorespiratory endurance* is the ability of the heart muscle to adapt to stress and to recover quickly. *Flexibility* involves the range of motion you have in joints, muscles, tendons, and ligaments. *Body composition* is the ratio of lean body mass to body fat. Many test batteries are available to assess your level of physical fitness.

Physical exercise enhances well-being and provides numerous benefits. Exercise is nature's best tranquilizer and the best means of coping with the day-to-day stress that we all encounter. In addition to release from anger, stress, anxiety, and depression, exercise gives you more energy! Many people who can hardly get through the day because they are so fatigued have difficulty understanding how they could gain additional energy by expending it through exercise. If you feel tired all the time yet you eat and sleep properly and do not have any medical problems, then try regular exercise. You will be amazed at the fact that you have to spend energy in order to generate more!

Exercise improves your moods and your outlook on life; you look healthier and serve as a good role model for those with whom you work. Exercise improves your posture and the condi-

tion of your heart and lungs and enhances the production of red blood cells. Exercise lowers blood pressure, makes the digestive system more efficient, and maintains or even increases bone mass. Exercise delays the aging process and is the most effective way to maintain normal body weight. Considering all the physical and psychological benefits that exercise provides, you cannot afford not to exercise!

GETTING ORGANIZED

Most of us feel we don't have enough time each day to accomplish everything that we need to do. In fact, the most commonly used excuse for not getting exercise is not having time! Somehow, we all find time to sleep, although perhaps not enough; we find time to eat, even if we may not eat the right foods; and we find time to bathe. Accomplishing everything each day requires a plan, and failure usually results from having no plan.

Setting Goals

Setting goals is simply a process of identifying what you wish to accomplish. Goal setting is the primary mechanism for motivation. You may wish to start with an overall subjective statement of your philosophy, expressing your own personal reasons for what you want to achieve. For example, you may wish to become one of the top experts in your field. Your goals, as opposed to your philosophy, are objective statements about specific achievements that you hope to attain, and they are stated in a manner that allows you to quantitatively evaluate them. You can improve every aspect of your life if you learn to set and attain goals to manage your time more efficiently.

The beneficial effect of goal setting on accomplishment is one of the most replicated findings in the psychological literature. Difficult, challenging goals lead to better performance

Exercise is an important means of preventing self-sabotage.

than do easier ones. Setting goals for your personal as well as your professional life will contribute to your feeling of control over your life and will provide a sense of purpose for your efforts. Every goal that you set must be yours; if you try to attain goals that others set for you or if you use others' achievements as guides for your own aspirations, you will not experience the senses of mastery and control that come with attaining your own personally formulated goals.

As you begin to incorporate goal setting throughout your day-to-day routine, remember that attaining a goal or failing to reach one has nothing to do with your self-worth. Few, if any of us, accomplish everything we set out to do. Self-worth comes from within you and is based on what you decide to believe about yourself. In fact, personal growth comes from failure, so having a setback now and then only contributes to your growth!

You have total freedom to set your own goals. To put them in the proper perspective, you need to establish a beginning point. This means that you must evaluate where you need to improve in order to set goals. Begin by making a list of things that you would like to accomplish. Next, order your priorities, then outline all the things that you need to know or learn or do in order to attain your goals.

State your goals in positive terms. If one of your goals is to eliminate junk food from your diet, you should state your goals to eat properly and to monitor your nutrition meal by meal. If you occasionally fall short and have a "Big Mac attack," you can renew your positive goals rather than feel guilty because you failed. Regrouping and reaffirming your goals is easier when they are stated in positive terms.

Be specific about what you wish to accomplish. Remember to state your goals in measurable terms so you can continuously evaluate your progress. Goals should also be realistic in light of your present situation, yet they should be challenging. For example, if your ultimate goal is to lose 20 pounds, you should set a short-term goal of losing at least 2 pounds per week. Los-

ing 20 pounds is too far from where you are starting, and you may become discouraged and give up long before you attain your goal. Pursue your goals one day at a time, and evaluate them regularly for feedback, adjusting them as needed.

Set goals for short, intermediate, and long terms. For example, a long-term goal can be one you have for your entire career. Your intermediate goals may be those you wish to accomplish during the year or within the next few months. Your short-term goals are set day by day as you work toward the attainment of the long-term goals.

Planning for Attainment

You must be committed to the attainment of your goals, so that you change "I should" to "I will." Instead of thinking, "I should lose some weight," say, "I will lost some weight." Then develop your day-by-day goals to establish your plan for accomplishment.

Tell others what your goals are; this helps keep you focused and motivated. Write your goals down, stating them in specific and positive terms that you can evaluate. Each day, list exactly what you have done toward attaining your goals. If your list is short, then you are not putting forth sufficient effort to reach your goals. Keep a daily log of your short-term goals and evaluate them in writing on a regular basis.

Barriers to Goal Attainment

Lack of knowledge about how to attain your goals can prevent your success. You may need to set goals about what you need to study and learn in order to reach a higher level of accomplishment. If you need certain skills to continue to make progress, you will have to set goals to acquire them.

You may be thwarted in your attempts to attain your goals by fear of failure. Stating realistic goals that are in keeping with your present level of accomplishment and your situation helps to reduce that fear.

Absence of support from friends and superiors sometimes bars you from reaching your goals. You can gain support by telling others about your goals and discussing your progress with them. Seek out their support when you feel you have slipped back or have not made the progress you expected.

As you proceed with your goal-setting strategies, learn to label your behavior, not yourself. Also, remember that the only behavior you can change is your own, not your co-workers' or your supervisor's. As you change your behavior, you can slowly change yourself as well. You can set goals to change those behaviors that get in your way and continue to sabotage your efforts. When you view any lifestyle or career as a series of steps, you can effectively change the behaviors that are counterproductive to your desires. Setting goals provides you with a strategy for making things happen the way you want.

- Set your goals just for you.
- Make your goals specific to your behaviors.
- State your goals in realistic and positive terms.
- Set measurable goals so you can evaluate your progress regularly.
- Pursue your goals one day at a time.

If you employ these five guidelines, all aspects of what you desire to accomplish can be broken down into goals. Goal setting provides you with a plan to attain whatever you desire. Many rewards await you when you learn to incorporate goal setting throughout your life, not the least of which is an increase in your senses of mastery and control over your life. Success in goal setting leads to stronger self-confidence and allows you to assume responsibility for your own behavior and motivation. Success in attaining goals in one aspect of your life leads to success in setting and attaining goals in other aspects.

OPTIMAL AROUSAL

All of us can remember situations when just thinking a stressful thought produced a racing heart, irregular breathing, sweating, and other physiological manifestations of fear. We literally think (and worry) with our whole bodies, not just between the ears! Thinking and worrying produce muscular tension; the more anxious and worried we become, the more muscle tension we experience. We have no automatic tension regulators in our bodies; consequently tension builds throughout the day unless we learn to control and regulate it.

Muscle tension works in only one direction; it can only pull, which it does by shortening and thickening. Voluntary muscles are arranged in pairs and when a muscle gets tense, the opposite muscle sets up countertension to hold the body segment in place. This "double pull" can build up formidable levels of tension over much of the body yet remain unidentified by most people. This double pull explains why one can become "scared stiff" or "rigid with anger" or have tension headaches, backaches, sore muscles without physical activity, and other physical manifestations of tension.

To avoid too much tension buildup, you must learn to relax. Once trained in relaxation, you will be able to regulate and lower muscular tension under any conditions when your muscles produce too much tension. You must practice relaxation on a regular basis just as in learning any other skill. In general, the techniques of relaxation fall into two categories. One category, *muscle to mind*, focuses on the physical aspects of relaxation. Jacobson's (1964) scientific neuromuscular relaxation or progressive relaxation is in this category. The objective is to train the muscles to become sensitive to any level of tension and to release that tension consciously. The other category, *mind to muscle*, involves the cognitive or mental approaches to relaxation.

Benson's (1976) relaxation response, meditation, autogenic training, and imagery all approach relaxation from the mind-to-muscle perspective. Either approach is effective; the point is to disrupt the stimulus-response pattern of the nerves leading to the brain or away from the brain. Learning to reduce the sensation in either half of the circuit will interrupt the stimulation necessary to produce unwanted muscular tension.

Learning to Relax: Muscle to Mind

Harris and Harris (1984) provided an overview of effective muscle-to-mind techniques that utilize breathing exercises as well as muscle tensing and relaxing to reduce tension. As with all relaxation techniques, you should get into a comfortable position in a quiet, warm climate before beginning the exercise.

Breathing Exercises

Breathing properly is relaxing, and it facilitates performance by increasing the amount of oxygen in the blood. Unfortunately, many individuals have never learned deep, diaphragmatic breathing. Those who have learned it often find their breathing patterns disrupted under stress. With practice, breathing is one of the easiest physiological systems to control. Learning to take a deep, slow, complete breath will usually trigger a relaxation response. This relaxing, complete breath is the basis for a variety of breathing exercises.

Complete Breath. Proper breathing comes from the diaphragm, which is the thin muscle that separates the lung and abdominal cavities. During inhalation the diaphragm should move slightly down, thus pushing the abdomen out and creating a vacuum in the lungs. This fills the lungs from the bottom. To practice a deep, complete breath, imagine that the lungs have three levels. Concentrate on filling the lower level first by pushing your diaphragm down and forcing your abdomen out. Fill the middle level by expanding your chest cavity and raising your rib cage and chest. Finally, fill the top level by raising your chest and shoulders slightly. Filling all three levels should be one continuous, smooth process. Hold your breath for several seconds, then exhale by pulling your abdomen in (which pulls the diaphragm up) and lowering your shoulders and chest to empty your lungs. Finally, pull your abdomen in farther to force out the last bit of air from the lungs. Let go of all muscular action at the end of the exhalation so the abdomen and the chest are completely relaxed. You should take at least 30 to 40 deep breaths each day. Associating deep breathing with events that naturally occur during the day will facilitate practice. Each time the phone rings, take a deep breath, exhaling fully and completely before answering. Breathe deeply and completely while stopping at red lights or during other routine breaks in the day. This technique is good to use during any situation in which you need momentary relaxation and regaining of composure.

Sighing With Exhalation. Sighing aids in reducing tension. In fact, you may unconsciously sigh when you are under a great deal of stress. Inhale slowly and then hold your breath for 10 seconds, feeling the tension building in your throat and chest. Exhale through your mouth and sigh as you let go of the tension in the rib cage. Do nothing about inhaling; let that happen naturally. Hold your breath and repeat the sigh with the exhalation as you force the air out of your lungs. Feel the stillness at the moment directly after fully exhaling and sighing. If you can feel this quietness, you are learning how to relax. Practice again, but without holding your breath. Anytime you find yourself in a stressful situation, try to recreate this moment of quietness, peacefulness, and calmness by practicing this breathing exercise.

Concentration Breathing. Focus your attention on your breathing rhythm, inhaling and exhaling. If your mind wanders to some other thought between inhaling and exhaling, redirect your attention to your next breath, letting the intruding thought pass through your mind. Think of becoming more relaxed with each breath. This is also a good exercise to practice if you have difficulty concentrating.

Progressive Relaxation

Working under the assumption that an anxious mind cannot exist within a relaxed body, Jacobson (1964) developed progressive relaxation. This technique consists of a series of exercises that involve contracting a specific muscle group, holding that contraction for several seconds, then relaxing. These exercises progress from one muscle group to another. The purpose of the muscle contraction phase is to help you reach an awareness of and sensitivity to muscular tension. The letting go, or relaxation, phase teaches an awareness of what absence of tension feels like and teaches that this absence can be voluntarily induced by passively releasing the tension in a muscle.

Learning to Relax: Mind to Muscle

According to Harris and Harris (1984), meditation and visualization are two mind-to-muscle relaxation techniques. In meditation, you use a mental device called a *mantra* to help shift your mind away from logical, externally oriented thought, which creates arousal and tension. A mantra is a nonstimulating, meaningless, rhythmic sound of one or two syllables that you regularly repeat while meditating. The mantra provides a focus of attention on something that

is nonarousing and nonstimulating. The passive attitude of "letting it happen without effort" is the most important element in learning to meditate. Distracting thoughts or "mind wandering" may occur, but this is to be expected and does not mean that the technique is being performed incorrectly. When these thoughts occur, simply redirect attention to the mantra, letting all other thoughts move on and making no attempt to attend to them or to continue them.

Relaxing through the use of imagery or visualization means that you use your imagination to elicit a relaxation response. As an example, you might imagine that you are lying on a warm, sandy beach listening to a continuous rhythm of waves breaking on the beach. Or you might visualize yourself by a mountain stream or in a place where you always feel warm and secure. Use whatever image produces a sense of comfort and relaxation; you can use this technique anytime and anywhere.

Experiment with all types of relaxation techniques and find the one that works best for you. The idea is to be able to consciously reduce excess tension created by stress and worry. When you learn to relax you will discover that you are much less irritable, more efficient, more productive, and nicer to be around. You also have more energy and are able to get through each day with greater ease.

CONTROLLING CHATTER IN YOUR HEAD

Each of us continually engages in "mental chatter" or self-talk. If these chats are accurate and in touch with reality, we function well. If they are irrational and untrue, they cause anxiety and emotional disturbances, and our performances suffer. In most situations, our inner thoughts focus on the differences between our best performances and our worst performances. Our thoughts generally go beyond what is actually happening. We may think of similar situations, what happened to us in them, how they affected us, what we did about them, and what the outcomes were. Then we begin to jump ahead of the situations we are in, anticipating the outcomes before they happen and losing focus on the situations at hand. If we anticipate unpleasant outcomes, our thoughts can run away, leading to disastrous consequences. Self-fulfilling prophecies have a way of predicting outcomes!

Directing self-talk toward the positive aspects of any situation is the best strategy for setting the stage for a positive outcome. Developing a sense of control over the situation and how you expect the situation to evolve is critical to the outcome. You can, through self-talk, perceive a potentially aversive situation as much less threatening. Your thoughts generate specific emotions such as fear, anxiety, and depression, which are manifested physiologically as stress.

You need to become aware of what thoughts you process in certain situations and how those thoughts affect you. If they are detrimental, you need to change them. Identify those that encourage and increase worry and thereby produce anxiety and stress. Change them to positive and encouraging statements that will reinforce your sense of mastery and control.

If negative thoughts interfere, let them pass on and don't attempt to deal with them. If anxious thoughts come, do not dwell on them—switch to positive ones. If you can learn this technique, you will never reach the panic stage!

Goals can provide a source of positive self-statements. Your concentration also directly relates to your self-statements. An awareness of your thoughts will indicate where your attention is focused. When you focus your thoughts on what you fear may happen to you, you are reduced in your abilities to anticipate, interpret, and process relevant external cues and information. To stay securely focused on the present moment, you must learn to concentrate and attend to what is going on around you. You cannot be preoccupied with what has already happened nor with what the outcome will be.

The ability to switch channels with your thoughts involves the skill of thought stopping, being able to eliminate a certain thought. Learning the skill involves concentrating on the undesired thought briefly, then suddenly stopping that thought and clearing your mind. You can use a cue such as a timer buzzer, saying *stop* out loud, or snapping your fingers.

For practice, select a particular thought that you want to extinguish. Close your eyes and try to imagine the situation in which you have that negative thought. Practice interrupting that thought until you can eliminate it at will. When you have accomplished this, practice substituting a positive thought that is relevant to the situation. Thought stopping takes time to learn; the thought will return again and again, and you will have to interrupt it again and again. Learn to extinguish it just as it begins and switch channels to focus on a positively reinforcing thought.

Negative, fearful, and panicky thoughts precede negative, fearful, and panicky emotions. Learning to stop thoughts that lead to those states will provide mastery and control that will reduce overall anxiety and stress levels and increase your effectiveness.

Ellis (1971) developed a system to counter irrational ideas and beliefs. The basic thesis of his system, called rational emotive therapy, is that events themselves do not elicit emotions. Thoughts that you have after the event generate your emotional response to the event. Only you can control your own thoughts and direct them in such a manner to avoid undesirable emotional responses.

Psychological Barriers or Self-Limiting Thoughts

Our personal beliefs and expectations about outcomes have a great deal to do with the actual outcomes. As beliefs and thoughts about our performances change, the limits of our performances actually do change! Excellence in any pursuit is largely a matter of believing we are

> ## *Guide to*
> ## *Promoting Positive Thoughts*
>
> 1. The situation does not make me anxious; the situation does not do anything to me. I cause the anxiety and fear because I say or think things to myself that produce worry and anxiety about how I will do in the situation. I must keep my self-talk positive.
>
> 2. To think that things will always be the way I want them to be and that they will occur in a certain manner is to believe in magic. Situations differ because so many factors influence and produce situations. To expect that things will always be the same is to ignore causality. I must be objective and realistic in my evaluation of the ever-changing situation.
>
> 3. I feel the way I think; therefore, I must change how I think to change how I feel. I must control my thoughts and direct them to a positive, constructive state.
>
> 4. Everyone is fallible. Accepting this, and using a framework of goal-setting strategies (i.e., short-term, intermediate, and long-term goals), I can adjust to setbacks and failures. When I attain my goals, that success will sustain me over failures I experience.

capable. At the same time, each of us must commit to maximizing our abilities, working hard, and preparing for the situation.

A classic example of self-limiting thoughts was demonstrated in the attempt to break the 4-minute-mile barrier. Until Roger Bannister accomplished it, no one thought it could be done. Bannister, a medical student, knew what was required to reach that goal and keenly understood his physical capabilities. He knew he could break the barrier and directed his goals accordingly. When he accomplished his goal and ran a mile in less than 4 minutes, over 50 more men managed to accomplish the same goal within the next 2 years. A belief that you can accomplish a certain mission, accompanied by realistic goals, can lead to peak performances and accomplishments under all conditions. The inner thoughts or dialogues of successful individuals differ considerably from those of the unsuccessful. Positive thoughts make a significant contribution to ongoing success.

MOVIES IN YOUR MIND

Once you learn to relax, clear all the debris from your mind, and direct your thoughts in a positive manner, you are ready to utilize the most potent mental strategy identified to date. This strategy, mental imagery or mental rehearsal, can prepare you for every situation you will ever face.

To increase the effectiveness of mental imagery, you must learn concentration skills so that you can maintain your attentional focus as long as needed to rehearse the situation for which you are preparing. An exercise that will help you develop concentration ability requires a string about 10 inches long. Attach a small weight (or ring or key) to the end of the string to form a plumb line. Stabilize the elbow of your dominant arm on a desk or table while dangling the string gently between your thumb and forefinger. Your arm and hand should be at a 45-degree angle. Get comfortable, relax, and focus your attention on the weight at the end of the string. Concentrate on the weight as it moves in a clockwise circle. Let the movement happen without any overt movement of your hand or arm. You will note that the weight begins to move in that pattern without any movement or effort on your part beyond concentrating on the direction you wish the weight to move. This exercise demonstrates quite readily how you ''think with your muscles.'' As a matter of fact, you cannot think without some muscle response at some level!

This string exercise can include practice in a counterclockwise pattern or a pendulum pattern away from your body and back, or back and forth parallel to your shoulders.

Using mental imagery strategies in preparing for upcoming events works effectively for several reasons. First, the body is literal; it knows if it has "been there before." The more often you imagine what you have done or wish to do, the more familiar this experience becomes; you experience déjà vu. The déjà vu effect occurs because you cannot think or imagine without some level of physical response. When you imagine an action, your central nervous system sends impulses in a pattern associated with that action. The more you practice this in your imagination, the more efficient and effective the subsequent imagination or action becomes. You can use this strategy in preparation for any upcoming situation—a presentation, an interview, or a new proposal. Overall, mental rehearsal is the most effective way to build confidence that leads to maximizing your potential. You can always prepare by imagining the upcoming situation taking place just the way you desire it to unfold. You can use this strategy for personal as well as career-oriented situations. Clear mental rehearsals can direct your thoughts and feelings, keeping you focused in your efforts and maximizing your chances of achieving your goals with minimal energy output.

A FINAL WORD

If you wish to do the best job you can in every endeavor, you need to commit to maximizing your potential. This involves getting yourself into top physical condition by exercising regularly, eating properly, resting adequately, and managing stress. Maximizing your potential also involves setting realistic and measurable goals, which provides you with a sense of mastery and control as well as contributing to self-confidence. Commitment leads to conditioning, which leads to control, which leads to confidence. All of these behaviors are within your reach if you regularly practice the skills and strategies included in this chapter. As you obtain mastery and control and learn self-regulation of your responses, things will fall into place for you. You will be far more productive with less effort, and you will feel completely in control in pressure situations.

LEARNING ACTIVITY

Go to the library and find information on Jacobson's (1964) relaxation technique and Benson's (1976) relaxation response. Try each of these methods of relaxation. Which works the best for you?

REFERENCES

Benson, H. (1976). *The relaxation response*. New York: William Morrow.

Ellis, A. (1971). *Growth through reason*. Palo Alto, CA: Science and Behavior Books.

Harris, D., & Harris, B. (1984). *The athlete's guide to sport psychology: Mental skills for physical people*. Champaign, IL: Leisure Press.

Jacobson, E. (1964). *You must relax*. New York: McGraw-Hill.

PART III

THE BODY
OF KNOWLEDGE

CHAPTER 17

Twentieth-Century Sport in the United States

M. Joy Sidwell
Bowling Green State University

Mary Jo Kane
University of Minnesota

Sport permeates the American culture; it is an immense and lucrative business enterprise involving both the public and private sectors. Sport continues to need qualified administrators with strong backgrounds in management theory who understand sport. Sport managers today face many of the same or similar problems that sport managers faced during earlier periods of sport development in the United States.

Understanding the sport enterprise requires a knowledge of how sport developed in this country. This chapter offers a brief overview of American sport in the 20th century.

EARLY 1900s

Between 1901 and 1910, over 8 million immigrants arrived in the United States bringing dreams of prosperity. However, free or inexpensive land had become scarce, and new immigrants had to compete with established citizens for jobs and homes. Mass production had come into its own and required skilled workers, but the middle class benefited the most from this form of production. The new immigrants were left with the unskilled and less

desirable jobs, and many faced hardships greater than those they had left in their native countries (Noverr & Ziewacz, 1983).

Early 1900s basketball team

Youth Sport

Against this backdrop youth sport programs emerged. The Public School Athletic League of New York, established in 1903, was an important voluntary sport group founded by educators and wealthy citizens in an effort to counter the deplorable conditions of urban slum life. This and other similar organizations offered adult-managed sport for children, programs that founders hoped would effect social control, improve values, raise physical fitness levels, and acculturate immigrant children (Riess, 1984). Soon, additional organized sport programs began to develop.

Many people acknowledge the 1920s as America's golden age of sport. This was a time when sport began to mature, a time of innovations and sports heroes. Mandell referred to this period as one of "sports escapism" (Mandell, 1984).

National Game

Baseball became the national game. Players began to conduct themselves in a more professional way in order to widen interest and make baseball a family game. Ban Johnson, president of the American League, deserves much of the credit for improving the status of the game (Noverr & Ziewacz, 1983). The World Series was begun in 1903 to maintain spectator interest in the game throughout the season (Baker, 1982). The game also became more offensive, and spectators thrilled at the skill and flare of such players as Babe Ruth.

One blight on the game was the "Black Sox" scandal of 1919, when several Chicago White Sox players were charged with throwing the World Series to the Cincinnati Red Stockings. The eight accused players were found not guilty but were banned from the game for life (Baker, 1982).

Black baseball was boosted in 1902 when the National Negro Baseball League was formed, followed by establishment of the Eastern Colored League in 1923. Both leagues had the same problem—a few of the teams in each league were considerably stronger than the others and repeatedly won the championships (Rust & Rust, 1985). However, the Negro leagues stabilized, and players received salaries and achieved recognition (Rust & Rust, 1985). Many of the teams were the pride of their communities, providing entertainment and diversion.

Intercollegiate Athletics

College football remained a popular spectator sport. The first Rose Bowl game was played in 1902, with the University of Michigan defeating Stanford 49-0 (Baker, 1982). In response to demand, numerous football facilities were built or expanded. The Yale Bowl opened in 1914 with a seating capacity of 80,000, quite large considering the size of the school.

At this time football was still a dangerous sport, even with the new rules that had been instituted. President Theodore Roosevelt, a sport enthusiast and advocate of rugged individualism, met with three Ivy League representatives to urge them to make football safer. As a result, in 1905 about 30 college and university representatives gathered to discuss the problems of college football. At a second meeting even more institutions were represented, and they formed the Intercollegiate Athletic Association (ICA). The organization's name was changed in 1910 to the National Collegiate Athletic Association (NCAA). Its purpose was to oversee all sports but without regulatory control or enforcement procedures (Chu, Segrave, & Becker, 1985).

The 1920s marked a golden era for college sports. Institutions of higher education formally recognized intercollegiate athletics as a part of education. Such recognition and funding assisted the growth of athletics to an extent that would have been impossible previously. College football became big business and consequently became much more commercialized. But many began to criticize football and raise serious

1915 college football team

questions concerning whether the game actually contributed to the goals of higher education. However, football revenue paid for other sport programs and facilities on campus; consequently, college football continued its trend toward commercialization. A Carnegie Report entitled "American College Athletics," released in 1929, contained the results of a 3-year study of athletics on college and university campuses and detailed abuses in college sport, most involving football. The report urged college administrators to assume control and eliminate abuses, but the report actually did little to change the situation (Chu, Segrave, & Becker, 1985).

Professional Sport

Professional football struggled to find a formula for success due to a lack of spectator acceptance and organizational ability (Noverr & Ziewacz, 1983). At this time professional football was far less popular than the college game. The National Football League was formed in 1921 to remedy this situation, but by 1926 the number of pro teams had dwindled from 22 to 12, with only two teams making money. The turning point was in 1925 when Red Grange, an outstanding University of Illinois player, signed with the Chicago Bears and drew many spectators to the games (Noverr & Ziewacz, 1983).

Minorities

Minority players in the early 1900s were mostly isolated in their own institutions and leagues. Charles Follis was the first black professional football player, signing a contract in 1904 to play for the Shelby Blues in Shelby, Ohio. Paul

The high jump in the 1920s

Robeson, Phi Beta Kappa scholar, was a great collegiate player at Rutgers and also a professional player, turning pro in 1920. He played with three different teams and after completing his football career became a lawyer, a Shakespearean actor, and a famous singer. Jim Thorpe, Native American and an exceptional athlete, played collegiate football at Carlisle University in Pennsylvania. Thorpe participated in the 1912 Olympics, where he won medals in the pentathlon and decathlon. Shortly after his outstanding performances, officials discovered that Thorpe had played baseball for a minor professional league during one summer in college, thereby violating his amateur standing. The International Olympic Committee stripped him of his medals and removed his records from official Olympic history, although they were reinstated 20 years after his death (Rust & Rust, 1985).

Boxing

Boxing, another major spectator sport, also struggled for acceptance and legal standing in some areas of the country at this time due to its brutality and its association with gambling (Riess, 1984). Jack Johnson, the first black heavyweight champion, defeated Jim Jeffries, who had come out of retirement as the "great white hope." Johnson humbled the out-of-condition Jeffries in the ring that night in 1910 and touched off race riots across the country, resulting in several blacks being killed or injured by whites. Due to a variety of legal problems and racial acrimony, Johnson fled the country and settled in Europe. Johnson continued to fight and lost the title to Jess Williard in 1915. Jack Dempsey took the title from Williard in 1919 when the two met in Toledo, Ohio. Dempsey held the title until 1926 when he was beaten by Gene Tunney (Noverr & Ziewacz, 1983).

Horse Racing

Horse racing was outlawed in some areas because of its association with gambling. Still, the sport had spectator appeal. Black jockeys, who had ridden well in several Kentucky Derbys, stopped racing after 1911 following the closing of the race tracks in New York—after the state legislature outlawed all race track betting—and following the racial backlash caused by Johnson's defeat of Jeffries in the ring (Rust & Rust, 1985).

Women in Sport

Women's sport and athletics began to emerge in the 1920s. Women's basketball, played on a divided court was a truncated and far less strenuous version of the men's game but remained a popular team sport. The modifications to women's basketball found widespread support, especially among female physical educators who worried about women's health and masculinization; the divided basketball court lasted into the early 1970s (Twin, 1985). Everything possible was done to prevent women's sport from becoming as competitive as men's.

Women participated mostly in individual and dual sports, which were considered more feminine and therefore were more socially acceptable than women's sports (e.g., basketball) had been in the previous century. Of course, even these sports were modified in various ways. Women's tennis matches, for example, were reduced from three out of five sets to two out of three sets in deference to women's presumed lack of endurance.

Most female physical educators discouraged competition, even in sports that were considered feminine. The emphasis was on the social aspects of play, not on winning. Schools insti-

tuted play days to fill the competitive void and to prevent interscholastic competition. These events emphasized social interaction, with participants divided and games modified in such a way that serious competition was out of the question.

Some women, however, had the courage to successfully compete in sports and endurance events. Among these was Gertrude Ederle, who in 1926 at age 19 became the first woman to swim the English Channel. Helen Wills, publicized as "attractive and feminine," was an excellent, unemotional tennis player, who in 1927 won her first of eight singles titles at Wimbledon.

During World War I, women proved they could successfully handle heavy industrial tasks that had previously been the domain of men, and some women applied this strength and determination to team sports. Mildred "Babe" Didrikson was "discovered" at age 15 and began playing basketball for the Golden Cyclones, an insurance company team. She participated in AAU basketball tournaments, which began in 1926. She achieved her greatest accomplishments, however, at the 1932 Olympic Games in Los Angeles.

THE DEPRESSION

The Great Depression, beginning in 1929 and extending well into the 1930s, adversely affected some sports, in most cases causing cutbacks but not total curtailment. The America's Cup yacht race, on the other hand, changed its venue from New York to Newport, Rhode Island, and became a popular part of the social calendars of the wealthy (Baker, 1982).

Professional Sport

Of the professional sports, baseball was the hardest hit during the depression, with the minor leagues bearing the brunt of the economic crisis. Many teams disbanded and others were purchased by major league clubs, resulting in the formation of the farm system that exists today (Baker, 1982). In an attempt to economize and keep teams afloat, owners reduced major league salaries. For example, Babe Ruth's salary dropped from $80,000 in 1930 to $35,000 in 1934, but still was the highest salary in the major leagues; the average player earned only a fraction of this amount. When the economic situation began to improve, baseball recovered more quickly than other sports due to changes in rules, increased promotional activities, fan loyalty, and managerial skill (Noverr & Ziewacz, 1983). Another boost occurred in 1935, when the first night game was played in Cincinnati, drawing larger crowds of working people (Noverr & Ziewacz, 1983).

Intercollegiate Athletics

College sport was not spared during the economic crisis. Football gate receipts declined as much as 40 percent at some institutions, necessitating cuts in everything from scholarships to equipment. Attendance began to improve around the mid-1930s, and new bowl games were added—the Orange Bowl in 1933 and the Sugar Bowl in 1937 (Baker, 1982). Following the depression era, college football rapidly returned to the race toward greater commercialization.

As the economic picture began to improve, professional football grew more stable financially and more popular with spectators. A large part of this increase in popularity was due to rule changes that increased the offensive action. A professional football draft was instituted in 1936 to select the best players from the college game; however, the first draft pick (from the University of Chicago) refused to play pro ball (Noverr & Ziewacz, 1983).

Boxing

Joe Lewis caught the attention of the boxing world during the 1930s. About 3 years after his first professional bout and victory, he became the world heavyweight champion. Racism still affected boxing, and Lewis's managers carefully prepared him for the role he was to play. In 1936 he lost to a German challenger, Max Schmelling, a symbol of Hitler's Germany. They met again in 1936, and the "Brown Bomber" won— 70,000 fans attended and thousands of others tuned in on their radios. Lewis became a national hero to both blacks and whites (Noverr & Ziewacz, 1983).

Olympics

Despite the depression, the 1932 Olympic Games in Los Angeles were a success, due in part to public and private donations. Some 1,500 athletes from 34 countries competed after receiving assurances that they would receive housing, food, local transportation, and entertainment for a fee of $2 each day (Baker, 1982). Many world and Olympic records were shattered in Los Angeles. The standout of the Games, Mildred "Babe" Didrikson, won gold medals in javelin and 80-meter hurdles but after setting a world record in the high jump was forced to accept a silver medal because officials claimed she "dove" over the bar (Lucas & Smith, 1978). Following the Olympics she moved on to basketball and softball and finally became a professional golfer. Unfortunately, questions concerning Didrikson's femininity plagued her throughout her life, even after her marriage to George Zaharias, a professional wrestler. Society was not yet ready to accept such a talented female athlete.

The 1936 Olympics in Berlin, often referred to as the "Nazi Olympics," were held amid controversy. The National Socialist Party had come to power in 1933 on a platform of Aryan supremacy. Non-Aryans, especially Jews and Negroes, were persecuted, and Jews were excluded from sport organizations and sport facilities (Mandell, 1984). Because of these practices, some Americans questioned whether the United States should participate in the Games. After the Germans assured USOC president Avery Brundage that they would not discriminate against Jewish athletes and spectators, the United States entered the Olympic Games. Many performances were outstanding, but none surpassed that of Jesse Owens, a black track and field star and a member of the Ohio State University track and field team. At the 1935 Big Ten meet, he had broken three world records (broad jump, 200-yard dash, and 220 hurdles) and tied his own world record in the 100-yard sprint—all in slightly over an hour (Rust & Rust, 1985). At the Olympics he won four gold medals while setting new Olympic records in the 200-meter sprint, 400-meter relay, and broad jump and tying the record in the 100-meter sprint (Baker, 1982). He returned to New York City to a tickertape parade and racial prejudice. According to Baker, "Several commercial offers failed to materialize, requiring Owens to engage in degrading races against dogs, horses, and cars" (Baker, 1982).

1940s

World War II had a somewhat democratizing effect in this country due to changes in military regulations. Whites were exposed to black athletes and their considerable skills, but change was painfully slow. Possibly the most notable event occurred in baseball, the most popular professional sport. In 1945 Jackie Robinson, a four-sport letter winner at UCLA, was signed by Branch Rickey to play for the Montreal Royals

for $400 per month. In 1947 Robinson became a member of the Brooklyn Dodgers and thus the first black in major league baseball. Rickey, who wanted a talented black player who could keep his cool when bombarded with racial slurs from spectators as well as other players, carefully selected Robinson to fill this role. Robinson filled the bill and agreed to Rickey's terms. Finally, in 1949, both agreed that Robinson would be allowed to openly express his feelings, and he did so, often amid criticism from the press (Lucas & Smith, 1978). This was also the year Robinson won the National League's most valuable player award.

Professional football, however, was the first major professional team sport to desegregate following the war. The Rams, after moving from Cleveland to Los Angeles after the 1945 season,

Baseball has endured as a popular sport since the Civil War

signed two black players from UCLA (Lucas & Smith, 1978).

The 1940s also witnessed the establishment of the All-American Girls' Baseball League, which played between 1943 and 1954. Chicago Cubs owner Phillip K. Wrigley, Branch Rickey, and a few other entrepreneurs joined together to found the league after learning that the major league season might be cancelled because of a shortage of men brought on by World War II. Wrigley began hiring women for full-time jobs as ball players at salaries ranging from $50 to $125 per week for the season (Gerber, Felshin, Belin, & Wyrick, 1974). At one point, the league had 10 teams located in five midwestern states and two exhibition/farm teams. Faced with a somewhat limited talent pool and increasing costs, the league was reduced to eight teams in 1949. The women had a professional sport, but at a cost women would not agree to pay today: They were expected to conform to strict behavior and appearance codes that included chaperons and short-skirted uniforms that emphasized femininity.

1950s

Sport in the 1950s was set against a background of the Korean Conflict, the Soviet Union's successful launch of Sputnik, and McCarthyism and the communist scare. A landmark Supreme Court decision in 1954, Brown v. the Topeka Board of Education, struck down the "separate but equal" doctrine in the public schools, legally clearing the way for desegregation in the educational systems of this country. Many public officials, however, defied the ruling.

Youth Sport

Youth sport, after a rapid rise in the schools of this country during the early 20th century, began to come under attack by educators who were concerned with the emphasis placed on winning and the physical and emotional strain that they believed was associated with highly competitive sport programs. Educators wanted these school-based programs replaced with physical education programs for all children, resulting in the elimination of many competitive sport programs.

The educators' desires ran counter to those of many children and parents who still wanted the competitive programs. Community organizations stepped in to offer such programs, which were typically led by volunteers rather than professional physical educators.

During the early 1950s, the controversy still raged and some expressed concerns about the appropriateness of state, national, and international championships for youth. Many people criticized Little League Baseball, an organization that was established in 1939 and by 1952 had a half million male participants (Martens, 1978).

Intercollegiate Athletics

This decade was also important in the development of collegiate athletics. Football, in particular, became highly commercialized and competitive. Television, an important factor in the popularity of football, increased the game's spectators and consequently its commercialization. Initially the NCAA objected to the televising of college football games, believing it would detract from gate receipts. NCAA officials soon realized the commercial benefits to be gained and removed their objections.

As many anticipated, the increased popularity of college athletics, the emphasis on winning, and the commercial growth potential brought on more abuses. These were not limited to football, but also involved the "point shaving" scandals in basketball during the early part of the decade. The NCAA attempted to counter the illegalities with new rules and penalties, but to little avail (Chu, Segrave, & Becker, 1985).

The NCAA began to exert more control over sports in the 1950s

Professional Sport

Of the professional sports, baseball suffered the most during the 1950s. The game was slow compared to other professional team sports, and attendance declined. Television was one factor that adversely affected the traffic at the turnstiles; an increase in daytime network programming reduced one segment of spectators—the number of women attending games (Noverr & Ziewacz, 1983). In 1953, the game's organization was restructured and teams were allowed to move, making it a nationwide game, with the West Coast acquiring major leagues teams in 1958 (Spears & Swanson, 1983). These moves helped attract new fan support, and cities became in-volved in the construction of facilities to house the teams (Noverr & Ziewacz, 1983).

Professional football, on the other hand, came of age in the same era that baseball struggled to find a formula for commercial success. Several changes made the game more interesting for spectators. The NFL reorganized in 1950 and divided into two conferences, the National and American Leagues; the two leagues competed in a championship playoff each year (Spears & Swanson, 1983). Another change involved the use of a two-platoon system that allowed for more player specialization, more finesse, and longer player careers (Noverr & Ziewacz, 1983). The passing game also came into its own, offering more exciting offensive and defensive play.

Professional football and television seemed to be made for each other. The Los Angeles Rams became the first NFL team to televise its complete season schedule in 1950, resulting in a significant decrease in home game attendance. The following season, home games were blacked out locally to encourage ticket sales. The plan worked, and other teams followed suit (Noverr & Ziewacz, 1983).

Basketball continued to seek a niche in the world of professional sport. Significant changes, which were necessary in order to improve spectator appeal, were instituted during this time. One important change was the addition of the first black players in the National Basketball Association (NBA), signed in the 1950-1951 season. These talented players and those who followed them changed the style of play, making the game more exciting for fans. Rule changes also increased the pace of the game. Players increased in size and finesse, with players over 6 feet in height becoming the norm.

Women in Sport

The status of sport for girls and women during the 1950s showed little change from the previous

2 decades. The Division of Girls' and Women's Sports still espoused the philosophy of participation for all, in the form of play days, sport days, and other invitational social/play encounters. The organization's only concession to reality (approximately one third of the colleges provided varsity programs for women) was the approval of intercollegiate sports, provided they did not usurp the resources of programs that provided sport and physical activity for the larger number of other female students (Gerber et al., 1974).

The number of professional women athletes during this period was few, with most still participating in the safe "feminine" sports. Among the best known of this group was Maureen Connolly, who won the U.S. Open in tennis in 1951 at age 16. Between 1952 and 1954 she was the top tennis player in the world.

Another outstanding woman athlete was Althea Gibson, a powerful black tennis player who grew up in Harlem under adverse conditions. She picked up the rudiments of the game and was allowed to play at the Cosmopolitan Tennis Club, located in an affluent black section of Manhattan. Her abilities quickly became evident, and she was able to take lessons. Later she came to the attention of two black physicians, who became her mentors. She completed high school, practiced her game, and played in tournaments. Following high school she attended Florida A & M on a tennis scholarship.

In 1950, Gibson became the first black woman to play in the National Indoor Tournament. The next several years she suffered from discrimination at the hands of the white amateur tennis establishment. She persevered, with the assistance of several people, and became the first black woman to win the French Open. In 1957 she took the Wimbledon title in singles and doubles, repeating both in 1958. After her hard-fought tennis career, she went on to become a professional golf champion (Rust & Rust, 1985).

In the 1970s, women and girls found more opportunities to participate in sports.

THE 1960s AND 1970s

The American sport scene of the 1960s and 1970s reflected the larger social changes that were taking place throughout the entire country. Noverr and Ziewacz (1983) refer to this time as an era of turmoil and change. It was also a time of great social upheaval and conflict marked by such historic events as the Vietnam War, the civil rights movement, and the feminist movement. Traditional values were challenged by the nation's youth, the hippies of the counterculture movement. Against this social backdrop, the sport world also experienced a time of conflict and change, and the traditional beliefs of the athletic establishment were called into question. For example, several professional athletes such as Jim Bouton and Dave Meggasey wrote books that shattered the myth of sports as the breeding ground for the "all-American boy." These exposés revealed that racism, sexism, and drug abuse were rampant in professional athletics. In addition, two major events happened during this period that forever marked the 1960s-1970s as an era of radical social change in sports. The first event was the black revolt at the 1968 Olympics, and the second was the passage of Title IX of the Educational Amendments Act of 1972.

Black Revolt

The civil rights movement of the 1960s pushed for an end to discrimination and called for equal rights for blacks. Protests on college campuses and riots in inner cities reflected the anger of many blacks at widespread racial injustice. This anger and protest spilled over into the 1968 Olympics in Mexico City. Led by prominent black activist and athlete Harry Edwards, a number of black athletes threatened to disrupt the Olympics. The disruption came during the victory ceremony of the 200-meter dash. Tommie Smith and John Carlos won the gold and bronze medals, respectively, of this event. During the "Star-Spangled Banner," both athletes lowered their heads and raised black-gloved fists in a black power salute. Their protest was met with great anger by the sport establishment. Both Smith and Carlos were suspended from the United States team and ordered to leave Mexico (Rust & Rust, 1985).

Title IX

Title IX was a federal law that prohibited sex discrimination in athletics under the Educational Amendments Act of 1972. The women's movement of the early 1970s brought about dramatic changes for many American females. Historically, a woman's role was limited to such domains as homemaker and mother. But the women's movement encouraged females to expand into traditional male roles such as doctor, lawyer, and athlete. Within this social atmosphere Title IX was born. Title IX stated that females should have equal access to sport participation, scholarships, and facilities. Proponents of Title IX argued that this legislation would create unlimited opportunities for girls and women to fully participate in the world of athletics (Wendt & Carley, 1983). Female sport involvement has increased dramatically since the passage of Title IX; before Title IX, fewer than 300,000 females were involved in high school athletics, but today the figure is almost 2 million (Becker, 1986). However, Title IX has not achieved the goal of equality for females in sport, and in some cases, it has actually led to fewer opportunities. Although advances have been made, women's athletics still lags far behind men's athletics. According to Christine Grant, women's athletic director at the University of Iowa, women's programs are cut back at a much greater rate than men's programs: "Nationwide, women never did receive equal opportunity, but when it comes to cutting back, suddenly women are more than equal" (cited in Hogan, 1988, p. 7). Even today, on far too many high school and college campuses, women's teams still have to arrange their schedules and practice times to accommodate the men's teams.

One area where Title IX has had very negative consequences for women is coaching. Here, women have not only failed to gain new opportunities, but they have lost what they already had! Before Title IX, over 90 percent of the coaches in women's collegiate athletics were female. More recent statistics indicate that this number has dropped dramatically, to approximately 52 percent (Acosta & Carpenter, 1985). In terms of career opportunities in coaching, Title IX has helped males far more than females.

In spite of these negative consequences, the passage and implementation of Title IX have directly impacted on the field of sport management. As Zeigler (1987) points out, organized athletics and physical activity have grown into such large and complex enterprises that an ever-increasing demand for sport managers now exists. What Title IX provided for sport management is a vast, new sport world where both the participant and public need to be served. For example, sport management can serve the many young girls and women who now participate at every level of sport and physical activity as coaches, trainers, and athletic directors. Moving beyond direct participation, the sport management field can provide marketing and management of women's sport to the general public. As we move toward the 21st century, women's sport and sport management, both relatively new phenomena, can offer each other a great deal.

Violence in Sports

The 1960s and 1970s also marked a period of violence, which included the assassinations of John Kennedy, Robert Kennedy, and Martin Luther King. This time also included violent confrontations—concerning the war in Vietnam—between college students and police and national guardsmen in places such as Chicago and Kent State. All of these events serve as painful reminders of this very violent era in American history. The sport world was not without its share of violence and bloodshed. During the 1972 Olympics in Munich, Germany, Arab terrorists murdered nine Israeli athletes. In professional sports, the level of player violence reached frightening proportions (Noverr & Ziewacz, 1983), such as with the case of professional football player Daryll Stingley. Stingley was a promising wide receiver when he was hit in the back by a severe blow from an opponent's helmet. As a result, Stingley is now a paraplegic.

The trend of increasing sport violence continued into the 1980s. Severe injuries, often the result of player violence, became such a problem in professional sport that careers often ended prematurely. For example, in 1983 the average

College basketball: Is it sport, business, or both?

playing career of an NFL football player was 4.6 years; by 1986, it was 3.6 years (Zimmerman, 1986). League officials in pro basketball, football, and hockey tried to decrease the eruption of player violence by imposing stiffer penalties and fines. Violence on the courts and playing fields often spilled over into the streets, where fan violence resulted in serious injury and, on rare occasions, even death.

Social Awareness

The 1960s and 1970s were not characterized only by confrontation and violence; these decades also marked an emergence of great social awareness. Part of that awareness was an increasing sensitivity to the needs of disabled citizens. In the 1960s, our society began to expand services and programs to both physically and mentally handicapped individuals. A basic philosophy that developed during this time was that policies should be created that encouraged citizens with disabilities to more fully participate in all aspects of life (Compton, 1985a), including sport and physical activity. The U.S. government officially recognized the need for physical recreation as a therapeutic device in 1965: The Vocational Rehabilitation Act allocated funds to provide training for professional preparation in therapeutic recreation (Compton, 1985b). Also during this time period, the Joseph Kennedy, Jr. Foundation created and sponsored Special Olympics, a landmark program for mentally retarded/developmentally delayed citizens. Started in the mid-1960s, Special Olympics has become an international event with over 4,600 athletes participating in events such as gymnastics, swimming, and track and field (Haskell, 1987).

Perhaps the most significant event that created sport opportunities for individuals with disabilities during these decades was the Amateur Sports Act of 1978, which proposed to promote and coordinate amateur athletic activities throughout the United States (DePauw & Clarke, 1986). Part of this act's objectives and purposes was a commitment to increasing opportunities for individuals with disabilities to compete in athletic events held for able-bodied individuals.

In addition to the Amateur Sports Act, the Handicapped in Sports Committee helped to encourage wide-scale participation in sport and physical activity by individuals with disabilities. This committee, now known as the Committee on Sports for the Disabled, was instituted by the United States Olympic Committee (USOC) to promote and encourage amateur athletic involvement for people with both physical and mental handicaps. According to DePauw and Clarke (1986), some of the committee's more significant accomplishments in support of sport participation for the disabled have been

As social awareness increases, sport participation becomes possible for more diverse segments of the population.

- receiving $100,000 from the USOC for planning the 1984 International Games for the Disabled,
- recommending that the United States Olympic Training Facilities in Lake Placid, New York, be made accessible to athletes with disabilities, and
- proposing and endorsing the development of a sports medicine manual specifically designed to deal with medical problems faced by athletes with disabilities.

In spite of this tremendous progress, disabled individuals still lag far behind their able-bodied counterparts in terms of involvement in sport and physical activity. For example, even though a number of national organizations were created in the 1960s and 1970s to increase sports and leisure participation for citizens with disabilities, a 1975 national survey indicated that in 61 communities that responded to the survey, only 3 percent of the disabled population received any recreational services (Compton, 1985b). We hope that in the future, the social awareness and sensitivity toward the disabled that emerged during the 1960s and 1970s will continue to grow.

1980s

Sport in the 1980s can be characterized as "the best of times and the worst of times." Positive and negative trends that emerged in the 1970s came to fruition in the 1980s. The best of times has been reflected in a period of unparalleled growth in the sport world. This is particularly true for professional sport, which has seen a tremendous expansion of corporate sponsorship (Gerrie, 1986). In addition, the 1980s were marked by spiraling television revenues and player salaries. The worst of times stemmed from a number of abuses during this decade, ranging from recruitment violations in college basketball and football to widespread illegal drug use in both professional and collegiate athletics.

The Best of Times

Sandomir (1987) pointed out that in the 1980s, for the first time in history, the sport economy became part of this country's gross national product (GNP). In fact, sport economists state that rising attendance and participation rates have resulted in a sport economy that is growing at a faster pace than the overall GNP (Sandomir, 1987). The sport economy includes such factors as gate receipts, concession sales, corporate sponsorships/endorsements, and television revenues. One figure that indicates how enormous the sport industry became in the 1980s is the total revenue generated from gate receipts: $3.1 billion during the 1986-1987 season. Although this figure is impressive by itself, Sandomir (1987) stated that gate receipts account for only one fifteenth of the overall sport economy!

Two other factors that showcase the growth of the sport industry during this time are corporate endorsements or sponsorships and television contracts. Corporate sponsorship blossomed during the 1984 Summer Olympics in Los Angeles. In the past, the cost of staging the Olympics had become so burdensome that many potential bidders had begun to shy away from hosting the Games. But the commercialization (through corporate sponsorship) of the 1984 Summer Olympics was so successful that it resulted in a $15 million surplus for the Los Angeles Olympics' Business Committee (Sullivan, 1984). Corporate involvement in sporting events for 1986-1987 alone topped over $800 million (Sandomir, 1987). One example of this was the $1.3 million Sunkist paid to sponsor the Fiesta Bowl (Lynn, 1987). Endorsements from the corporate world also skyrocketed during this time. While the Chicago Bears were on their way to winning the Super Bowl in 1985, William "The Refrigerator" Perry received over $2 million in endorsements.

Finally, television revenues also generated enormous growth for the sport world in the

1980s. Professional football provides an excellent example. In 1972, Pete Rozelle, the commissioner of the NFL, reported that the three major television networks would collectively pay the NFL $60 million a year for 4 years, or $2.5 million per franchise per year (Harris, 1986). This unprecedented sum was topped by an even larger figure in the 1980s: $2 billion over a 5-year period or $14 million per club annually (Harris, 1986). And this was before a team ever walked out onto the playing field and collected any gate receipts!

Owners weren't alone in making big money. Players' salaries also increased steadily during the 1980s. In professional football, Eric Dickerson of the Indianapolis Colts was the highest paid player, earning $1,741,000 in 1987. Kirk Gibson negotiated a contract with the Los Angeles Dodgers for $4.5 million over a 3-year period. Although both of these cases are examples of star athletes who are among the highest paid in their profession, average professional athletes also earn considerable salaries: In professional baseball, the per-player average was $410,732 for the 1987 season ("Baseball Salaries," 1987).

The tremendous growth of sport and physical activity into a major business enterprise has resulted in a need for trained, business-oriented sport marketers and managers. In this sense, the evolution of sport into big business has a direct connection with the field of sport management. As the buying, selling, and packaging of sports have moved into the sophisticated world of corporate America, a parallel need has arisen to adequately train young professionals interested in more than just the Xs and Os of sports. Sport management is filling this need by providing young women and men with a background in administration, communication, accounting, promotion, journalism, and advertising. Individuals with both the educational and hands-on experiences that apply directly to the administration and management of sport can combine a knowledge and love of sport with a solid business foundation and find success in sport management. As Ashyk (1988) points out, as the business of sports grows, so too will the opportunities for those interested in sport marketing, administration, and management.

The Worst of Times

Just as the 1980s marked a period of growth and development, it was also a time when recruitment violations, drug abuse, and illegal signing with professional agents were widespread. The football program at Southern Methodist University violated so many rules that it received the "death penalty" in 1987, which meant the team could not play any football games for the entire 1987 season. It was the harshest penalty ever levied by the NCAA.

The 1980s also saw collegiate athletes in football and basketball sign with professional agents in violation of NCAA guidelines. With offers of cars, clothes, and bonus money, many agents signed players who were later put on probation or were forced to prematurely end their collegiate athletic careers. Former all-American wide receiver Cris Carter of Ohio State University was suspended from the team in 1987, his senior year, for signing with an agent before he graduated. This cost him an opportunity to make a great deal of money, because he would have been a first-round draft choice in the NFL's annual collegiate draft.

Another issue that plagued both professional and collegiate sports was drug abuse, especially abuse of anabolic steroids. Originally developed for medical use, steroids frequently are used by athletes who wish to build up their bodies. Steroids stimulate muscle growth in such a way that muscles develop faster and to a greater degree than conventional diet and training methods allow (Overdorff, 1987). However, prolonged steroid use has very serious side effects. A number of studies indicate that some of the common side effects include impotency,

Will Proposition 48 increase the number of student athletes who receive college degrees?

baldness, increased blood pressure, liver tumors, and heart disease (Utterback, 1987). The link between steroid use and heart disease appears to be so strong that Dr. William Taylor, a member of the International Olympic Committee's (IOC) drug control program, stated:

> Heart disease will be fairly common among steroid users. It may not be evident for a long time, but maybe ten or twenty years down the road. . . . It will be a standard procedure to ask any man with chest pains if he used steroids at some time in his life. (Utterback, 1987, p. D8)

Perhaps many of these abuses resulted from the "win at all costs" attitude that permeates professional sport. For example, many people have criticized college coaches and administrators who allegedly keep student athletes academically eligible only as long as they can "produce" on the playing field. Once their ath-

letic eligibility expires, these same athletes often leave college with no academic degrees and with few chances for success in the business world. Primarily because of this situation, many critics of men's intercollegiate basketball and football charge that the concept of "student athlete" is a farce.

Partly in response to this criticism, the NCAA and NAIA passed Bylaw 5-1 (J). This bylaw, commonly referred to as "Proposition 48," was designed to raise academic standards for incoming student athletes. A great deal of controversy surrounds Bylaw 5-1 (J). A number of leaders in the black community have argued that scores on standardized tests such as the ACT and SAT may be culturally biased (Spander, 1983). One study showed that 55 percent of all black students taking the SAT scored lower than required under Bylaw 5-1 (J) (Kantzor, 1985). By comparison, only 14 percent of all white students scored below the requirement. Perhaps the biggest criticism leveled at Bylaw 5-1 (J) is that no correlation exists between scores on standardized tests and graduation rates. To support this position, one academic institution (Prairie View A. & M.) pointed out that according to 1977 data on black student athletes, adherence to the academic standards set by Bylaw 5-1 (J) would have disqualified for admission almost 70 percent of those black athletes who eventually graduated (Cramer, 1986). As a result of these criticisms, the NCAA is reevaluating Bylaw 5-1 (J).

SPORT HISTORY AND SPORT MANAGEMENT

You may have begun this chapter wondering why you as a student of sport management need to know about 20th-century sport in America. This information is important because it increases your knowledge of where sport came from and how it evolved. Did you know that many people criticized intercollegiate sport in the 1920s for overemphasizing winning and commercialism? Or that the first black woman to win both the French Open and Wimbledon was Althea Gibson? You do now, and in that sense you have increased your knowledge of sport. Knowledge of the history of sport can also help you in a practical way. As a potential future sport manager, you may need to know, for example, about the basic educational requirements of Proposition 48 or that as a result of the Amateur Sport Act of 1978, federal money is available to organize and promote sport activities for disabled individuals.

As part of the next generation of sport managers, you will make history in the world of sport and physical activity. Knowledge of the past puts you in a better position to make a future that provides sport opportunities for all people, not just an elite few; insight into the history of sport can help eliminate past abuses. The future of sport depends upon the knowledge that you, the young professional, bring to it. An important part of that knowledge is the history of sport in America.

Although Title IX opened doors for athletic participation by women, equality between men's and women's programs hasn't yet been achieved.

LEARNING ACTIVITIES

1. Explain how the notion of competition was viewed by women involved in sport during the early 1920s.

2. Outline in-depth ways in which the Great Depression affected both professional and inter-collegiate athletics.

3. Discuss how the dramatic social changes that took place during the 1960s and 1970s were reflected in the world of sport with respect to Title IX and the black revolt in sport.

4. Using the section on violence in sport as a background, take the position that violence in sport is out of control. First, outline why you take that position and then offer specific suggestions for curtailing violence.

5. Describe how the 1960s and 1970s were also a time of social awareness and sensitivity. In particular, focus on the issue of the disabled population in sport and physical activity.

6. Discuss in-depth how the 1980s can be described as both the best and worst of times for sport.

REFERENCES

Acosta, R.V., & Carpenter, L.J. (1985). Women in athletics—a status report. *Journal of Physical Education, Recreation and Dance*, **56**, 30-34.

Ashyk, L. (1988, October 10). Executive searching has become her game. *Crain's Cleveland Business*, pp. 2, 17.

Baker, W.J. (1982). *Sports in the western world*. Totowa, NJ: Rowman and Littlefield.

Baseball Salaries '87. (1987, April 20). *Sports Illustrated*, pp. 54-69.

Becker, D. (1986, September 16). Courts kick the teeth out of Title IX. *USA Today*, pp. 1C-2C.

Chu, D., Segrave, J., & Becker, B. (1985). *Sport and higher education*. Champaign, IL: Human Kinetics.

Compton, D.M. (1985a). The status of recreation participation by disabled persons in America. *Inspire '85*, Conference sponsored by the National Council on the Handicapped, Washington, DC.

Compton, D.M. (1985b). The status of recreation participation by disabled persons in America.

In J. Kelly (Ed.), *International forum: Leisure, sports, cultural arts and employment for persons with disabilities* (pp. 11-19). Washington, DC: National Council on the Handicapped.

Cramer, J. (1986, May). Winning or learning? Athletics and academics in America. *Phi Delta Kappan*, **67**, k1-8.

DePauw, K.P., & Clarke, K.S. (1986). Sports for the disabled U.S. citizen: Influence of Amateur Sports Act. In C. Sherrill (Ed.), *Sport and disabled athletes*. (pp. 41-50). Champaign, IL: Human Kinetics.

Gerber, E., Felshin, J., Belin, P., & Wyrick, W. (1974). *The American woman in sport*. Reading, MA: Addison-Wesley.

Gerrie, A. (1986). A question of sport. *Marketing*, **27**, 59-61.

Harris, D. (1986). *The league: The rise and decline of the NFL*. New York: Bantam Books.

Haskell, A. (1987, July). [News release]. *Special Olympics International Newsletter*, p. 1.

Hogan, C.L. (1988, February 14). The eroding of Title IX. *Chicago Tribune*, Section 6, pp. 7-8.

Kantzor, K. (1985, November 8). Varsity racism? *Christianity Today*, p. 17.

Lucas, J., & Smith, R. (1978). *Saga of American sport*. Philadelphia: Lea and Febiger.

Lynn, D.M. (1987). If the shoe fits. *Public Relations Journal*, **43**, 16-20.

Mandell, R.D. (1984). *Sport: A cultural history*. New York: Columbia University Press.

Martens, R. (1978). *Joy and sadness in children's sports*. Champaign, IL: Human Kinetics.

Noverr, D., & Ziewacz, L. (1983). *The games they played: Sports in American history 1865-1980*. Chicago: Nelson-Hall.

Overdorff, J. (1987). *The abuse of steroids*. Unpublished manuscript, Bowling Green State University, Bowling Green, OH.

Riess, S. (1984). *The American sporting experience: A historical anthology of sport in America*. Champaign, IL: Leisure Press.

Rust, E., & Rust, A. (1985). *Art Rust's illustrated history of the black athlete*. Garden City, NY: Doubleday.

Sandomir, R. (1987, November). GNSP: The gross national sports product. *Sports, Inc.*, **1**, 14-16, 18.

Spander, A. (1983, February 14). A vote for NCAA's new rule 48. *Sporting News*, p. 13.

Spears, B., & Swanson, R. (1983). *History of sport and physical activity in the United States* (2nd ed.). Dubuque, IA: Wm. C. Brown.

Sullivan, R. (1984, August 27). Sports comeback of the year: The Olympic Games. *Sports Illustrated*, p. 11.

Twin, S.L. (1985). Women and sport. In D. Spivey (Ed.), *Sport in America: New historical perspectives*. Westport, CT: Greenwood Press.

Utterback, B. (1987, August 30). Deadly deception: Muscle mania stirs steroid epidemic and in the end, users must pay the price. *The Pittsburgh Press*, pp. D1, D8-9.

Wendt, J.C., & Carley, J.M. (1983). Resistance to Title IX in physical education. *Journal of Physical Education, Recreation and Dance*, **54**, 59-62.

Zeigler, E.F. (1987). Sport management: Past, present, future. *Journal of Sport Management*, **1**(1), 4-24.

Zimmerman, P. (1986, November 10). The agony must end. *Sports Illustrated*, pp. 16-21.

CHAPTER 18

Psychology of Sport and Exercise

Mary Jo Kane
University of Minnesota

Certain words and themes have appeared repeatedly in the previous chapters. Consider the topics that have been discussed with respect to career opportunities and preparation within sport management: marketing, personnel management, public relations, sales, scheduling, recruiting, and supervising. What do all of these have in common? People! Whether you are designing a fitness program, selling a program to the public, or hiring and supervising people to implement a program, you are first and foremost dealing with people. And dealing with people means learning how, when, where, and why they do what they do. How does this knowledge of human behavior apply to sport management? The following scenario provides an explanation.

The manager of a fitness club wants more women to attend an adult aerobics class and so decides to offer a special rate for women between the ages of 25 and 45. But the special rates would not apply between 4 and 6 p.m. on weekdays. Why not? Because many women are particularly busy during those hours. This example illustrates a critical element of an effective sport management program: Awareness of factors that influence participation in sport and physical activity is the cornerstone of any successful program.

Whether the career you want is in the exercise and sport sciences, sports information management, or sport organization management, you will ultimately be dealing with people. And knowing about people involved in sport and exercise is the business of sport psychology.

DEFINITIONS

Let me start with definitions of three terms: *psychology*, *sport*, and *sport psychology*. There are many definitions of all three terms; I have chosen the definitions here because they are current and inclusive and have been developed by experts in each area.

Psychology

Psychology (derived from the Greek words meaning "study of the mind and soul") has been defined as the scientific investigation of human behavior, which includes mental and emotional processes (Davidoff, 1980). The primary role of the psychologist, then, is to understand people's behavior in a variety of different roles and activities. Successful sport managers know, understand, and can predict human behavior.

Sport

Snyder and Spreitzer (1989), noted sport sociologists, define sport as activity meeting three criteria: (a) It involves competition; (b) it involves human physical movement; and (c) it is governed by systematic rules and regulations.

Many activities meet one or two of these criteria. Chess, for example, has highly complex rules and can be intensely competitive. But it does not require physical movement, and it is the physical dimension of an activity that is most relevant to the field of sport management.

Sport Psychology

An understanding of psychology and of sport leads to the conclusion that sport psychology refers to human behavior within sport and physical activity. Gill (1986) defines sport psychology as "the scientific study of human behavior in sport and exercise" (p. 6). Whereas the psychologist seeks to understand human behavior in all walks of life, the sport psychologist specializes in studying human behavior in sport and exercise. With these definitions in mind, we can now turn to the scope and nature of sport psychology.

THE SCOPE OF SPORT PSYCHOLOGY

In her text on the psychological dynamics of sport, Gill (1986) presents a comprehensive description of the scope of sport psychology:

Today, individuals with varied backgrounds in psychology, health sciences, and related fields, as well as those from physical education and exercise science programs, investigate sport psychology issues ranging from competitive anxiety to group cohesiveness. The application of sport psychology to physical education and competitive athletics remains prominent, but sport psychology, along with the other sport sciences, is extending increasingly into nontraditional settings such as corporate fitness, exercise rehabilitation, and health behavior programs. (p. xiii)

This description illustrates that sport psychology encompasses a wide variety of concerns related to sport and exercise. These concerns have traditionally involved both academicians and practitioners and have also traditionally taken place within the realms of physical education and competitive sports. Recently, however, sport psychology has expanded to include the ever-growing area of psychological well-being as related to fitness and exercise; this expansion has significant implications for sport/fitness managers.

THE NATURE OF SPORT PSYCHOLOGY

A common misperception among many people is that sport psychology is concerned with how to psych up or psych out athletes. Although these are important aspects of the psychology of sport, other psychological factors are equally important to an adequate understanding of involvement in sport and exercise.

Three major areas of sport psychology are (a) the effect of psychological variables on performance in sport and physical activity, (b) the association between psychological well-being and fitness, and (c) applied sport psychology. The first area focuses primarily on how specific psychological variables such as personality and motivation enhance performance. Sport psychology is also concerned with how and why involvement in sport and exercise influences psychological development. Thus, the second major area—the influence of sport and physical activity on psychological well-being—examines the psychological consequences of participation. For example, how does involvement in a fitness program affect self-esteem? Applied sport psychology, the third major area within the field, emphasizes ways in which sport psychologists can educate coaches, athletes, and exercise enthusiasts in specific psychological or "mental" skills such as imagery and relaxation techniques.

PSYCHOLOGICAL VARIABLES AND PERFORMANCE

The key objective in this area of sport psychology is to understand how certain psychological variables influence performance in competitive athletics. This section will look at three major psychological variables that influence successful sport performance: personality characteristics; arousal and anxiety; and achievement motivation.

Personality

Personality differences among athletes and ways these differences may affect performance in sport have been among the most popular and widely examined topics in sport psychology (Fisher, 1976). The following scenario is typical in competitive athletics and is an example any coach can relate to.

Mary and Susan are talented basketball players with equal physical and natural abilities. They both perform well in practice, but during games Mary becomes very aggressive and rises to the challenge, whereas Susan becomes easily intimidated and plays poorly. We can attribute these differences to the personality characteristics of both individuals: Mary has an aggressive personality, whereas Susan's personality is much more passive. This is an example of attributing a specific sport behavior to an individual's personality type (Cox, 1985).

The effort to describe, explain, and predict human behavior in sport in terms of personality is an important part of sport psychology. The majority of research in this area has sought to identify a personality profile that is uniquely athletic (Gill, 1986). Is there such a thing as an "athletic personality"? More importantly for competitive athletics, do specific personality traits lead to success in sports? Sport psychology has attempted to answer these questions by examining (a) level of athletic involvement and (b) sport type.

Level of Athletic Involvement

Examining the level of athletic involvement simply entails comparing athletes to nonathletes with respect to personalities. Do athletes have personality traits or characteristics that differ from those of nonathletes? Studies show that athletes are more socially outgoing or extroverted than nonathletes (Cooper, 1969; Hardman, 1973; Morgan, 1980b). Athletes also tend to be more independent than nonathletes (Schurr, Ashley, & Joy, 1977). Finally, a number of studies found that athletes are much less emotionally tense and anxious than nonathletes (Hardman, 1973; Morgan, 1980b; Ogilvie, 1976).

Type of Sport

The second personality issue focuses on the type of sport with which the athlete is associated. Do athletes who participate in one type of sport differ from athletes in another type of sport? Sport "type" has typically been classified in one of two ways: (a) team sports (e.g., basketball and baseball) versus individual or dual sports (e.g., swimming and tennis) and (b) combative sports (e.g., basketball and wrestling) versus noncombative sports (e.g., volleyball and gymnastics).

When comparing athletes according to participation in team versus individual sports, researchers found team sport athletes to be more emotionally anxious, dependent, extroverted, and objective than individual sport athletes (Cratty, 1981; Schurr et al., 1977). Singer (1969) discovered that tennis players were much more dominant, aggressive, achievement oriented, and autonomous than were baseball players.

With respect to personality differences between participants in combative and noncombative sports, athletes in the more aggressive sports such as football score significantly higher in mental toughness, dominance, and endurance (Berger, 1970; Vanek & Cratty, 1970). However, noncombative sport athletes score higher in ego strength, tactical ability, and the ability to delay aggression (Berger, 1970; Schurr et al., 1977).

In spite of these findings, many authors remain highly skeptical about the relationship between personality and sport. For example, Fisher, Ryan, and Martens (1976) argued that personality traits have little if any relationship to athletic involvement and performance. Gill (1986) pointed out that for every study that finds runners to be more introverted than volleyball players, another study finds no difference or even finds contradictory results. Are these inconsistent and contradictory findings a result of no association between personality and sport, or have we simply studied the association in the wrong manner? Both Morgan (1980a) and Kane (1970) stated that common problems within the research, rather than with the relationship itself, have resulted in inconclusive findings. One common problem illustrates this point. Research studies define the word *athlete* in many different ways. Some studies have defined an athlete as any member of a varsity team, whereas others have classified athletes as those belonging to professional sports teams. Contradictory findings that emerge from these two types of studies

Researchers have found that athletes in team sports and athletes in individual sports differ in personality.

may result from different definitions of *athlete* rather than from no association existing between personality and sport. Therefore, before we can accurately determine if and how personality affects sport, we need to standardize our definitions. Only then can we assess whether a relationship exists between personality and sport and how that relationship may affect performance enhancement within competitive athletics.

Arousal and Anxiety

Athletes often say they had a poor performance because they could not get psyched up for the game. Other athletes say they did poorly because they were so psyched up they became too tense and anxious to perform. Both of these cases are examples of arousal or anxiety affecting sport performance.

Arousal and anxiety are always present during sport competition. The stress and worry over performance evaluations, the fear of failure, and

Arousal and anxiety always exist in athletic competition.

the never-ending cycle of winning and losing are all cornerstones of the competitive sport process. How arousal and anxiety influence sport performance is a major concern within sport psychology. Is a high state of arousal beneficial? Or do the benefits of arousal depend upon the person and the situation? One major theory may explain the association between arousal and effective sport performance.

Gill (1986) stated that the arousal/performance theory currently favored by most sport psychologists is the *inverted-U theory*, which proposes that performance steadily increases as arousal increases—up to a point; beyond that point, performance progressively decreases as arousal continues to increase. Figure 18.1 illustrates the arousal/performance relationship according to the inverted-U theory.

This theory appeals to our logic, because our personal experiences in sport often confirm the inverted-U theory. We know that athletes who are understimulated or bored will not give their best performances. At the same time, athletes who are overstimulated become too tense and anxious, and this may also lead to subpar performances. The key for any coach or athlete is to find that peak level where arousal helps to psych you up but doesn't psych you out. This peak level of arousal is often referred to as the optimal zone of arousal (Cox, 1985).

Sport psychologists have identified three factors that can affect people's abilities to reach their optimal levels of performance: individual differences, complexity of the task, and skill level of the performer.

The key point here is that skilled performers do not eliminate arousal; they control it (Gill, 1986). Thus, the ability to control anxiety and arousal becomes a key factor in reaching the optimal zone of peak performance.

Achievement Motivation

A third factor affecting sport performance is achievement motivation. Two areas that sport

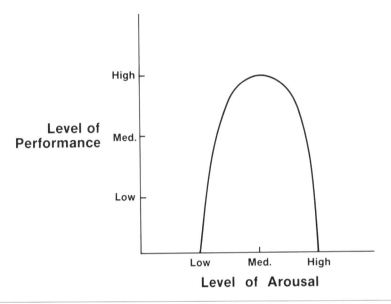

Figure 18.1   The arousal/performance relationship according to the inverted-U theory.

psychologists have focused on with respect to achievement motivation are (a) factors that contribute to people having high or low achievement motivation and (b) the relationship between achievement motivation and sport performance.

Obviously, the need to achieve has a tremendous impact on sport involvement and performance. Some people seem to have greater needs to achieve than do others; some thrive on competition, yet others go to great lengths to avoid it. A number of theories of achievement motivation have attempted to explain this need to achieve. The Atkinson (1964) theory is one highly regarded model of achievement motivation. Because it involves a complex mathematical approach to explaining the need to achieve, a simplified version of the model will be presented.

Atkinson (1964) stated that achievement motivation is the result of combining two personality characteristics: the motive to achieve success (Ms) and the motive to avoid failure (Maf). Everyone has both characteristics, because we all like to achieve success and avoid

Achievement motivation is one of the factors affecting sport performance.

failure. Individuals who are high in Ms and low in Maf are considered high achievers; success in sport is very important to them. According to Gill (1986), these people strive hard for success by seeking out challenging achievement situations. They are not preoccupied with failure. In contrast, people low in Ms and high in Maf are considered low achievers because they avoid being placed in highly competitive sport situations. Their fears of failure exceed their desires to achieve success. Even though being successful matters to those high in Maf, the anxiety and pain that they associate with failure may cause them to shy away from competitive situations.

How do the motives to achieve success or avoid failure actually affect sport performance? In an effort to answer that question, researchers in sport psychology have focused on risk-taking behavior. High achievers (those high in Ms) like to engage in a sport situation in which the risk taking, or chance of success, is in the intermediate range. Low achievers (those high in Maf) prefer a competitive situation that is either very easy or very difficult. A famous study by Atkinson and Litwin (1960) illustrates this point. The researchers asked college students to indicate from which distance they wanted to attempt a ring toss exercise (1 to 15 feet). The high achievers chose an intermediate distance, whereas the low achievers stood either very close or very far away. This pattern makes sense in the way people play sports. Athletes with a high need to achieve would stand far enough away to create a challenge that would mean something if they were successful. But low achievers, or athletes preoccupied with failure, would create a risk situation in which they could not fail. By standing very close, they would greatly increase the probability of success; by standing far away, they would have a built-in excuse if they did not succeed.

Many athletes can relate to this situation. If you are a very competitive athlete and therefore have a high need to achieve, you want to compete against someone who is at least as skilled as you; you feel that beating a lesser opponent is not really an achievement. But if you cannot cope with the possibility of failure, then you play an opponent you can either always beat or never beat. Using this strategy, you avoid the shame and humiliation that often accompany failure.

The need to achieve is also related to the competitiveness of the sport situation. For example, research by Ryan and Lakie (1965) showed that Maf people (low achievers) actually outperform Ms people (high achievers) in neutral or noncompetitive situations. When the competition increases, however, Ms individuals consistently outperform Maf individuals. The authors offered this explanation for these performance differences:

> The more anxious individual (Maf) appears to do well in a noncompetitive situation when he is not threatened or under pressure, but when placed in competition his anxiety or fear of failure tends to interfere with performance. In contrast, the competitive situation seems to motivate the individual with a high desire to succeed (Ms), energizing and improving his performance. (p. 345)

To adequately understand achievement motivation in sport, we must consider both the personality of the athlete (Ms vs. Maf) and the type of sport situation (high vs. low competition) in which he or she engages.

PSYCHOLOGICAL WELL-BEING THROUGH EXERCISE AND FITNESS

A second major area addressed by sport psychology is how involvement in exercise may influence psychological well-being and mental health. Three important issues directly relate to this topic: (a) self-concept, (b) depression and anxiety, and (c) exercise addiction. Information presented in this section shows that involvement in exercise and fitness programs can have both positive and negative consequences for psychological well-being.

Self-Concept

Self-concept, or self-esteem, generally involves the images or views that people have of themselves. This self-perception often includes social identities (e.g., social status, occupation, and family position) and physical characteristics (e.g., height, weight, and body type).

Self-esteem is heavily influenced by body image (Wylie, 1979). Thus an individual who exercises regularly or who is physically fit should have greater self-esteem and thus greater psychological well-being. Although this is a very appealing and logical connection, little scientific support exists for the relationship between physical fitness and self-concept. Research that has examined the impact of exercise and fitness on positive self-concept has resulted in inconsistent and contradictory findings (Sonstroem, 1984). For example, a typical study would assess individuals' self-concepts and then measure their fitness levels to determine if those who were high in physical fitness were also high in self-concept. Although some studies found a positive relationship between physical fitness and self-esteem (Collingwood, 1972; Dowell, Badgett, & Landiss, 1970), other studies found no relationship at all (Heaps, 1978; Leonardson & Gargiulo, 1978). However, one finding was consistent throughout many studies: Self-esteem was positively related to a person's perception of his or her fitness level, rather than to the actual fitness level. For example, an individual may have been rated physically fit as a result of performance on a standard fitness measurement (e.g., 12-minute run/walk test). However, being physically fit would not automatically result in high self-esteem unless the person actually believed or perceived that he or she were physically fit.

This pattern may explain another consistent finding in research on this topic: Involvement in intervention exercise programs for individuals with low self-concepts can increase self-esteem, but certain conditions should be met in order for that to happen (Holberg, 1978). Research has indicated that participation in exercise programs has been very effective in enhancing the self-esteem of those individuals already low in self-concept (Sonstroem, 1984). However, this same research has shown that physical exercise alone will not automatically lead to significant increases in self-esteem. The participants have to believe that they are becoming more physically fit in order for their self-esteem to increase (Heaps, 1978).

Given these results, any well-designed exercise program should include three elements: longer and more intensive programs, positive feedback, and success experiences. An individual who is involved in an intensive and thorough program that includes feedback from leaders and experience with success can develop the real connection between exercise and psychological well-being. In this type of program, the participant comes to believe that physical fitness involves more than the results on a treadmill test. It is the feeling of increased competence (as a result of becoming more physically fit) that actually leads to an increase in self-esteem (Felker, 1974; Heaps, 1978; Iso-Ahola, 1980).

These findings have enormous implications for sport and fitness management. It is not enough to simply make facilities and equipment available. An ongoing, structured program that enables people to set and surpass goals, receive positive feedback, and thereby gain new senses of competence will be most effective in ensuring psychological well-being through exercise and fitness.

Anxiety and Depression

The influence of exercise on the reduction of both anxiety and depression is another important topic in sport psychology. The physiological benefits of physical exercise have been firmly established (Folkins & Sime, 1981). According to Mihevic (1981), the psychological benefits of exercise are also widely touted, but have considerably less scientific support. For example, Post and Goodwin (1973) found that depression did decrease in moderately depressed patients after involvement in an exercise program. Working with college-age women, Folkins, Lynch, and Gardner (1972) also discovered that participation in a semester-long jogging program led to a decrease in anxiety and depression levels. However, Morgan, Roberts, Brand, and Feinerman's (1970) extensive study on anxiety and depression in both women and men did not find a reduction of tension and depression in the participants after 6 weeks of regular exercise.

In spite of this conflicting evidence, exercise is increasingly recommended for the clinical treatment of anxiety and depression (Mihevic, 1981). Perhaps this is because of the "feel-better phenomenon" that participants in exercise programs consistently report. However, we should not assume that any kind of exercise for any type of person will significantly alter anxiety and depression. Research indicates that the type or intensity level of the exercise (vigorous vs. moderate or light) plays an important role in the reduction of anxiety and depression. For example, light or moderate levels of exercise have not been associated with decreases in anxiety and depression (de Vries, 1981). In contrast, several studies show that vigorous exercise leads to significant reductions of anxiety and depression in both highly anxious and "normal" individuals (Cox, 1985).

Vigorous exercise is defined as aerobic or rhythmic activities such as jogging, cycling, or bench stepping that are performed for 30 to 40 minutes per session, 3 to 5 days per week. In addition, the activity must be performed at a minimum of 60 to 70 percent of maximal aerobic power (Raglin & Morgan, 1985). A study with both clinically depressed and nondepressed college students illustrates this point (Brown,

Ramirez, & Taub, 1978). The researchers measured the depression levels of people before and after they engaged in vigorous exercise (jogging), light exercise (softball), or no exercise. They found that people involved in the jogging program reported much less anger, fatigue, and tension and much more cheerfulness and energy following exercise. In contrast, the individuals in the softball program as well as those doing no exercise at all showed no significant reduction of depression. These results were found for both nondepressed and clinically depressed individuals.

Although it is important to discover that participation in vigorous exercise coincides with reduced anxiety and depression, we cannot say that vigorous physical exercise causes the reduction of anxiety and depression. Unfortunately, many professionals and practitioners often make this claim (Raglin & Morgan, 1985). This belief can be very misleading, because the reduction in anxiety or depression that frequently follows exercise could quite possibly result from being mentally distracted, not from being physically active.

We all know that exercise allows people to become temporarily diverted or distracted from the pressures of everyday life. In fact, Bahrke and Morgan (1978) suggested that this element of distraction in exercise, rather than a physiological response, may ultimately reduce anxiety and depression. Their study illustrates this point. They measured the anxiety levels of three different groups of people who had been involved in either physical or nonphysical activities. The *physical* group consisted of people who walked on a treadmill at 70 percent of maximal aerobic power. The two *nonphysical* groups consisted of people who were either meditating or quietly resting. All three groups had significantly less anxiety following their activity. This finding challenges the popularly held belief that physical exercise alone is responsible for anxiety reduction.

Do these results mean that we don't need involvement in regular physical exercise or that simply doing nothing, or quietly resting, will achieve the same results as exercise in terms of alleviating anxiety and depression? No, because vigorous physical exercise is also associated with physiological changes (e.g., an increase in cardiovascular efficiency) that do not occur during passive or nonphysical activity. These physiological changes are particularly important for anxiety reduction. Compared to the effects of meditation or quiet rest, physical exercise may result in longer periods of reduced anxiety and depression (Raglin & Morgan, 1985).

Exercise Addiction

Frequently physical activity can lead to undesirable results. Recently we have discovered that some people become so committed to regular exercise that they actually become "addicted." Using jogging as an example, this section will identify the symptoms of exercise addiction, discuss who may be at risk, and explore ways to avoid becoming addicted to exercise.

Millions of American women and men are serious, committed runners. When they first became involved in their running programs, they often experienced negative physical side effects such as shortness of breath, fatigue, and muscle soreness. But gradually, they began to experience the sensation of feeling better, or a "runner's high," which can last 2 to 5 hours following exercise (Morgan, 1979). As with other addictions, however, the dosage (in this case mileage) must be increased periodically to maintain the same sense of euphoria. During this process some runners fall into a vicious trap of abuse and overuse. As Bittker states, the exercise addict begins to experience "runner's gluttony":

We may begin running 'just to stay in shape' but soon are seduced by the sense of clarity, energy, and self-esteem accompanying the daily run. Having achieved reasonable conditioning, we run farther and faster in an attempt to find our peak. It is at this point that our tragic flaw emerges. Our gluttony may once again conquer us. (cited in Morgan, 1979, pp. 58-59)

How do we know when we are addicted to running? What are the symptoms of an exercise addict? Morgan (1979) states that two criteria identify the exercise addict. First, the person must believe that she or he cannot function properly without daily exercise. Second, when the person is deprived of exercise, she or he will experience withdrawal symptoms such as depression, anxiety, restlessness, insomnia, constipation, muscle tension, and loss of appetite (Morgan, 1979).

The key ingredient for determining if individuals are addicted to exercise is whether they continue their activities at the expense of other important aspects of their lives. For example, do they continue to exercise even though they are risking serious or permanent injury? Does their exercise routine take time away from job responsibilities and family obligations? If so, the individuals lose an important psychological benefit of exercise: They may no longer feel a sense of competence and control over themselves and their lives, because exercise is now controlling them!

No magic formula says that if you run over 50 miles a week, you are an addict. Different people require different levels of exercise. Someone who runs 10 to 15 miles a week may be an addict, yet someone who runs over 100 miles a week may not. Avoiding addiction depends upon a balanced perspective about running that sees exercise as a means to an end, not an end in itself (Morgan, 1979). This balanced or healthy perspective can be very difficult for some people to achieve. If a large part of one's ego or identity is associated with exercise, then keeping it properly ranked in priority may become a challenge. For example, to people who have previously been overweight and out of shape and who have used running as a way to slim down and tone up, exercise may be much more than a daily activity. These people may equate their new, healthy bodies with their new, healthy self-concepts. Under these circumstances, placing exercise in its proper perspective can be very threatening.

Nevertheless, exercise addiction is a problem that should be remedied. It can cost people their families and careers. Individuals who find themselves becoming too preoccupied with exercise can take steps to avoid the dangers of addiction. One approach is to incorporate variety into an exercise routine, which is important for two reasons. First, variety is better physiologically because of the balance it provides. Second, a variety of activities may help psychologically by eliminating the tendency to become too dependent upon only one particular exercise.

A second approach is discipline, that is, the discipline to take time off (at least one day a week) from training. This may be difficult at first, but the same discipline and control that were used to adhere to exercise initially can also help achieve a balanced restraint.

APPLIED SPORT PSYCHOLOGY

Applied sport psychology is the newest subfield in sport psychology. This is an area in which many sport psychologists are beginning to apply their knowledge by working directly with coaches and athletes. Additionally, sport psychologists are beginning to train and educate sport and exercise enthusiasts in a number of psychological or "mental" skills (Gill, 1986).

The following example explains what is meant by a mental skill. All of us have "choked" in an athletic contest or "gone blank" during an important exam. We probably had the physical or mental abilities to perform successfully; we just didn't perform up to par because of mental mistakes (Harris & Harris, 1984). These mental mistakes are often the difference between winning and losing. Many coaches say that mental ability is 80 to 90 percent of the game. If this is true, why do physical educators spend so much time on physical skill development and technical strategy sessions but so little formal time on developing mental skills? This is what applied sport psychology is all about: developing mental skills and techniques that will help both competitive athletes and exercise enthusiasts manage stress, control anxiety, and improve concentration and self-confidence (Williams, 1986).

Several important points relate to the development of mental skills and techniques. First, none of these skills work unless practiced on a regular, systematic basis. Just as you wouldn't expect to develop your physical abilities without following a regular routine, you also can't expect to develop a visualization (or imagery) skill without regular practice. Second, practicing mental skills cannot replace practicing physical skills; they complement and supplement each other. Third, becoming proficient in a psychological skill will not guarantee success. For example, being able to control your anxiety through a relaxation technique will not automatically lead you to success any more than practicing a jump shot will guarantee a winning basket. However, learning a psychological skill can consistently create an ideal mental climate that allows an athlete to perform at his or her best (Williams, 1986). Finally, the benefits of learning a psychological skill can be applied to a number of "real life" situations, not just to performance in sport and physical activity. For example, a technique such as mental rehearsal or imagery that allows you to visualize success can be just as effective in the classroom as on the basketball court (Harris & Harris, 1984). In fact, many of the mental skills used by sport psychologists are also emphasized in such fields as stress and time management.

Imagery

Imagery is one psychological or mental skill that sport psychologists use extensively today. Although imagery (also known as mental rehearsal or visualization) has been studied for years by psychologists, sport psychologists and athletes are just beginning to examine the effects of imagery on sport performance (Gill, 1986). Elite athletes have used imagery for years. Jack Nicklaus has talked about visualizing the arc and placement of the golf ball before he ever takes a swing. Chris Evert has stated that before every competition, she visualizes her tennis match in great detail, including her opponent's strategy.

If you wish to effectively enhance your imagery skills, you must consciously practice on a regular, systematic basis. By doing so, you can more highly develop all of your senses. This is important for success in sport, which involves a series of constantly changing situations and images that involve every one of the senses. Therefore, the better you develop your bodily sensations and awareness, the more effective you may become on the playing field (Harris & Harris, 1984).

IMPLICATIONS FOR SPORT MANAGEMENT

The information in this chapter raises a number of implications for the field of sport management. Perhaps the most important implication is that both sport psychology and sport management ultimately seek to understand how and why people participate in sport and exercise. Think about some of the issues and questions that this chapter has raised; many apply equally to both areas. For example, why does one person reach an optimal level of performance under a certain degree of arousal, yet another person collapses under the same amount of pressure? How can two very successful, world-class athletes have entirely different kinds of personalities? How do people's motivations to succeed affect the ways they perform in competitive athletics? Why does someone who previously was overweight and who had a negative self-concept successfully participate in a fitness program yet still have low self-esteem?

All of these psychology-related questions and their answers can easily be applied to sport management. For example, knowing that some people are motivated only by very challenging situations whereas others may be so afraid of failure that they avoid any kind of competitive setting can have practical implications for the sport management practitioner. A common problem illustrates this point. Many people may be interested in playing basketball in your Thursday night program. You know from sport psychology that some people need to be highly competitive, whereas others just want to play for fun. So you offer two different kinds of programs and emphasize their differences in your marketing and promotions campaign.

Or you may notice that many people sign up for a fitness program but drop out within the first 2 or 3 weeks. If you design a program that builds in both short-term and long-term goal setting, participants' motivations to stick to the program may increase dramatically.

It is hoped that this chapter has provided thought-provoking information that will be useful to the athlete, exercise enthusiast, and future sport management professional. It is also hoped that the issues, questions, and concerns raised here have created a new awareness of the importance of sport psychology and its very direct link to sport management. Finally, it is hoped that this chapter will serve as a catalyst for further inquiry into this new and ever-expanding area.

LEARNING ACTIVITIES

1. What is meant by the term *applied sport psychology*? How does this apply to someone interested in a career in sport management?

2. Explain how someone could become addicted to exercise. What signs would you look for to determine if one of your clients was a fitness addict? What would you do if the symptoms indicated addiction?

3. You are the manager of a fitness center, and a local agency has asked that your staff test the physical fitness levels of a group of disabled children. The agency also wants to know if any relationship exists between physical fitness and self-esteem. How would you respond to that question? What suggestions would you make for developing a fitness program that may increase the children's self-concepts?

REFERENCES

Atkinson, J.W. (1964). *An introduction to motivation*. Princeton, NJ: Van Nostrand.

Atkinson, J.W., & Litwin, G.H. (1960). Achievement motivation and test anxiety conceived as a motive to approach success and motive to avoid failure. *Journal of Abnormal and Social Psychology*, **60**, 52-63.

Bahrke, M.S., & Morgan, W.P. (1978). Anxiety reduction following exercise and meditation. *Cognitive Therapy and Research*, **2**, 323-333.

Berger, B.C. (1970). *Effect of three sport environmental factors upon selected personality characteristics of athletes*. Unpublished doctoral dissertation, Columbia University, New York.

Bittker, T. (1977). Runner's gluttony. *Runner's World*, **12**, 10-11.

Brown, R.S., Ramirez, D.E., & Taub, J.M. (1978). The prescription of exercise for depression. *The Physician and Sports Medicine*, 35-45.

Collingwood, T.R. (1972). The effects of physical training upon self-concept and body attitude. *Journal of Clinical Psychology*, **28**, 583-585.

Cooper, L. (1969). Athletics, activity and personality: A review of the literature. *Research Quarterly*, **40**, 17-22.

Cox, R.H. (1985). *Sport psychology: Concepts and applications*. Dubuque, IA: Wm. C. Brown.

Cratty, B.J. (1981). *Social psychology in athletics*. Englewood Cliffs, NJ: Prentice-Hall.

Davidoff, L.L. (1980). *Introduction to psychology*. New York: McGraw-Hill.

deVries, H.A. (1981). Tranquilizer effect of exercise: A critical review. *The Physician and Sports Medicine*, **9**, 47-53.

Dowell, L.J., Badgett, J.L., & Landiss, C.W. (1970). *A study of the relationship between selected physical attributes and self-concepts of entering male freshmen at Texas A & M University* (Project 153Q8). College Station, TX: Texas A & M University, Research Council.

Felker, D.W. (1974). *Building positive self-concepts*. Minneapolis: Burgess.

Fisher, A.C. (1976). *Psychology of sport*. Palo Alto, CA: Mayfield.

Fisher, A.C., Ryan, E.D., & Martens, R. (1976). Current status and future directions of personality research related to motor behavior and sport: Three panelists' views. In A.C. Fisher (Ed.), *Psychology of sport* (pp. 400-407). Palo Alto, CA: Mayfield.

Folkins, C.H., Lynch, S., & Gardner, N.M. (1972). Psychological fitness as a function of physical fitness. *Archives of Physical Medicine and Rehabilitation*, **53**, 503-508.

Folkins, C.H., & Sime, W.E. (1981). Fitness training and mental health. *American Psychologist*, **36**, 373-389.

Gill, D.L. (1986). *Psychological dynamics of sport*. Champaign, IL: Human Kinetics.

Hardman, K. (1973). A dual approach to the study of personality and performance in sport. In H.T.A. Whiting, K. Hardman, L.B. Hendry, & M.G. Jones (Eds.), *Personality and performance in physical education and sport* (pp. 71-122). London: Kimpton.

Harris, D.V., & Harris, B.L. (1984). *The athlete's guide to sports psychology: Mental skills for physical people*. Champaign, IL: Leisure Press.

Heaps, R.A. (1978). Relating physical and psychological fitness: A psychological point of view. *Journal of Sports Medicine and Physical Fitness*, **18**, 399-408.

Holberg, A. (1978). Effects of participation in the physical conditioning platoon. *Journal of Clinical Psychology*, **34**, 410-416.

Iso-Ahola, S.E. (1980). *The social psychology of leisure and recreation*. Dubuque, IA: Wm. C. Brown.

Kane, J.E. (1970). Personality and physical abilities. In G.S. Kenyon (Ed.), *Contemporary psychology of sport: Second International Congress of Sports Psychology* (pp. 131-141). Chicago: Athletic Institute.

Leonardson, R.R., & Gargiulo, R.M. (1978). Self-perception and physical fitness. *Perceptual Motor Skills*, **46**, 338.

Mihevic, P.M. (1981). Anxiety, depression and exercise. *Quest*, **33**, 140-153.

Morgan, W.P. (1979). Negative addiction in runners. *The Physician and Sportsmedicine*, **7**, 57-70.

Morgan, W.P. (1980a). Sport personology: The credulous-skeptical argument in perspective. In W.F. Straub (Ed.), *Sport psychology: An analysis of athlete behavior* (2nd ed.) (pp. 330-339). Ithaca, NY: Mouvement Press.

Morgan, W.P. (1980b). The trait psychology controversy. *Research Quarterly*, **51**, 50-76.

Morgan, W.P., Roberts, J.A., Brand, F.R., & Feinerman, A.D. (1970). Psychological effect of chronic physical activity. *Medicine and Science in Sports*, **2**, 213-217.

Ogilvie, B.C. (1976). Psychological consistencies within the personality of high-level competitors. In A.C. Fisher (Ed.), *Psychology of sport* (pp. 335-338). Palo Alto, CA: Mayfield.

Post, R.M., & Goodwin, F.K. (1973). Simulated behavior states: An approach to specificity in psychobiological research. *Biological Psychiatry*, **7**, 237-254.

Raglin, J.S., & Morgan, W.P. (1985). Influence of vigorous exercise on mood state. *The Behavior Therapist*, **8**, 179-183.

Ryan, E.D., & Lakie, W.L. (1965). Competitive and noncompetitive performance in relation to achievement motivation and manifest anxiety. *Journal of Personality and Social Psychology*, **1**, 344-345.

Schurr, K.T., Ashley, M.A., & Joy, K.C. (1977). A multivariate analysis of male athlete characteristics: Sport type and success. *Multivariate Experimental Clinical Research*, **3**, 53-68.

Singer, R.N. (1969). Personality differences between and within baseball and tennis players. *Research Quarterly*, **40**, 582-587.

Snyder, E.E., & Spreitzer, E.A. (1989). *Social aspects of sport* (3rd ed.). Englewood Cliffs, NJ: Prentice-Hall.

Sonstroem, R.J. (1984). Exercise and self-esteem. In R.L. Terjung (Ed.), *Exercise and sport sciences reviews*, **12**.

Vanek, M., & Cratty, B.J. (1970). *Psychology and the superior athlete*. London: Macmillan.

Williams, J.M. (1986). *Applied sport psychology*. Palo Alto, CA: Mayfield.

Wylie, R.C. (1979). *The self-concept: A review of methodological considerations and measuring instruments* (Vol. 2). Lincoln, NE: University of Nebraska Press.

CHAPTER 19

Sociology of Sport

Eldon E. Snyder
Bowling Green State University

Sport is one of the most pervasive institutions in our society, permeating the social universe from the macrosocial level down to the individual. We can document the prevalence of sport in modern society in terms of news coverage, financial expenditures, number of participants and spectators, movies, books, themes in comic strips, hours consumed, sports equipment sales, and time samplings of conversations. In short, the institution of sport is linked to many aspects of human social behavior and social institutions. Thus, it is appropriate to view sport, and consequently sport management, from a sociological perspective. This chapter focuses on two areas: (a) the nature of sport and (b) social factors that help explain our attraction to sport. Obviously, the latter level of analysis is particularly important for the marketing and managing of sport.

THE NATURE OF SPORT

Most people will agree that football, basketball, baseball, tennis, golf, and gymnastics are sports. Yet, some people are likely to object to including hiking, fishing, and walking under the label of sports. In everyday discourse a broad range of activities are often considered as sports—including all of the previously listed activities and more. The following definition can help sharpen our understanding of sport: Sport is a competitive, human activity that requires skill and exertion and is governed and regulated by institutionalized rules. This definition does not, of course, give us absolute clarity in our consideration of activities that are defined as sports. For example, we may not agree on the degree or level of competition, the amount of physical exertion, or the degree of formality of the rules. We can agree, however, that card games are competitive, are governed by rules, but require very little physical skill or exertion of energy. Likewise, running or swimming obviously require considerable physical exertion, but they would not be considered sports unless they take place within a regulated and competitive context.

Play is a closely related concept and is frequently confused with sport. In fact, we often equate the two words in such expressions as, "She plays basketball" and "He is a good tennis player." Singer (1976) defines play as

an enjoyable experience deriving behavior which is self-initiated in accordance with personal goals or expressive impulses; it tolerates all ranges of movement abilities; its rules are spontaneous; it has a temporal sequence but no predetermined ending; it results in no tangible outcome, victory or reward.'' (p. 40)

Thus, play is an activity that is rewarding because it is primarily fun and enjoyable; the satisfactions come from the activity itself rather than from victories, trophies, recognition, prestige, monetary benefits, and bragging rights.

The competitive orientation of the world of sport suggests a contest for extrinsic rewards beyond the mere joy of the activity itself. From junior high school athletics to the professional levels of sport we see an increased emphasis on the external rewards that go to the winners. Yet, many sport activities involve a mixture of intrinsic, playful elements and the extrinsic, competitive motif. Thus, a continuum of play and sport can help us conceptualize sport. In this conceptualization, play shades off into sport as the following transformations occur (Edwards, 1973; Snyder & Spreitzer, 1989):

1. The physical activity becomes less subject to individual discretion and spontaneity accordingly decreases.
2. Explicit rules, roles, and regulations become central to the physical activity.
3. The physical activity is not separated from the routine of daily life.
4. The individual's accountability for his or her quality of performance in the physical activity is emphasized.
5. The outcome of the activity (victory) extends beyond the participants in the physical activity.

6. The motivation for participation becomes more extrinsic and is affected by social expectations.
7. The physical activity consumes greater amounts of the individual's time and energy because of the seriousness of the activity—that is, the participant begins to lose control over the activity's flow.
8. The physical and mental demands of the activity exceed simple leisure and recreational proportion.

Admittedly, play and sport as outlined here are ideal types. Many activities are not "pure" play or "pure" sport. Consequently, a range of physical activities can be distributed on a continuum as shown in Figure 19.1.

Thus, performance in high school intramural basketball is not spontaneous because rules, roles, and responsibilities are involved. Yet, constraints of the school varsity basketball team are more formal than those of the intramural sport. Likewise, many adult physical activities are of the nature of informal or semiformal sport. Perhaps the term *leisure sports* is appropriate for sports that contain a mixture of play and sport characteristics. It is also clear that sport shades off into a species of work for participants in major collegiate and professional athletics. However, even for the professional athlete, the intrinsic aspect of sport may overlie the extrinsic core. Figure 19.2 sketches some physical activities that range from play to formally organized sport. The calibration of this scale is not very precise, and variations will exist depending on the type of activity, the community, and the school context of the sport.

Figure 19.1   Physical activities continuum.

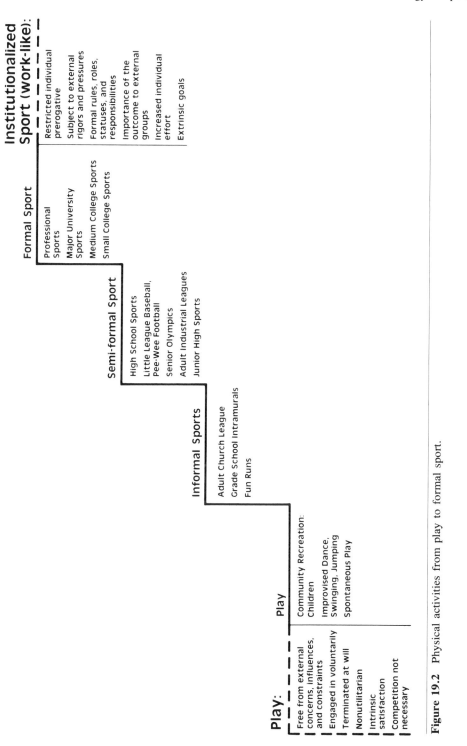

Figure 19.2 Physical activities from play to formal sport.

ATTRACTION TO SPORT

The management of sport activities, facilities, and enterprises depends upon people becoming involved in sport. Thus, it is important to understand why people are attracted to sport. An attraction implies commitment or motivation to become involved in sport activities and adherence to a program—either as a participant or spectator.

Initially, many people are socialized into sport as children. Socialization occurs within the social milieu that is likely to include parents, siblings, school, peers, and mass media. In the early childhood years the opportunity to learn the rules and skills of various sports often comes from family and neighborhood friends. In elementary and junior high school, children continue to refine their skills and develop a perception of their athletic abilities relative to those of other children. If this self-evaluation includes

Initial socialization into sport often occurs in childhood.

Parental interest in sport → Others' encouragement for sport participation → Participation in sport → Perceived ability in sport → Adult participation in sport

Figure 19.3 Variables affecting adult participation in sport.

less perceived ability than most other children of the same age, the child is likely to turn to other activities that provide more personal gratification. The self-evaluation of physical skill is further reinforced or modified by the formal evaluations given by teachers and coaches. This socialization into (or away from) sport during childhood is often significant to one's level of adult sport participation. The causal linkage of some variables associated with adult involvement in sport is shown in Figure 19.3.

Other Role Commitments

This diagram is not, however, a complete picture of the variables associated with adult participation in sport. Obviously, many who were encouraged in their youth to participate in sports are not regularly engaged in sport activities as adults. One's athletic role is also influenced by such other role commitments as family, work, community, and leisure activities. Configura-

tions of these roles vary not only from individual to individual but also by stages of the life cycle. Table 19.1 provides data from a study of three adult samples: participants in a 10K run, participants in a racquetball tournament, and a cross section of the general population (Spreitzer & Snyder, 1983). The pattern of the findings is clear. The runners and racquetball players generally placed a high value on their respective forms of physical activity; consequently, they typically saw no conflict between this leisure role and their roles as spouse, parent, and worker. The respondents from the general population, on the other hand, were much more likely to view their jobs or families as preempting any discretionary time that might be available for physical activity. Further, the rates of agreement with the following item are particularly interesting as a measure of commitment and attraction to sport: *I lack the will power to adhere to a regular exercise regimen*—general population 53 percent, racquetball players 24 percent, and runners 14 percent.

Table 19.1   Attitudes Toward Work and Leisure as Related to Adult Sports Participation

	Percentage agreeing with statement		
	Runners (N = 316)	Racquetball players (N = 201)	General population (N = 112)
I find that my leisure activities are more satisfying to me than my work.	61	62	48
My personal identity is realized more in my work than in my leisure activities.	38	42	61
If I were to describe myself, you would get a better understanding of me through my leisure activities than through my work.	48	48	26
I am too involved with my family to do very much physical activity.	7	5	29

Note. Data from "Correlates of Participation in Adult Recreational Sports" by E. Spreitzer and E. Snyder, 1983, *Journal of Leisure Research*, **15**, pp. 27-38.

It is evident that commitment and attachment to sport incorporate some tenets of exchange theory. That is, the motivation to participate in sport is strengthened when the activity results in rewarding and satisfying experiences, but motivation disappears when the activity results in failure, criticism, or embarrassment; costs in time, money, or energy; or conflicts with other roles. In general, people attempt to maximize their rewards relative to the costs or investments (cost:benefit ratio) in their activities and interactions with other people (Turner, 1987).

Social Factors

Numerous studies have documented the effect of socializing agents such as parents, siblings, teachers, and coaches who influence individuals' initial and continued involvement in sport contexts. Furthermore, adults as well as youth cite the social influences of friends as factors in their continued involvement in sports. As a consequence of the satisfactions that flow from social attachments, mutual esteem, and companionship, this social support factor is primary in many people's sport involvement. This is positively illustrated with leisure sports played in a club context or with friends, where the relationships are pleasant and enjoyable.

Research on the social world of shuffleboard players demonstrates the importance of friendship networks among tournament players (Snyder, 1986). They frequently travel to tournaments with other players—usually as couples—and much of their social lives and conversations relate to shuffleboard. The following excerpt from an ethnographic account of shuffleboard players illustrates the social dimension (Snyder, 1986).

> As one player noted, "Our best friends are shufflers, we're closer to them than our own relatives." When another player was asked about social relationships in shuffleboard, he said, "Oh yes, most of our friends are also shufflers." When asked if they talk

about shuffleboard, he replied, "You better believe it. We often go with three other couples to eat out and they also shuffle. When we get together it's 'If I had made this shot or if I had made that shot.' I guess we have to cry on each others' shoulders." Another serious shuffler said, "Shuffling is where you make your friends. That's the nice part of shuffling." (pp. 244-245)

On the other hand, negative social influences—failure, criticism, too much pressure to win, and feelings of inadequacy and embarrassment—promote aversive socialization from sport roles.

Intrinsic Rewards

Other factors promoting an attraction to sport roles include the sheer intrinsic enjoyment, pleasure, ecstasy, and fun of physical exertion in competitive sport contexts and the sense of efficacy that results from a competent performance (Deci, 1973). The human being is an active animal who enjoys performing a task that is challenging yet within his or her capacity to perform (Csikszentmihalyi, 1975). This consideration of intrinsic satisfactions rests primarily in the playful aspects of sport most evident in informal sport. This perspective might be further explained by looking at play as a form of information seeking and as competency motivation (Ellis, 1981). The theory of play as information seeking suggests a human need to interact with the environment in order to achieve optimal levels of satisfaction, arousal, and interest. Play is thus seen as a type of behavior concerned with maintaining a stimulating flow of information; once a person has satisfied the more pressing needs of survival, he or she tends to seek out environmental interaction of a more challenging or complex variety. We can also view play as a form of arousal seeking. Here the focus is on the human propensity for curiosity, challenge, exploration, investigation, and wonder. The arousal-seeking theory views the human as having a need to produce effects in the environment and to gain satisfaction from demonstrating competency.

Research conducted by Thompson and Bair (1982) among weight lifters reveals aspects of intrinsic satisfaction. Although many of the lifters indicated they were motivated by extrinsic desires such as better physical fitness and getting in shape for particular sports, "most of the participants derived a sense of accomplishment and intrinsic satisfaction in having achieved the ability to lift a particular weight, or perform a specific exercise a certain number of times" (p. 196). Similarly, Nash (1979) recognized the intrinsic dimension of running in a "fun run." A fun run is organized without regard for winning or prizes; rather, "people are supposed to enjoy themselves, each according to their own individually defined motivation for running. . . . To simply participate and to run as far as one can in the presence of others who intrinsically feel the goodness of the fun may be eventful" (Nash, 1979, p. 205).

Extrinsic Rewards

Central to sport roles is extrinsic motivation in the form of victories, trophies, recognition, prestige, money, awards, favors, and other ego-gratifying outcomes associated with successful athletic performances. Conversely, if performances are unsuccessful in these outcomes, we would expect the sport role to lack satisfaction and the participant to possibly disengage from the role. Given the present structure of formal sport, the core values often emphasize this extrinsic motif. In general, a more serious stance toward the importance of winning is equated with a greater investment of identity and commitment in the sport role. The following comments by a woman tournament shuffleboard player illustrate her senses of identity, well-being, and accomplishment that represent extrinsic satisfactions (Snyder, 1986):

Extrinsic rewards are associated with successful athletic performance.

Here in Ohio I'm classified as an expert. I've just been elected to the Shuffleboard Hall of Fame. I'm so thrilled over that. I've won the nationals, singles and doubles. You have to do a lot of winning. You have to qualify and be nominated by a club. The Akron Club nominated me. The committee voted for me according to my record. Not everyone gets in, only the best. There are a lot of great players in the Hall of Fame. Some have passed on, but their pictures remain in there. (p. 249)

The extrinsic dimensions, evident in all forms of competition, are personally satisfying and provide a continued motivation to participate.

Self-Identity

Through interaction within sport contexts, an individual develops a self-perception of his or her athletic ability. This perception represents the core of one's sport identity. Research indicates that perceived athletic ability is a primary predictor of adherence to physical conditioning regimens (Snyder & Spreitzer, 1984). Likewise, studies indicate a variety of social factors outlined previously and correlate intrinsic and extrinsic satisfactions (or dissatisfactions) with one's sport identity (Snyder & Spreitzer, 1984; Spreitzer & Snyder, 1983). If an individual's sport experiences lead to a low perception of his or her sport ability, continued participation in sport is unlikely. Indeed, the lack of success in the sport role may contaminate the broader image of self. It is clear that we strive to manage and enhance our self-image (Becker, 1971). McCall and Simmons (1978) noted the following.

Those actions that are not consonant with one's imaginations of self as a person in a particular social position are regarded as embarrassing, threatening, and disconcerting; if possible, they will be discontinued and superseded by actions more in keeping with one's view of self. (p. 67)

Closely related to one's perceived athletic ability is actual innate athletic ability. Based on studies of characteristics such as intelligence, height, weight, and music ability, we know that most people have average athletic abilities and if the rewards are sufficient may achieve a relatively high level of athletic achievement. Yet, some individuals are talented and perform very well with ease. Their payoffs will be greater, and generally these individuals continue with higher-than-average levels of attachment to sport. Conversely, a few people have very few athletic abilities and enjoy few extrinsic satisfactions in sport. If they participate in sports, their involvements are likely supported

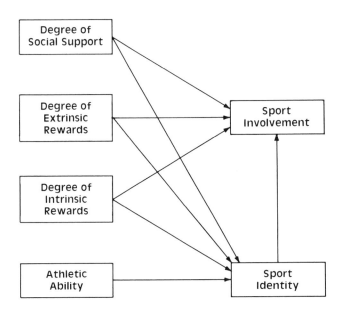

Figure 19.4 A theoretical model of sport involvement, probable causal variables.

by heavy doses of social support and the intrinsic dimension.

Figure 19.4 illustrates the probable causal variables that help explain an attraction to the sport role.

IMPLICATIONS FOR SPORT MANAGEMENT

The nature of sport is based on three elements: It is competitive; it is a human activity that requires skill and exertion; and it is governed and regulated by institutionalized rules. This definition helps clarify our understandings of the levels of sport and related behavior. An athletic event is by definition competitive, and the outcome is uncertain. Consequently, this uncertainty promotes excitement, challenge, and the desire to achieve the optimal level of competence and performance in order to win. These characteristics are manifest in the attractions of sport that are described in the form of intrinsic and extrinsic payoffs.

Interaction in sport requires an expenditure and investment of such variables as time, energy, and money. An attraction to sport is reinforced when we associate it with a maximizing of the social, extrinsic, and intrinsic rewards relative to the costs. Additionally, variations in an individual's perceived athletic ability will likely reflect that person's past experiences in sport contexts as well as his or her innate athletic ability. These factors provide a greater understanding of people's participation in sport organizations.

To successfully manage and market sport, you must understand the basic social factors that are associated with sport and fitness activities. Of particular importance is the analysis of the meanings people attach to sport; as a manager of sport and fitness programs, you can use this knowledge to make your programs attractive to people of all ages. The public's consumption of sport goods and services is likely to parallel the stages of sport involvement outlined in this chapter. The specific stage of consumer participation and demand will reflect consumers' interpretations of meanings associated with the sport product or service. People must view the product, service, or activity—as with other forms of behavior—such as a job, a hobby, or organizational membership—as sufficiently valuable and worthy of investment of time and money (Snyder & Spreitzer, 1989). In general, people will "buy into" sport if they feel it "sells" these satisfactions.

LEARNING ACTIVITIES

1. Discuss in small groups your "sport life history." Identify the social factors, self-perceived abilities, and extrinsic and intrinsic rewards that encourage or discourage your participation in sport.

2. Interview five people who are very involved and five people who are not involved in sport activities; analyze the reasons the interviewees give for their degrees of involvement.

3. Interview members of a racquet, golf, tennis, or swimming club to determine their reasons for belonging to the club. Also interview the manager or managers of the sport club to determine the reasons they believe are important for people's involvements in the club. Compare the views of members and managers.

4. Interview several students or other adults who are very involved in music, art, speech, or other nonsport activities; determine the social factors, self-perceived abilities, and extrinsic and intrinsic rewards that influence their participation in these activities. How are their motivations similar to those of sport participants?

REFERENCES

Becker, E. (1971). *The birth and death of meaning*. New York: The Free Press.

Csikszentmihalyi, M. (1975). *Beyond boredom and anxiety: The experience of play in work and games*. San Francisco: Jossey-Bass.

Deci, E. (1973). *Intrinsic motivation*. Rochester, NY: University of Rochester.

Edwards, H. (1973). *Sociology of sport*. Homewood, IL: Dorsey Press.

Ellis, M. (1981). Motivational theories of play: Definitions and explanations. In G. Luschen & G. Sage (Eds.), *Handbook of social science of sport* (pp. 479-491). Champaign, IL: Stipes.

McCall, G., & Simmons, J.L. (1978). *Identities and interactions*. New York: The Free Press.

Nash, J. (1979). Weekend racing as an eventful experience. *Urban Life*, **8**, 199-217.

Singer, R. (1976). *Physical education: Foundations*. New York: Holt, Rinehart and Winston.

Snyder, E.E. (1986). The social world of shuffleboard. *Urban Life*, **15**, 237-253.

Snyder, E.E., & Spreitzer, E. (1984). Patterns of adherence to a physical conditioning program. *Sociology of Sport Journal*, **1**, 103-116.

Snyder, E.E., & Spreitzer, E. (1989). *Social aspects of sport*. Englewood Cliffs, NJ: Prentice-Hall.

Spreitzer, E., & Snyder, E.E. (1983). Correlates of preparation in adult recreational sports. *Journal of Leisure Research*, **15**, 27-38.

Thompson, W., & Bair, J. (1982). A sociological analysis of pumping iron. *Free Inquiry in Creative Sociology*, **10**, 192-196.

Turner, J. (1987). Toward a sociological theory of motivation. *American Sociological Review*, **52**, 15-27.

CHAPTER 20

Sport Philosophy and Social Responsibility

Joy T. DeSensi
University of Tennessee–Knoxville

A main purpose of philosophy is to assist individuals in evaluating their beliefs so the actions that follow are logical and consistent. Philosophy is a process that should lead to understanding. We explore and evaluate questions within the areas of metaphysics, ontology, epistemology, ethics, and aesthetics by using the philosophic process. Philosophic investigation and reflection offer us ways of thinking about issues and behavior. Philosophy is the most general form of human understanding and offers an inclusive perspective of humankind. The process of philosophy is the "effort to transform the obscure, the ambiguous and the indeterminate into the evident, the explicit and the understandable" (Bressen & Pieter, 1985, p. 1).

This chapter will not cover all there is to know about sport philosophy. You should take courses specifically addressing sport philosophy, social theories, and sport sociology in order to grasp the implications that these areas have for sport management. As managerial responsibilities test your decision-making abilities, sound analytical and critical philosophical questioning applied to the management setting will help you make the best decisions.

The field of sport has a great need for social awareness and responsibility in the midst of all the theories, techniques, styles, and models of management. As a sport management student, you will soon be in a position to effect change. Understanding sport and management from a philosophical perspective will assist you in developing a sense of social responsibility and beliefs based on reason.

This chapter will explore the value of philosophy and philosophical questioning in sport and sport management; the relevance of sport philosophy and the importance of philosophical training; and philosophy and action in sport management.

THE VALUE OF PHILOSOPHY AND PHILOSOPHICAL QUESTIONING

Numerous philosophers have attempted to define and describe the nature of philosophy. Concepts concerning truth, beauty, God, freedom, right and wrong, good and evil, existence, reality, being, and life's meaning can create unsettled feelings and thoughts. These rational, cognitive, or conceptual activities of individuals characterize the process and product of philosophy. More specific questions stemming from these basic life questions emerge in specific settings. In this case, the questions relate to the concepts of sport within our society. The spectator, participant, and practitioner all have potential to emerge in sport with questions and reflections of meaning, definition, and justification. Other definitions of philosophy reveal that it is the love of wisdom, a process of thought, a product of logical discourse, and a human endeavor that leads us to the truth, meaning, freedom, justice, virtue, humanness, choices, and a way of life (DeSensi, 1985).

Philosophy plays an extremely important role in the development of personal beliefs, values, and actions. The reflective, analytical, and speculative features of the philosophic process offer individuals mechanisms for problem solving as well as contemplation. Katen (1973) notes that a balance should occur in one's philosophical thinking and philosophical existence. ''Thinking and experiencing should blend into a continuum and provide a richly unified existence'' (Katen, 1973, p. 346). Many consider philosophy to be profound thinking; it is actually profound living. One's life should be unified by a combination of philosophical thought and philosophical behavior.

How does the concept of philosophy relate to sport management? We find that through intellectual conflict and argument we generate new theories and questions and ultimately initiate action and change. Such examination may give rise to questions regarding the worth of sport/fitness programs; the concept of profit maximization and social responsibility; the responsibilities of sport franchises to a community; the rights of spectators and athletes; moral and political actions in sport; and ethics and managerial practices.

In the pursuit of finding and understanding philosophical truths, you should be able to take a position, analyze it from a number of perspectives, manipulate it, and then make appropriate applications in real life settings. Learning to ask questions is necessary in order to adequately apply philosophical methods. The process involves identifying concerns, refining problems, attaining argumentative rigor, acknowledging connections, and noting presuppositions. Such creative, synthesized literacy is necessary for each individual to achieve in order to find the wisdom and truths associated with one's life beliefs.

Philosophy, then, is a practice and is not limited to those we call philosophers. Rather, philosophy is a human practice of reason that is appropriate and necessary for everyone. Developing a broad sense of understanding and reason within the area of sport management is critical to your pursuit of a position in this field. Familiarity with the major issues in our society and within the sport society from a philosophical perspective gives the sport manager an advantage in knowledge, understanding, decision making, and problem solving within the sport management setting.

In no other discipline do we have the opportunity to examine and practice perspectives that offer such breadth and depth in inquiry and analysis regarding the levels of sport participation, sporting opportunities for all populations, and sport management in general. The process of raising and exploring philosophical issues in the management of sport should be an exciting challenge for you. As a result of such practice, you can experience a harmonious blending of knowledge, understanding, and action.

THE RELEVANCE OF SPORT PHILOSOPHY

Philosophy is relevant in the study of sport, and ultimately in sport management, and is a continuously evolving process leading to knowledge and understanding in these areas. As you ex-

Thousands of people in the United States participate vicariously in sports.

plore definitions of play, games, sport, dance, and fitness activities, in addition to issues such as the body as subject or as object, ethics and moral behavior, the spiritual dimensions of the sport experience, the art of movement, and our own participation in such activities, you will find new meanings and explanations.

Elite sport has set the pace for the increase in participation in all sport and physical activities. Consequently, the services provided to individuals through public and private sport facilities, recreational sport programs, professional sport, and school, college, and university programs have increased. The increase in participation for many has been due to identification with the elite programs. Unfortunately, elite programs are available only to the elite performers. Most of the individuals in our society are not elite athletes but instead vary in ages, sizes, and degrees of interest and skill in certain sports. Many of us participate vicariously in elite sport as spectators, yet some groups in our society are excluded from sport altogether due to age,

sex, skill level, and physical, emotional, or mental handicaps. Programs such as the Special Olympics and the Senior Games attempt to provide opportunities for some individuals but are limited programs. Even with the Title IX legislation, sport opportunities for girls and women are still limited. Many of the activities and programs for youths are directed toward those who are highly skilled; thus those who do not have many abilities but greatly desire to play are without opportunities to participate. Each of these problems is directly associated with concerns dealing with human issues.

More opportunities are becoming available to many in our society, but many injustices still exist. It is easy to see, through philosophical reflection and contemplation, the development of thinking that has created and perpetuated or changed some of these situations. Philosophy offers us a way to examine basic problems of individuals and society. Sport managers can be practical philosophers in their work as they deal with critical issues for the sport participant and

Many children's sports programs are limited to the highly skilled participant.

spectator. As a sport manager, you must be able to ask pertinent questions regarding our lives and interactions with others, our realities, our values and beliefs, and our moral and political actions. All of us who purport to live and interact with others should question and explore such issues. The process of philosophy can help us to integrate ideas and seek answers to such problems as value judgments, administrative decisions, and problems plaguing the sport world. To ask philosophical questions of yourself as well as of participants or spectators makes this area of inquiry a part of the life process.

PHILOSOPHY AND ACTION IN SPORT MANAGEMENT: SOCIAL RESPONSIBILITY

Closely allied with the philosophical tenets of axiology and ethics is the concept of social responsibility. Social responsibility involves a moral, legal, or mental accountability on the part of individuals for the self and others. It denotes reliability and trustworthiness and is reflected in one's behavior. In addition, concern or regard for others also belongs within the context of social responsibility (DeSensi, 1987). The sport manager's development of an individual social awareness and social consciousness, and ultimately social responsibility, is an ethical trial in today's world. Within such an examination, you as a sport manager must realize (a) the nature of the relationship between society and your particular sport management setting, (b) the formal organizations that are associated with the sport management setting, and (c) the responsibility of the particular sport organization or setting to society.

Focusing on the subjective meanings and significance of our sport world is difficult at best when the objective issues of win/loss records, high standards of performance for athletes, increased memberships for sports clubs, sport franchise stability, and increased revenue production are constantly top priorities for sport businesses. Perhaps the objective here should be to strike a balance wherein profit or achievement (in whatever form) is ethically and responsibly managed.

Robbins (1976) noted that in the process of planning within management, the selected objectives, in some cases, may relate to social awareness, or the act of being socially responsible and responsive. We tend to lose sight of the potential that the concepts of social awareness and social responsibility possess when we further discover that most nonprofit organizations are based on an awareness of very real societal needs. This is not necessarily the case, however, with for-profit organizations such as professional sport and, in some cases, intercollegiate sport.

The corporate business model's influence on the educational model of sport has been a point of contention for some time. The revenue-producing potential and managerial practices of the professional sports team setting have set the pace for college and university sports departments. The effects of this influence have been both positive and negative. Many colleges and universities have lost their credibility with the critics as they stand closely in the shadows of professional structures. We even hear overtones of the professional ranks when directors of college and university athletic programs talk about the similar power structures and the labor force. We have been hesitant to acknowledge the businesslike structures of our athletic departments. Such organizations have had to hide behind a facade and purport a certain philosophy that in many cases has opposed the business model. For example, the NCAA as well as some athletic departments have purported concerns for athletes and schools when in fact money-making ventures were the primary concern. More recent legislation from the NCAA does in fact address the issues of the college athlete. The athletic organizations on college and university campuses are different from the other struc-

tures on the same campus. This department should not have to contend one philosophy of operation and actually work under the guise of another; athletics in most educational settings is a business and should be run as such. As soon as the organizations responsible for sport in the athletic setting acknowledge the similarities and differences (i.e., the production status, the emphasis of the win/loss record, and the need to increase profit), the sooner more sound foundational philosophies can be established for such organizations.

One focus of social responsibility within the athletic setting has to do with ensuring that every athlete receives an education. In the current structure, athletic departments are caught in a paradox. The department attempts to please several conflicting social groups (i.e., players, alumni, administrators, and the NCAA), and the attempt to balance an educational model of athletics with that of a business model becomes infeasible in certain cases. Perhaps the models should not be restricted to an "either/or" case. The business and educational models of athletic

What social responsibilities do professional sport franchise managers have?

programs may possess separate aims and objectives; however, such aims and objectives may not necessarily be mutually exclusive. An attempt to balance this thinking is a check on the ethical standards of the athletic organization. The attempt to keep a balance without losing sight of primary goals may allow the attention to social responsibility to exist within an otherwise objective and goal-directed world. True concern and regard for the individual athlete, the college or university program, those involved with such programs, and its community of spectators are great considerations within the concept of balancing the business and educational models at this level.

A common view of the professional sport level is that it is "big business." Within the concept of big business is the economic impact generated by such teams. According to Hemphill (1983), "the pursuit of profit maximization has taken first place while sport management and labor have forsaken the public interest in favor of monetary self-interest" (p. 2). Issues such as the revenue generation potential of the sport franchise, the public interest in sport, and the social responsibility of the franchise owner to the community are called into question.

Some sport franchise owners are aware of the social implications and meanings their franchise holds for a community. On one hand, fans become emotionally attached to and strongly identify with the home team, but in addition, the city depends on the revenue generated by a sport franchise. Hemphill (1983) points out that the sports team owner has three indirect obligations to the community: franchise location stability, team performance quality, and unpredictability of performance outcome. The owner's recognition of these points and action toward such ends ensures that the needs of the public are considered and that the franchise can be profitable.

Some professional team owners regard their teams as objects or toys to play with and manipulate. Many of these individuals know nothing about sport or its management and are more in-

volved in the cartellike power structures of business manipulation than in serving the community with socially responsible actions. Flint and Eitzen (1987) further substantiate this point by stating the following:

> Because sport is still categorized as simple play, the power of wealthy capitalist owners can be overlooked as simple aberration or eccentric pastime. Although the meritocratic recruitment arguments are held high by the owners as well as the participants (players or consumers), little attention is given to the contradictory fact that owning a team is not based on merit but on enormous wealth. (p. 25)

These same authors go on to note that the concept of ownership "defines a full range of economic relations, from entrepreneurial freedom of operation to the refined security of monopoly capitalism; from the independent pursuit of self-interest to the control of market exigencies by an interlocking corporate directorate" (p. 18). It seems that a socially responsible sport operation can be achieved if responsible individuals make changes that enhance the long-term operation of the professional sport franchise rather than sacrifice public interests for monetary interests.

Sport and fitness programs are increasing in number to meet the exercise and fitness demands of society. Such clubs are not exempt from the concept of social responsibility. As with the intercollegiate and professional sport settings, certain legal and professional standards help keep this area in check. Social responsibility is the obligation that the owners and managers of the clubs have to their public or clientele. Such responsibilities might include a clean and safe environment; qualified and, in some cases, certified personnel to ensure safe practices in exercise prescription and adherence; good equipment in respect to functional assessment, safety evaluation, and performance and stress tolerance; flexible hours of availability; appropriate facilities and equipment for both women and men; fair membership costs; information concerning risks of activities; adaptability to the changes in society; programs and accessibility for all populations; and general care and concern for the well-being of the clientele. While maintaining responsibility for these features of a health club, owners and managers can ensure an environment that is conducive for the programs it sponsors, the people it serves, and the overall sport management setting. Being socially responsible to the needs of the public goes hand in hand with survival in the business world.

Another area within the concept of social responsibility is the interaction between individuals. Whether friendships grow out of social or business contexts, they involve definite responsibilities. Even the relationships that are developed solely for business reasons demand responsible attitudes. Business cannot exist for very long without mutual trust and goodwill among business associates.

I-Thou and I-It Relationships

One example of putting philosophical beliefs and a sense of social responsibility into practice may be explained by Martin Buber's theory of "I-Thou" and "I-It" relationships. According to Buber (1970), a philosophical anthropologist, the most important aspect of the world is the meeting of the individual (I) and the other (Thou). Any sport setting is basically amoral; only when we interact within that setting do values, beliefs, and actions influence the occurrences and interactions with other individuals. To Buber, real life is encounter. The importance of this belief is not grounded in *whether* we meet and consider the other individual, but rather *when*. Buber notes that the ultimate responsibility of individuals to each other is one of love, but he does not interpret the concept of love in

the usual way. Rather, according to Buber, love means that individuals need to accept others and relate to them as unique human beings. Buber indicates that we can enter into a living relationship with another individual, with nature, or with objects. The way in which this meeting or encounter occurs is either in the realm of an I-It relationship or an I-Thou relationship.

The premises of Buber's theory of relationship are relevant and applicable to all settings in sport as well as in management. Within the I-Thou relationship, the individual lives as a subject among subjects. This relationship is not limited to relations with other individuals, but includes one's relationship to God, nature, and intelligible forms. Within the I-Thou encounter, we view the other as a unique individual and take a stand in mutual relationship with her or him. Characteristic of this encounter are the concepts of mutuality, directness, presentness, intensity, and ineffability. Through the concept of *mutuality*, we experience mutual regard and a sense of humanness for the other individual. Within *directness*, no foreknowledge of the individual interferes with the relationship. *Presentness* offers the incredible importance and emphasis on the "here and now"; within this characteristic, only that which occurs at the moment is important. *Intensity* is interpreted to mean that more and more of the individual becomes involved in the interaction or relationship. *Ineffability* basically acknowledges that a very special encounter has occurred between individuals and that in reality such a relationship is silent and cannot easily be explained. This relationship is considered the deepest, most meaningful interaction of which an individual is capable. It occurs by *will* (a psychological readiness) and *grace* (a gift or spontaneous occurrence) rather than by planning for the encounter.

Within the I-It encounter, we live as objects among objects and tend to use, manipulate, and experience others. The I-It world is indirect and exists in the contexts of time, space, and causality. This view of the world is objective and frequently serves as a means to an end. The I-It relationship is purposeful and becomes a means of securing knowledge and other needs as a necessary way to sustain life. Sport and management settings are filled with objective relational aspects and needs such as product marketing, profit maximization, and win/loss records, for example. The I-It world is a necessary realm in which we must survive. Buber indicates however, that we cannot live in this realm alone. Without authentic relationships with others, our world and life would be lacking (Progen & DeSensi, 1984). Acceptance of an authentic interaction with others is vital to the sport and management world. Perhaps the I-Thou and I-It contrast can help explain how we tend to relate to those individuals in our society who are within special populations. Reflection on the objectiveness of our interactions with the aged, youth, the handicapped, and minorities may well reveal a discriminatory pattern within the sport and sport management settings. Our greatest social responsibility is to provide programs, facilities, and the necessary personnel for sport programs in their broadest sense.

I-Thou relationships are not incompatible with sporting activities.

LEARNING ACTIVITIES

1. What roles do philosophical understanding and questioning play in sport management?

2. Social responsibility within sport management settings can take several forms. Choose specific sport management settings and analyze how the sport organization, business, or team can be socially responsible. What responsibilities does a sport manager have to maintain the integrity of the sport setting?

3. Equal opportunity in sport and similar activities for all populations in our society (e.g., men, women, the aged, the handicapped, and children of all races and skill levels) does not presently exist. Discuss changes that would allow for equal opportunities for these groups in the various sport settings in our society.

4. Choose a sport management setting. Discuss how the manager who practices social responsibility and the manager who does not practice social responsibility would manage the setting.

5. How can the concepts of profit maximization and social responsibility in a sport be compatible?

REFERENCES

Bressan, E.S., & Pieter, W. (1985). Philosophic processes and the study of human moving. *Quest*, **37**, 1-15.

Buber, M. (1970). *I and thou* (W. Kaufman, Trans.). New York: Scribners & Sons.

DeSensi, J.T. (1985, June). *Preparing physical education teachers: Perspectives from the sub-disciplines—Philosophy*. Paper presented at the Association Internationale des Ecoles Superieures d'Education Physique conference, Garden City, NY.

DeSensi, J.T. (1987, May). *Social responsibility and the management of sport*. Paper presented at the meeting of the North American Society for Sport Management, Windsor, ON.

Flint, W.C., & Eitzen, S. (1987). Professional sports team ownership and entrepreneurial capitalism. *Sociology of Sport Journal*, **4**, 17-27.

Hemphill, D. (1983). *The social responsibility of a professional sport franchise to a community*. Unpublished manuscript.

Katen, T.E. (1973). *Doing philosophy*. Englewood Cliffs, NJ: Prentice-Hall.

Progen, J.L., & DeSensi, J.T. (1984). The value of theoretical frameworks for exploring the subjective dimension of sport. *Quest*, **36**, 80-88.

Robbins, S.P. (1976). *The administrative process: Integrating theory and practice.* Englewood Cliffs, NJ: Prentice-Hall.

CHAPTER 21

History of Management Thought

Robert L. Minter
University of Michigan–Dearborn

Prior to the turn of the century, a manager had little information to help in effectively operating a business. Due to the lack of literature during this period, managers had difficulty finding answers about planning, organizing, and controlling the business operation; measuring work performance; delegating tasks; designing the organization and its workflow for maximum efficiency and overall effectiveness; motivating personnel; improving overall productivity; determining an equitable wage and salary system; and setting prices for products or services.

Only since the beginning of the 20th century have major advancements in management thought and principles been developed, recorded, and published. This chapter will summarize management literature into units of information often referred to as *movements* or *schools of thought*.

MANAGEMENT MOVEMENTS

Three movements we can identify are often referred to as the administrative/scientific management movement, the behavioral management movement, and the contemporary management movement. Table 21.1 highlights leading contributors and their major contributions to each of these movements.

Table 21.1 Leading Contributors to Management Thought

Name	Major contribution
Administrative/Scientific Management Movement	
Henri Fayol (1841-1925)	Was one of the first to develop a theory of administration containing principles that could be taught to managers.
Frederick W. Taylor (1856-1915)	Introduced time-study techniques to develop work standards. Referred to as "the father of scientific management."

(Cont.)

Table 21.1   (Continued)

Name	Major contribution
Henry Gantt (1861-1919)	Developed a task-and-bonus system of wages, graphic charting techniques for industrial/business use, and methods of production control.
Max Weber (1864-1920)	Was foremost contributor in the development of a theory of bureaucracy.
Frank Gilbreth (1868-1924)	Developed the method of motion study to improve upon human efforts in the work place.
Mary Parker Follett (1868-1933)	Contributed to area of applying social sciences to industry.
Lillian Gilbreth (1878-1972)	Developed psychological principles to help management understand work behavior.
Chester I. Barnard (1886-1961)	Led in stressing the importance of understanding the informal organization, communication networks, role of authority, and decision-making processes.
James Oscar McKinsey (1889-1937)	Focused attention on the importance of budgeting as a major instrument of management.

Behavioral Management Movement

Kurt Lewin (1890-1947)	Developed theories and conducted research on group dynamics and group participation.
Fritz J. Roethlisberger (1898-1974)	Conducted pioneer research on human factors in management, later known as the Hawthorne experiments. A number of human relations principles emerged from this study.
Douglas McGregor (1906-1964)	Developed the "Theory X–Theory Y" managerial leadership model, which revolutionized the management/leadership concept.
Abraham Maslow (1908-1970)	Introduced a five-tier need hierarchy motivation model that pioneered the way for future motivation concepts.
Frederick Herzberg (b. 1923)	Developed a maintenance/motivation theory. Often referred to as the "father of job enrichment concepts."
Victor Vroom (b. 1932)	Developed an expectancy model of motivation, which provides a probability estimate that a given level of effort will result in a given outcome of performance.
David C. McClelland (b. 1917)	Introduced the achievement/motivation model, which specifically deals with high and low achievers in the work setting.

Contemporary Management Movement

Ludwig von Bertalanffy (1901-1972)	Proposed a theory of general systems and subsystems that aided in explaining behavior in an organizational context.
Fred E. Fiedler (b. 1922)	Developed first of the contingency theories proposing that successful leadership depends on the match between the manager's leadership style and the demands of the situation.

Name	Major contribution
Victor Vroom (b. 1932)	Developed a contingency theory focusing on how a manager makes decisions. This theory assumes that the nature of problems vary and should be solved by different decision-making strategies.
Peter Drucker (b. 1909)	Developed the concept of management by objectives (MBO).

Establishing specific dates as boundaries for each of the movements is somewhat arbitrary. For our purposes, we can say that the administrative/scientific management movement was dominant between 1850 and 1945; the behavioral movement was dominant between the 1930s and the mid-1970s, and the contemporary movement began in the early 1970s and continues to the present. The literature associated with these schools of thought reveals that the principles, theories, and concepts of management are derived from diverse fields or academic disciplines, as indicated in Table 21.2. The body of information contributing to the development of management thought is eclectic in nature.

Table 21.2 Disciplinary Bases for Management

Discipline	Special emphasis
Industrial engineering	Measurement and analysis of physical factors to achieve work efficiency
Economics	Allocation of scarce resources with orientation to the future
Financial accounting	Recording, reporting, analyzing, and auditing of past transactions
Public administration	Formation of a rational hierarchy for the accomplishment of activities
Legal profession	Development of a consistent course of action based on precedents to achieve stability, order, and justice
Statistical methods	Employment of probability theory to infer facts from samples and to handle uncertainty
Mathematics	Construction of models that explicitly state one's assumptions, objectives, and constraints
Psychology	Scientific investigations concerning human needs, perceptions, and emotional factors
Sociology	Study of interrelationships within and among work groups

(Cont.)

Table 21.2   (Continued)

Discipline	Special emphasis
Anthropology	Cultural variations and discoverable patterns of behavior from history and environment
Organizational communication	Study of formal and informal communication networks within organizational settings

Note. From Joseph L. Massie, *Essentials of Management*, 4/e, © 1987, p. 27. Reprinted by permission of Prentice-Hall, Inc. Englewood Cliffs, New Jersey.

Administrative/Scientific Management Movement (1850 to 1945)

The thrust of thinking in the administrative scientific concepts was usually not concerned with the welfare and working conditions of employees. The movement emphasized what management should do to maintain order, cut costs, and increase productivity through improved organization and management. Unions emerged during this period, mainly due to the negative working conditions and to the resulting employee dissatisfaction.

The contributions to management thought during this era were concerned primarily with

- increasing efficiency and effectiveness with which work was designed and accomplished;
- giving management, rather than workers, control over planning and coordination of work;
- instituting pay structures and incentive systems;
- ensuring mandatory employee obedience (i.e., the interest of the employees or work groups should not supersede the organization's objectives);
- motivating employees primarily through monetary rewards; and

- creating division of work and job specializations.

The major thrust of the management literature during this period was to develop a single set of universal management principles applicable to all situations.

The Behavioral Management Movement (1930s to mid-1970s)

Many disciplines contributed to the development of this school of thought, and research in psychology, sociology, anthropology, and communication added to this base of knowledge. The behavioral management movement focused on the employee as well as on management. Unlike the administrative/scientific management school, the behavioral movement was primarily concerned with the human aspect of managing the enterprise. The movement stressed the importance of human relations, employee attitudes and feelings, and the impact the informal organization can have on the day-to-day performance of employees.

Major contributions of the behavioral management school concentrated on improving the management of human resources in the areas of employee selection, employee counseling, employee compensation and incentives, work group behavior, organizational communication,

Labor unions were formed to combat unsafe working conditions that existed during the administrative/ scientific management period.

human relations, employee job satisfaction and productivity, working conditions, job enrichment, and managerial leadership.

The behavioral management movement was the precursor of the field of human resource management. The human relations concepts emphasized company training programs, fringe benefit packages, social activities (e.g., picnics and employee interest clubs), and employee participation in management decisions that upgraded employee work.

A major problem emerged during this movement, which the literature has referred to as "pseudo human relations." A great deal of human relations hype during this period suggested that management should make employees "feel important." The underlying theory that many managers bought from the human relations movement in the 1940s, 1950s, and 1960s

was the assumption that a strong positive correlation existed between employee morale and employee productivity. That is, as morale increases, so does productivity. This theory was debunked in the early 1970s. Current research indicates that, at best, the correlation is spurious.

The human relations fad seldom addressed the true natures of worker alienation, job dissatisfaction, job enrichment, and overall organizational health-related problems. However, other activities and theories that emerged during the behavioral movement counteracted the human relation faddists and provided management with sound principles and techniques.

The administrative/scientific management focus was less concerned about employee feelings, attitudes, and compatibility with the work environment than with management of the formal organization in terms of profits, efficiency, and cost-saving measures. The primary concern of the administrative/scientific movement was the "bottom line."

The impact of both the administrative/scientific and behavioral management movements has been enormous in terms of modern-day managerial thought.

The Contemporary Management Movement (1970s to Present)

We can trace the development of contemporary management thought to both of the previous schools. The contemporary movement, however, focuses on developing concepts and theories that shapers of the administrative/scientific and behavioral management movements either excluded, only lightly touched upon, or were not aware of when developing their concepts.

Contributors to the contemporary school developed quantitative procedures to aid managers in making decisions under conditions of uncertainty relative to both short- and long-range planning. Although statistical procedures were applied to the area of quality control in the 1930s, computer and software developments within the past decade have made statistical concepts "user friendly" for management decision making.

The contributions of *systems theory*, *decision theory*, *human resource theory*, and *contingency theory* are associated with the contemporary management movement.

Systems Theory

Systems theory views the organization as an open system. The theory assumes that (a) the organization is composed of interdependent subsystems and that a change in any subsystem (e.g., department, work unit, or work procedure) will have intended and unintended consequences for other subsystems within the organization; (b) the organization is dynamic and constantly undergoing change (both planned and

unplanned); (c) the organization strives for homeostasis, or balance; (d) the total organization has multiple objectives that might conflict with one another; and (e) the organization is continually receiving inputs (e.g., money, people, raw materials, and ideas) that are transformed into new outputs such as products, services, ideas, and other materials.

The manager must be able to manage the transformation processes that change the inputs to outputs. The effective manager must also learn to cope with multiple interactions that exist on a daily basis relative to the tasks to be performed, the employees, the formal organization and its policies, and the culture of the informal organization.

Decision Theory

Decision theory focuses on problem-solving and decision-making styles of managers. Although decision theory had its beginning in the 1950s, the concept gained momentum early in the contemporary management movement of the 1970s. Decision-making models provide rules (the ideal) for managers to follow in their problem-solving and decision-making activities. Decision theory has made contributions in such areas as identifying approaches to the problem-solving process; providing decision-making strategies for managers under conditions of certainty and uncertainty; providing a framework for identifying problem-solving styles; utilizing linear programming concepts to find the best solution to a problem; and developing decision matrices to determine various forms of payoffs for respective decisions.

Contemporary mathematical developments along with decision theory have created a new analytic specialty called *operations research management*, commonly referred to as OR. OR is a mathematical modeling approach using statistical and computer-based tools that permit the decision maker to manipulate a number of complex variables. Linear programming, for example, can be applied to determine what combination of products, services, and raw materials are necessary to accomplish the objective. OR also emphasizes the utilization of project teams composed of the organization's experts and specialists to solve complex problems.

The National Aeronautics and Space Administration (NASA), for example, uses OR strategies to explore space. Spacecraft cannot be designed and launched without the use of complex mathematical calculations, computer-based decision models, and project teams consisting of many experts from diverse fields of specialization.

Human Resource Management Theory

Human resource management theory (HRM) views the organization's human resources as investments that can profit both the company and the employee if appropriately managed. The implementation of HRM philosophy establishes personal growth opportunities and planned career experiences for employees. These activities attempt to maximize employee personnel needs and potential for career enhancement and overall organizational effectiveness.

The HRM approach contrasts greatly with the scientific management era, when managers viewed the employee mainly as a factor of production and designed work to be as simple and routine as possible in order to assume maximum output.

Contingency Theory

Contingency theory takes into consideration the situation and environment in which the work is performed. Unlike the administrative/scientific management school, contingency management assumes that there is no one best way to manage or lead an enterprise—a manager has no universal prescriptions, principles, or techniques that will work in every situation.

Staff development programs are common in companies that use human resource management theory.

Contingency theory maintains that the organization's structure, processes, and situational characteristics must fit together. To understand this theory you must view *contingency variables* as aspects of the situation that might influence the desired outcome. The manager must determine what factors to manipulate to bring about the desired change.

Let us assume that the structure of a task can significantly influence the supervisor's behavior as well as employee job satisfaction. By changing the task structure, the manager may be able to improve his or her style of leadership as well as improve employee job satisfaction.

THE FUTURE

Industry requires approximately 10 to 12 years to utilize a new management theory or principle after it is made public. With the exceptions of the computer and software packages that are constantly being developed for management utilization, few new management concepts have developed since the early 1970s. The current period we are experiencing will probably be viewed as the incubation period for management thought, a period that is allowing managers to experiment with concepts developed over the past decade. This exploratory phase will doubtless result in a flurry of new management theories and principles in the near future.

The period between now and the year 2000 will provide sport management professionals with opportunities to experiment with the many management theories and principles that have emerged from the three schools of management thought. This experiential phase will no doubt spur sport management professionals to contribute new concepts to this growing body of literature.

LEARNING ACTIVITIES

1. Read each of the following concepts. Then determine which school of management thought is most closely associated with each concept by checking one of the following: A—administrative/scientific management school, B—behavioral management school, or C—contemporary management school. Do this independently for all items in the exercise. Then form small discussion groups to share your answers.

Concept	Description	A	B	C
(1) Theory Y	A fitness club manager assumes that employees are trustworthy, are not inherently lazy, and seek job challenges and self-actualization.	____	____	____
(2) Theory X	An athletic director assumes that employees are generally lazy, require close supervision, cannot be trusted, will not assume responsibilities on their own initiatives, and are mainly motivated by money.	____	____	____

(3) Time-and-motion study

A fitness director uses a stopwatch, film, videotape, or other methods of observation to assess employee work efficiency.

_____   _____   _____

(4) Organization-sponsored clubs, events, and social activities

An organization provides company-sponsored social activities to improve employee morale (e.g., bowling teams, ski clubs, camera clubs, investment clubs, and travel clubs).

_____   _____   _____

(5) Management by objectives (MBO)

A company uses a system whereby supervisors and their employees mutually establish performance goals with specific targets and deadlines. This is usually done on an annual basis, at the end of each year. Employees are rewarded for results achieved.

_____   _____   _____

(6) Human relations training

An organization emphasizes effective human relations between supervisors and their employees. Typical training subjects may be communication, employee morale, employee discipline, leadership, and employee counseling. Although human relations training is emphasized, it does little to change the nature of employees' jobs.

_____   _____   _____

(7) Self-actualization

A club manager maximally utilizes human resource potential by providing employees opportunities to participate in planning and designing their jobs.

_____   _____   _____

(8) Human resource planning (HRP)

An organization has an established human resource planning system that provides for employee career planning, identifies possible career tracks within the organization (i.e., related jobs that lead to career advancement), and identifies employee potential for future advancement opportunities.

_____   _____   _____

(9) Job rotation	A club manager allows employees to rotate from one job to another. Each job is of equal complexity. Job rotation is practiced to alleviate boredom and to assume properly trained employees are available as backups for other jobs at similar pay levels.	____ ____ ____
(10) Close monitoring of employee time	A company requires nonmanagerial employees to use a time clock to record when they arrive at work, take rest breaks, take lunch breaks, and leave at the end of the day.	____ ____ ____
(11) Profit motive	An organization has an abundance of employee grievances relative to unsatisfactory working conditions and has not made improvements in the work areas in years. Management believes that any profits should go back to the investors rather than be used to update and modernize equipment and work places.	____ ____ ____

2. Form small discussion groups of not more than five individuals, then identify actual situations in sport and fitness that demonstrate the descriptions in Exercise 1.

Answers to Exercise 1: (1) B; (2) B; (3) A; (4) B; (5) C; (6) B; (7) B; (8) C; (9) B; (10) A; (11) A.

SUGGESTED READINGS

Administrative & Scientific Management Movement

Barnard, C.I. (1938). *The functions of an executive*. Cambridge, MA: Harvard University Press.

Donald, J. (Ed.) (1931). *Handbook of business administration* (James O. McKinsey chapters). New York: McGraw-Hill.

Fayol, H. (1949). *General and industrial management* (Constance Starrs, Trans.) London: Pitman.

Gantt, H.L. (1910). *Work, wages, and profits*. New York: Engineering Magazine.

Gilbreth, F.B. (1917). *Applied motion study*. New York: Sturgis & Walton.

Gilbreth, L.M. (1914). *The psychology of management*. New York: Sturgis & Walton.

Henderson, A.M., & Parsons, T. (Trans.) (1947). *The theory of social and economic organization* (Max Weber chapters). Glencoe, IL: The Free Press.

Metcalf, H.C., & Urwick, L. (Eds.) (1941). *Dynamic administration: The collected papers of Mary Parker Follett.* London: Pittman.

Taylor, F.W. (1947). *Scientific management: The principles of scientific management.* New York: Harper & Bros.

Behavioral Management Movement

Cartwright, D. (Ed.) (1951). *Field theory in social science.* New York: Harper.

Herzberg, F. (1966). *Work and the nature of man.* Cleveland, OH: World Publishing.

Lewin, G.W., & Allport, G.W. (Eds.) (1948). *Resolving social conflicts.* New York: Harper.

Maslow, A. (1962). *Toward a psychology of being.* Princeton, NJ: D. Van Nostrand.

Maslow, A. (1965). *Eupsychian management.* Homewood, IL: Irwin-Dorsey.

McClelland, D.C., Atkinson, J.W., Clark, R.A., & Lowell, E.L. (1976). *The achievement motive.* New York: Appleton-Century Crofts.

McGregor, D. (1960). *The human side of enterprise.* New York: McGraw-Hill.

McGregor, D. (1966). *Leadership and motivation.* Cambridge, MA: The MIT Press.

Roethlisberger, F.J. (1939). *Management and the worker.* Cambridge, MA: Harvard University Press.

Vroom, V. (1964). *Work and motivation.* New York: John Wiley & Sons.

Contemporary Management Movement

Bertalanffy, L.V. (1972). The history and status of general systems theory. *Academy of Management Journal*, **15**, 407-426.

Fielder, F.E., Chemers, M., & Maher, L.M. (1978). *The leadership match concepts.* New York: Wiley.

Drucker, P. (1954). *The practice of management.* New York: Harper and Row.

Drucker, P. (1974). *Management: Task, responsibilities, practice.* New York: Harper and Row.

Redding, W.C., & Sanborn, G.A. (1964). *Business and industrial communication: A source book.* New York: Harper and Row.

Vroom, V. (1973, Spring). A new look in managerial decision-making. *Organizational Dynamics*, Spring, 66-80.

CHAPTER 22

Organizational Behavior

Mary Kennedy Minter
University of Michigan-Dearborn

Due to the eclectic nature of organizational behavior (OB) as a field of study, we should view it from "macro" and "micro" perspectives. For example, *macrodimensions* refers to the "big picture" of an organization, such as its structure, production/service systems, external environment factors, mission, culture, and climate. *Microdimensions* refers to emerging behavior of individuals and groups within an organization and how those behaviors affect the organization and its management. The rationale in this overview is that we need to be aware of, and work toward an understanding of, the macroview of an organization in order to get a better focus on the microview of individual and group work behavior and how both dimensions interrelate in producing a dynamic organization.

Consider this brief example of a sport organization that represents "big business." Join me in visualizing a college football game. It is a sunny, crisp Saturday afternoon, and you have finally found a place to park (for $5) and have walked a mile to the stadium. You give your ticket to the gatekeeper and pass by the souvenir stands, where you can't resist buying a banner for your home team; then you buy a program from one of the many passing vendors. In front of the stadium entrance is the long row of food concession stands (you, of course, stock up with your favorite drink and snacks). Once inside, the aura of the crowd engulfs you, and yet you

can observe many parts of the football organization operating (in addition to those you've just passed through). The band is organizing on the sidelines for the pregame show. The security officers patrol the field, and you can see the doctors and emergency teams "in the wings." The cheerleaders, mascots, and student section leaders are all in action revving up the crowd for the big game. The referees are ready at center field. Last, but not least, both football teams are warming up with their coaches close at hand.

Now, this can all be called a macroview of what is really going on (and what has gone into the preparation for this moment). When the game begins, what macro- and microperspectives will you use as a spectator? Will you concentrate on who carries the ball and how far? Will you pay close attention to the offensive team and try to analyze the coaching strategies that the players execute as they protect the quarterback in the first-down thrusts? Will you criticize the coach of the defensive team for not having a more dynamic combination of players? Will you just concentrate on the cheerleaders? What would be different if you were working within that football organization? Keep this example in mind as you read through this chapter. Perhaps you will want to use the college football organization as another case study for practicing your OB analysis.

The college football organization makes a good case study of OB.

TERMINOLOGY

Following are definitions of three terms important to the topic of OB: *management*, *organizational behavior*, and the *contingency approach*.

Management

A commonly accepted definition of management is "working with and through individuals and groups to accomplish organizational goals" (Hersey & Blanchard, 1982, p. 3). This definition includes both the macro- and microperspectives of OB.

Organizational Behavior

Generally defined, OB represents the synthesis approach to management in that it recognizes the macrodimensions of the organization and the microimpacts of individuals and groups. OB is an interdisciplinary field of study in that it draws from the same disciplines as does management, especially psychology, sociology, anthropology, and organizational communication. To analyze organizations, OB specialists utilize theories, concepts, and research models from all three management schools of thought (i.e., administrative/scientific, behavioral, and contemporary).

We can think of OB as an applied approach to working with the behavioral and structural complexities of an organization in order to improve its effectiveness.

Contingency Approach

The contingency approach, which is especially helpful to OB practitioners, is the contemporary management orientation to analyzing management functions and organizational behavior. The contingency approach refers to a pragmatic view of organizations and management (i.e., a practical vs. an idealistic view). This view acknowledges that multiple variables and interdependencies that are inherent in the organization necessitate *situational management*. This means that one kind of management approach will not be effective in all situations or with diverse human behavior.

MACRO- AND MICRODIMENSIONS OF ORGANIZATIONAL BEHAVIOR

The contingency and OB approaches represent a way of thinking, analyzing, and managing organizational functions and resources. These concepts provide a framework for the macro- and microdimensions.

An analogy that may help you visualize the interrelationship of the macro- and microdimensions is that of the iceberg (see Figure 22.1). Scientists estimate that the tip of an iceberg is usually only one third of the larger mass lying beneath the water's surface.

From an OB perspective, the tip of the iceberg represents the formal organization, the prescribed processes and procedures (i.e., structure, subsystems, environment, development, and management) by which the organization should function. This formal organization is that part we can see documented in organization charts and procedural manuals. The microdimensions of the informal organization are illustrated in Figure 22.1 as the large mass under the water, which represents the cultural forces of the organization that keep the macrostructure "floating." This hidden mass of energy includes individual and organization behaviors and group dynamics.

CASE STUDY

The following case study[1] is presented to give you a situation to which you can practice relating the OB dimensions as you continue this chapter. The conclusion of the case study is presented at the end of the chapter, along with other OB exercises for you to consider.

I came out to California years ago after getting my B.S. degree in mechanical engineering from the University of Illinois. I accepted a job at a major aerospace corporation. But it wasn't long before I became more interested in surfing than in my job. First, I was into body surfing, then I learned how to use a surfboard and, for practice, a skateboard.

For the first year or so, I confined my surfing to weekends and after work . . . in those days we usually used much larger boards than today and we [my friends and I] constantly discussed and experimented with various models. My engineering interest and competence led me to ponder endless variations in design. Finally, I decided to do something.

I rented a garage a block from the beach, purchased some fiberglass, some tools, and other equipment. I made a few boards and tried them out. A number of times people offered to buy some of them. I sold some and more and more people began asking me to custom-make boards to their specifications or to make one of my own models. At the end of about thirteen months of this, I found myself with more orders than I could fill.

Finally, I made the big decision to quit my job and go into business for myself. I formed Windansea Surfboards, Inc., and

[1]*Note.* From *Contemporary Management* (2nd ed., pp. 112-113) by D.R Hampton, 1981, New York: McGraw-Hill. Copyright 1981 by McGraw-Hill. Reprinted by permission.

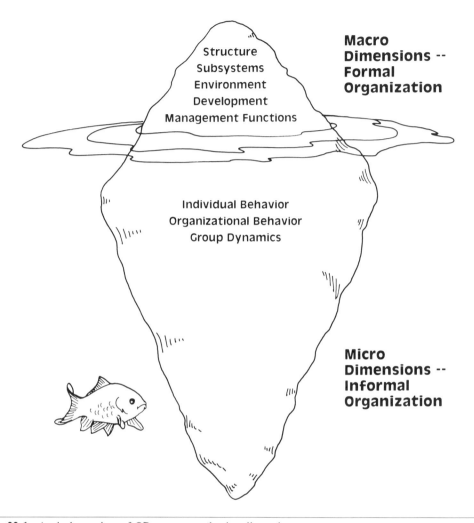

Figure 22.1   An iceberg view of OB: macro- and microdimensions.

operated it alone for six months. Business was even better than I expected, and I found it necessary to hire first one, then another employee. After two years, I had seventeen employees and had installed our operations in part of a rented industrial building.

The way we had things set up was pretty informal. We were still making custom boards for individuals or small batches of our own models. We rented a small store at the beach and displayed several models

there. The company continued in this way until, after nine years, it had over seventy employees, most of whom performed the several operations in making a complete surfboard.

While sales continued to rise, earnings were rising at a lesser rate. It began to dawn on me that something might have to be done to control costs and streamline operations. It seemed like a particularly good time to face our problems because it appeared that surfing was about to become substantially more popular, and we wanted to be in a good position to take advantage of the potential. As president, I retained a management and industrial engineering consulting firm and told them I wanted them to study our business from stem to stern and make whatever recommendations they felt appropriate for our manufacturing processes, financial planning, marketing, and management.

They made a comprehensive study of our market and our operations. They agreed that we were on the brink of a major increase in volume. They made a number of recommendations in finance and marketing. They also recommended a transformation of our manufacturing system so that instead of its being a shop where each worker made a complete board, it was to become more like a mass production factory where boards flowed from one end to the other in an integrated sequential process. We would make large batches of one model, then another, in this way. Most manufacturing employees would perform only a few repetitive operations.

They also proposed to rearrange and formalize the management of operations. For example, we had been operating without any particular person being responsible for either the planning of production or the inspection and quality control functions. Each employee was, for the most part, his or her own planner and inspector. The consultants, however, proposed to create a supervisor in charge of each of these functions. The supervisor of production planning would work out plans with the supervisor in charge of manufacturing operations. The supervisor of quality control would establish quality standards and use inspectors to check that they were being satisfied.

In short, it seemed that what they were proposing was, as I said, a mass- or large-batch production technology to replace our more self-paced system. To go along with this engineered system, they were proposing a more specialized and formal management system which would introduce new specialties and interpose a level of management between me and the workers.

I expressed some concern that even though I had a constantly changing work force, the jobs would become so much simpler that the few long-term employees I had might be extremely disappointed. The consultants seemed to have anticipated this because they proposed to promote four of my most senior and most valuable employees to the new management jobs. They said that I was correct and might disappoint some others, but that as we grew we might create more supervisory jobs. They also pointed out that it would cost less and take less time to train new employees for the simpler jobs.

I accepted their recommendations whole hog, but not without tossing and turning a few nights over the worry that there might be some problems we hadn't foreseen.

Anyway, within a year we had implemented virtually every one of the recommendations.

Several questions from an OB perspective arise from this case study. Before reading further, write down a few questions that come to your mind about this organizational situation. It will be interesting to compare these questions with others you pose throughout the remainder of this chapter.

MACRODIMENSIONS OF OB

Using the Windansea case study as a situational example, we can outline the macrodimensions of an OB approach as follows.

Organizational Structure

The original structure of the Windansea company was small in size and informal in its production system. The tasks involved in producing a surfboard were completed basically by one individual, so that the work was autonomous and each worker was essentially her or his own quality control inspector. The new structure significantly changed the design of the organization to a multiple-level one, with levels of management between the owner (or president) and surfboard makers, each of whom completed only part of the total surfboard product.

Outline an organizational chart for both the original Windansea structure and the new multiple-level structure. What do the different organizational charts indicate about potential problems in both kinds of organization? Remember that before the change in formal organizational design and structure, about 70 employees worked for one manager, the president.

Organizational Subsystems

A common definition of *system* related to organizations is "an integrated network of tasks and processes" (Hunsacker & Cook, 1986, p. 39). In contemporary management thought, an organization's systems are often defined as *open systems*, which means they interact with environmental forces. We will concentrate on the internal organizational systems but will also be aware of the external forces. For example, in the Windansea case, the decision to reorganize the formal system of production was influenced by the external factor that surfboarding was becoming more popular and the market for surfboards would increase.

Organizational systems are composed of subsystems, which are defined as smaller units within the total organization. Each subsystem has its own distinct network of tasks and processes and usually has its own management. In analyzing the behavior of the organization, one would observe and study the five common subsystems.

1. *Informational subsystem*—the way necessary information flows through the organization to accomplish the tasks and functions of the organization
2. *Materials subsystem*—the way materials flow through the organization to be transformed into products or services (e.g., an assembly-line operation)
3. *Technological subsystem*—the way nonhuman and nonmaterial processes provide support to the other subsystems (e.g., computers and equipment)
4. *Economical subsystem*—the way funds flow through the organization
5. *Social (human) subsystem*—the way human resources interact through the network of subsystems and contribute to organizational goals (Hunsacker & Cook, 1986, 42-43).

In an organizational behavior approach to management, the human (social) subsystem is emphasized.

Look at your organizational charts for the original Windansea company. What subsystem factors contributed to the desire for a change in the organizational structure? What formal subsystems exist in the new organizational structure?

Organizational Environment (External and Internal)

Many concepts and variables exist within this macrodimension of OB, only a few of which are outlined for this overview chapter. Contemporary behavioral psychologists have concentrated on the following organizational and environmental concepts.

External Environmental Factors

The organization is affected externally by markets (general), customers (specific), suppliers, regulators (governmental and others), and societal behaviors and norms.

Internal Environmental Factors

The organization is affected internally by organizational variables (e.g., tasks, goals, structure, policies, and managerial practices); technological variables (e.g., complexity, standardization, and variability); and work climate (affected by organizational variables, technological variables, and individual variables such as needs, motives, values, personal goals, and education or training).

Quality of Work Life

Another behavioral concept is *quality of work life* (QWL), which is contingent on the environmental variables previously outlined. For example, the work climate variables will impact the quality of work life and affect the worker's job performance and job satisfaction.

Job Design

Job design is an internal organizational variable that is a key factor in quality of work life. For example, in the Windansea case the original structure was based on an individual, autonomous job (task) design, whereas the new structure was to be a mass-production job design.

Organizational Culture

Organizational culture is a term related to the organizational environment dimensions and is often used synonymously with *organizational climate*. In essence, the cultural aspect of the organization refers to a culmination of all the variables mentioned thus far. Organizational culture encompasses the work group values, norms, and behaviors that emerge due to external and internal organizational variables and that, in turn, produce patterns of behavior unique to a particular organization.

How do you think the culture and work climate in the case study will change when the Windansea organization changes from its original structure to the new production system? What effects will the change have on the quality of work life?

Organizational Development

Organizational development (OD) is an approach to change that utilizes applied or "action" research to identify points where behavioral science and management techniques might aid in organizational improvement. The organizational development research approach, which encompasses the dimensions of OB, originated in the contributions of Kurt Lewin and his field theory research method in group dynamics.

In the Windansea case, the president of the company asks an outside consulting firm to analyze the organization and recommend changes. That action is an example of an OD approach. However, the case study does not provide the details of how the OD consultants researched the situation or how the intervention was managed. This kind of information is significant and would be needed in order to analyze the effectiveness of the OD approach in this case.

Organizational Management Functions

The last macrodimension interrelates with all the others previously listed. The standard management functions are commonly referred to as *planning*, *organizing*, *motivating* (*communication and leadership*), and *controlling*. These functions can be considered macrodimensions of an organization because they are broad conceptual factors that interact with the other macrodimensions: *structure*, *subsystems*, *environment*, and *development*. However, management functions are unique in that they represent a bridge or connection between the substance of the organization and the heart of the organization—the human resources. This idea of management as a coordinator of people for the purpose of accomplishing organizational tasks and objectives leads us into the concept of microdimensions of organizational behavior—the behavior of people as individuals and within groups.

MICRODIMENSIONS OF OB

The microdimensions of OB include theories and concepts about individual and group behavior and about how they interrelate with and affect the organizations. These concepts are emphasized because they represent the "dynamic life" of an organization.

Interrelationships and interdependencies of the concepts and processes occur within the contexts of individual behavior, individual and organizational behavior processes, and group dynamics.

Individual Behavior

The workers in an organization bring to that group their individual personalities and motivations. A common contemporary management question illustrates the importance of individual behaviors to the organization: Is there a "fit" between the formal organization (i.e., the way it was designed to function) and the informal organization (i.e., what employees actually do)? In other words, is there compatibility between

what the organization needs or wants and the employees' values, motivations, and job talents? This question implies another significant view of individuals within an organization. If an individual wants or needs to work in a particular organization but that organization's formal structure and culture do not fit the individual, then both parties will need to compromise. For example, in the Windansea case, the president decided to significantly change the organizational structure in order to increase earnings. This organizational change resulted in a much different organizational culture in which employees would work. We could predict that those employees who could adapt to the new climate or structure did so; others who preferred the autonomous, individualized production system would probably elect not to accept the new structure. The point is that the management of an organization has the right to structure the firm in ways that best suit the business needs, and employees have the right to select organizations that best fit their personal needs. However, if employment options for individuals are limited, then they (and the organization) will need to develop coping strategies in order to produce an effective, mutually acceptable organizational climate.

Self-Esteem and Attribution

Basic psychological concepts can help an individual understand and cope with the dynamic process of collaboration within an organization. For example, *self-esteem* refers to our personal, psychological judgments about ourselves regarding how worthy we feel in our general life experiences. Self-esteem has been defined as "the integrated summation of self-confidence and self-respect. It is the conviction that one is competent to live and worthy of living" (Branden, 1971, p. 110).

A more general personal concept encompasses the self-images we develop through our self-esteem perceptions and our social interactions.

The consequences of our personal and environmental (social) interactions can be perceived in many ways (e.g., as threats or as opportunities). However, we can cope with and reshape these personal/environmental relationships so that we can maintain effective levels of self-esteem and self-image in our relationships with others. This process of perceiving ourselves and our environments and trying to cope with (manage) both is referred to as *attribution*. A key to the attribution concept is a phenomenon called *locus of control*. For example, persons who perceive themselves as in control of their destinies are attributing their life outcomes to their internal strengths (e.g., self-esteem or image) and to their abilities to manage their own lives. The individual is the locus of control. In the opposite attribution pattern, people may perceive external factors as attributing most often to their successes or failures. The predominant attribution pattern we develop is observable in the way we perceive ourselves and our behavior with others.

---

1. *How can you use the concepts of self-esteem and attribution to analyze what changes in human behavior may occur with new Windansea organizational changes?*
2. *How may management and employees in the new Windansea organization need to cope in order to produce an effective work climate?*

Individual and Organizational Behavior Processes

The personality factors of self-esteem and attribution are inherent factors in our self-motivation behaviors. However, when the individual operates within an organization, the motivation for work performance becomes a more complex phenomenon. This complexity of an individual's motivation within an organizational context has been the basis for many theories and approaches to management and the OB field of study (e.g., Maslow's need hierarchy, McGregor's Theory X–Theory Y model, Herzberg's maintenance/motivation theory, and Vroom's expectancy model of motivation).

OB practitioners tend to focus on a microview of motivation within the context of different organizational processes. Within these processes, the following variables interact on an individual, group, and organizational basis: job performance (i.e., objectives, appraisal, and rewards), interpersonal relations and communication, leadership, power influence, problem solving, decision making, and career development.

We can analyze interpersonal relationships and communication patterns to help improve overall effectiveness. For example, we can study communication within an organization as a series of networks (e.g., task-related, informational, technical, or social) or as a vehicle for leadership, influence, or power.

Another process within organizational behavior is the problem-solving/decision-making activity, which is in turn interrelated to the key processes and variables of job performance, interpersonal relations/communication, leadership, and power/influence.

Career development is included in the list of key processes because it represents a contemporary microview of the individual within an organization. In this age of diversity among individuals and organizations, the concept of a "career" is, itself, a dynamic phenomenon. For example, a definite trend exists toward career clustering, whereby individuals can move among several different organizations depending on their "transferable skills." In an OB approach, career development is usually viewed as a process in which both the individual and the organization are responsible for input if both parties are to be effective.

Group Dynamics

OB practitioners also focus on the group dynamics within an organization. An OB approach would be to identify the formal group systems within an organization (e.g., department and task-related groups in a mass-production, assembly-line operation) and then to identify what informal groups have evolved that facilitate or hinder the production flow and total effectiveness of the formal system. We can analyze the structure of these formal and informal groups by identifying communication networks within them in order to determine how the groups function internally. Then we can analyze the relationships between department or work groups (intergroup) in a similar fashion to identify the dynamics of the situation.

The microdimensions of organizational behavior can, in turn, contribute to a better understanding of what is happening on the macrolevel in the dimensions of management functions (e.g., planning, organizing, and controlling), organizational structure, systems, environment, and development.

"WHAT HAPPENED"

(Conclusion of the Windansea Case)[2]

For the most part the changes worked out pretty well. Our volume of business did increase and our "mass production" set up with production planning and our quality control, with its standards and inspection, helped us produce the greater quantities we needed without any substantial loss of quality. We began to realize economics of sale from mass production better than we had been under our former system and our earnings gain began to keep up with our sales gains.

One thing I regret, though, is that we never again did seem to have the sort of pleasant atmosphere we had in the days when everybody was making complete boards. Things just became more factory-like. While we still have fairly good employee relations, the fact is that more individuals and groups gripe about various problems with their equipment, with inspection, with production quotas, and so on than before. Even though most of our present employees weren't here before the changes, I think the changes just make it more difficult to have good employee relations. Most of the old-time employees have been promoted, so they don't seem to have been hurt.

Frankly, the new organization worked so well that its success was a big factor in my agreeing to my husband's request that I take time off occasionally to have a baby. We now have two children, and Windansea continues to prosper.

---

[2]*Note.* From *Contemporary Management* (2nd ed., p. 131) by D.R. Hampton, 1981, New York: McGraw-Hill. Copyright 1981 by McGraw-Hill. Reprinted by permission.

LEARNING ACTIVITIES

1. What were your first reactions to the conclusion of the case study? For example, had you made some assumptions that proved not to be true? What were those assumptions?
2. What do such assumptions indicate to us about potential problems in analyzing organizational behavior? For example, what biases or stereotypes do we harbor that may affect our objectivity?
3. What may be some problems within the macro- and microdimensions of the newly organized Windansea Company of which its president is not aware (per the case study)?
4. What are potential microdimension factors that may arise in the future?
5. Write your own case study based on an experience in a sport-related organization. Analyze your case study from the two perspectives of OB—*macro* and *micro*. Share your case situation with your class members.

REFERENCES

Branden, N. (1971). *The psychology of self-esteem*. New York: Bantam.

Hampton, D.R. (1981). *Contemporary management* (2nd ed.). New York: McGraw-Hill.

Hersey, P., & Blanchard, K.H. (1982). *Management of organizational behavior* (4th ed.). Englewood Cliffs, NJ: Prentice-Hall.

Hunsacker, P.L., & Cook, C.W. (1986). *Managing organizational behavior*. Reading, MA: Addison-Wesley.

CHAPTER 23

The Future of Sport and Fitness

Annie Clement
Cleveland State University

Sport management is not new; people have worked as promoters, organizers, and athletic directors for years. The past several years, however, have witnessed a massive increase in the need for sport management professionals. Parks and Olafson (1987) illustrate these facts through their opening statements in the first issue of the *Journal of Sport Management*:

> Lest we be deluded by the notion that contemporary sport management is markedly different from the ancient art of staging athletic spectacles, let us consider for a moment the following description of the Games sponsored in 11 B.C. by Herod the Great, King of Judea and Honorary President of the Olympics (Frank, 1984):
>
>> "The games began with a magnificent dedication ceremony. Then there were athletic and musical competitions, in which large prizes were given not only to the winners but also—an unusual feature—to those who took second and third place. Bloody spectacles were also presented, with gladiators and wild beasts fighting in various combinations, and there were also horse races.
>>
>> Large prizes attracted contenders from all areas and this in turn drew great numbers of spectators. Cities favored by Herod sent delegations, and these he entertained and lodged at his own expense. What comes through most clearly . . . is that gigantic sums of money were spent" (p. 158).
>
> The success of such an extravaganza relied in all likelihood upon the organizational skills of the individuals charged with planning and executing the games. (p. 1)

Racquet clubs, spas, country clubs, employee and private fitness centers, and parks and recreation facilities with planned activities are everywhere. In an effort to meet the demand for organized physical activity, sport management has become a profession. Forecasts for the future mentioned throughout this chapter will illustrate the societal need for this type of sport professional. As a future sport manager, you are limited only by the extent of your imagination.

THE FORECAST

Hazel Henderson (1986) coined the phrase "The age of light" to identify the period following our "information age" of the late 20th Century. "The Age of Light is an image that reminds us that it is the light from the sun that drives the earth's processes and powers its cycles of carbon, nitrogen, hydrogen, and water and the climate machine'' (Henderson, 1986, p. 56). Although the information age focuses on technologies such as computers, robots, artificial intelligence, mass production, and competition, the age of light will concentrate on cooperation, reliance on nature, and using technology in a humane manner. Toffler (1980) similarly describes future cultures as cooperative rather than competitive, using technology as a means of interaction rather than a source of commercialism.

Careers in sport management in the immediate future (1990-2000) will be influenced by the information age—that is, by computers, robots, competition, commercialism, and production. In the extended future (2000-2020), careers will be influenced by cooperation, effective use of technology, and reliance on nature. Immediate-future careers will involve serving participants in their homes, fitness centers, spas, athletic clubs, marinas, corporate settings, and leagues. Careers will also include creating, programming, and selling technology, such as robots to be used as jogging partners. Sport management professionals of the extended future will include planners of weightlessness programs in space and managers of computer-generated interactive recreation centers. In the extended future, athletic opponents will often be life-size robots programmed to give the performer specific movement challenges.

Immediate Future (1990-2000)

Careers will change slowly as we progress from the information age to the age of light. For example, corporate fitness programs will give way to home-based skill and fitness training. As the importance of competition decreases, activities for all ages will change from team sport to individual endeavors. Persons requiring technical monitoring and exercise equipment that they cannot afford will continue to use hospital wellness facilities and public and private health clubs, and those requiring or desiring expert su-

pervision will save money by using facilities outside the home. But eventually only those seeking companionship and social interaction and those who cannot afford sophisticated equipment will use public, private, hospital, and corporate facilities.

Extended Future (2000-2020)

Futurists envision the demise of the traditional tax-supported elementary and secondary schools by the year 2020 (Perelman, 1986). This radical departure from the traditional educational organization is based on the premise that technical knowledge is most effectively acquired through working with a computer. Resources that fund today's schools will instead provide computers and other electronic technology as well as consultants to guide our uses of the technology. School buildings as we know them today will be eliminated. Although the computer may replace the school as a means of enabling students to acquire facts, the computer will not provide the opportunities for socialization and interaction that have become a hallmark of the schools. Socialization and interaction will be the major goals of a new type of community center or country club. These centers will assist clients in a social setting to incorporate their knowledge of content learned at home. Music, literature, art, theater, and physical activity will be the vehicles through which this synthesis will occur. Futurists also envision that athletic clubs for elite performers will assume many of the responsibilities that today's schools have for athletics. These clubs will sponsor contests and train teams for competition.

Demand for Higher Level Skills

As an individual's fitness and health move toward optimum levels, that person's demands for opportunities in skill acquisition and for leisure activities requiring physical skill will increase. The challenges of acquiring fundamental skills and motor patterns will fuel the same excitement in the 1990s that fitness and cardio-respiratory elements did in the 1980s.

Persons aspiring to professional employment as program planners, inventors of technology, or client consultants will be expected to possess advanced knowledge of kinesiology, biomechanics, motor learning, and physiology, as well as an understanding of technology. An advanced degree in exercise physiology will no longer be adequate for these positions; professionals will be expected to have studied all of the previously mentioned subjects. The public will expect a higher level of sophistication from human movement specialists and will fully recognize only those possessing doctoral degrees. A manager in the sport industry, as opposed to a human movement specialist, will obtain preparation similar to managers in other industries, and a bachelor's degree will be adequate.

Technology

Today's video and exercise machines can simulate game situations and stresses found in various physical activities. They can also record, analyze, and provide feedback on skill performance (Badzik, 1982; Garfield, 1985). As the acquisition of fundamental skills and patterns becomes important to the masses, preprogrammed computer software will read photographs or tapes of skill performance and give performers advice on how to improve. Some performers will choose to learn the basic contents of kinesiology and biomechanics, whereas others will employ consultants with expertise in these areas. The decision to engage an adviser or to learn the fundamentals independently will be similar to the decision to engage a tax consultant or to complete the return personally.

Robots will rehearse performers for competition or for recreational play. First, the learner will acquire the basic sport skills in an individual learning environment—a backyard or a public physical activity carrel. Upon acquisition of the

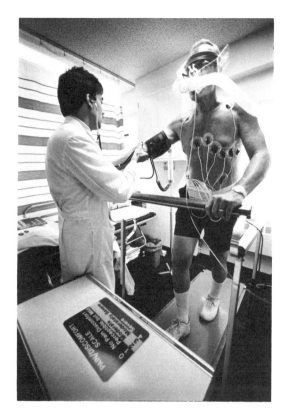

Exercise testing equipment such as this will become obsolete and will be replaced by fully computerized systems.

basic skills, the performer will work with a robot that will serve as an opponent. The robot, like today's tennis ball machines, will be equipped with sound and will be programmed to the level of competition appropriate to the learner's skill level. Robots will provide the novice's first game experience. The robot will be programmed utilizing sophisticated knowledge of imagery, feedback, and reward systems. As a result of this use of technology and knowledge, the robot may be programmed to stop at the first incidence of error or to continue to play a full game before corrections are made. Eventually the robot will record play and discuss errors with the client. The robot will be programmed according to its owner's personal desires. For example, a typical tennis player will select a disk for the robot that will provide a range of tennis shots, all backhand strokes, a lazy set of shots, or a high-speed rally. Also, telemetry equipment incorporated in the robot's intelligence will measure the intensity of the tennis workout. The performer will know the extent of cardiorespiratory output and the success of each skill executed as well as which muscle groups were challenged and which were neglected.

Weightlessness Activity

Zanger (1984), in her epilogue on the impact of the 1980s, signed off with this statement: "And then there is Tomorrow and Tomorrow will Bring ??? . . . Weightlessness Activities and Space Vacations and . . ." (p. 109).

Although nongravity physical activities are available today, they are seldom used. At this time, nongravity physical activities have been incorporated in astronaut training, actual space flight, and a few amusement parks, but the immediate future should see an expansion of weightless activities. Using the knowledge gleaned from NASA's research on weightlessness or "zero g" (Stine, 1985, p. 97) and from working with diving, underwater swimming, and trampoline activities, sport professionals will design a wide range of weightless activities. We will also turn our attentions to activities that ward off muscle and bone mass deterioration in the weightless environments. We will learn these activities in swimming pools and on trampolines and diving boards prior to space flight or extended visits to space platforms.

Competitive Arena

As technology provides average participants with opportunities to enhance their skill levels, they will begin to seek competitive arenas in which to test those abilities. This aspiration to elite athleticism will create a demand for Olympic festivals, road races, tennis tournaments, and

In the future there will be an increasing demand for opportunities for athletic competition.

numerous other sporting events to satisfy the competitive desires. Sport managers will play major roles in identifying and meeting the needs of the talented amateur athletes of the future.

Technology will equally influence professional athletics. The values of videography and computers to the professional athlete are obvious. Job tasks in coaching and athletic training will change, and these changes could affect role identification and preparation requirements for these positions. Professional athletes' salaries, currently starting on a downward trend, will provide the resources for the new cadre of advisers. Technology will enable us to teach and further prepare athletes, not just recruit athletes for collegiate and professional ranks. Basic skill acquisition and physical and psychological makeup of the player, rather than demonstrated team performance, may become the basis for selections.

By the year 2000, professional team owners will finance much of the basic research in sport. Results of this research will become more widely available and the accompanying applied technology will become less expensive, much as the decreasing cost of today's computers has allowed sophisticated programs to become available to the masses through local public libraries. These future trends will have a tremendous impact on all competitive sport.

ACTIVITY AND ENVIRONMENT

In the late 1970s and early 1980s, citizens of the United States demonstrated a renewed interest in personal health, longevity, disease, nutrition, and physical activity. Many of these patterns were similar to the principles held for years by Scandinavians, Canadians, and some Europeans. The masses took up running, cycling, racquetball, and tennis. People ran 10K races and marathons, often with only the goal of finishing. Generating this new enthusiasm were people from 26 to 65 years of age who also tended to be the more affluent or whose yearly incomes exceeded $25,000.

This enthusiasm for physical activity among a significant mass of the population gave rise to health spas, corporate and executive fitness centers, racquet and tennis clubs, and swimming pools, which appeared in shopping centers, office buildings, industrial parks, and hotels. A wild frenzy to attract a critical mass of people to these facilities has leveled off, and owners believe that although some of the attention of the 1980s should be attributed to a passing fad, much of the interest signals a trend. This trend has resulted in a demand for exercise/fitness delivery systems in homes, offices, and health care facilities.

Home

An exercise and fitness facility located in the home is usually a change in an existing bathroom or an addition to the bedroom or bathroom. Today's home spa contains a hot tub or whirlpool, stationary bicycle, rowing and jogging machines, minitrampolines, free weights, and space adequate for aerobics and exercise. It is usually designed to accommodate the family or those who live in the dwelling; however, dwellers are beginning to recognize the merit of the home spa as an environment for entertaining. Persons building new homes are not only building large bathrooms to accommodate these changes but are constructing spas off the dining or family rooms as an extension of the entertainment and living areas.

Results of research by manufacturers in the plumbing industry include the simulation of climate (e.g., sunshine, rain, storms, and wind) in shower/sauna systems; release of fragrance on demand; use of robots to scrub backs; and use of stereophonic sounds of waves, oceans, or overtures (Cornish, 1986). Innovations created to accommodate disabilities will be commonplace. As research and technology permit industry to expand our understandings of light, touch, and other sensations, we will incorporate these ideas in the spa/bathroom or body room of the future (Cetron & O'Toole, 1982). The room will be a body conditioning, fitness, and training center as well as a place to relax with friends and associates.

Personal fitness or fundamental movement advisers will be common. They will guide people in the design of comprehensive programs (including physiological, biomechanical, skill, and personality assessment), the purchase of equipment, and the renovation of space or the creation of new space. These advisers will also supervise home programs, give periodic evaluations, make recommendations about programs to be used, and offer nutritional advice. Some people will employ the advisers daily as motivators and to ensure that all training is under the supervision of an expert. Others will employ experts weekly to assess progress and recommend change. As the health care industry switches its focus from illness to wellness, the expenses of some of these services will be covered by insurance, and expenses of others will be legitimate tax deductions.

Bezold (1982) stated that in 1900 only 4 percent of the U.S. population, or 3.12 million people, were over 65 years of age. He predicted that by 2030, 57.6 million people, or 17 percent of the population, will be over 65. Based on these statistics, Bezold asserted that hospital use policies will change in the coming years; the elderly will be encouraged to remain at home and the health industry will move to a preventive mode rather than the illness model currently in operation. Bezold stated, "Treatment may focus on home care rather than on institutionalization of the elderly. . . . more exercise, improved nutrition . . . may ease mobility problems and make the elderly more self-reliant" (p. 15). Seniors and handicapped persons with recorded health deterioration will receive individual prescriptions created by personal fitness/skill advisers, physicians, and appropriate health care technical advisers. The federal and state governments will sponsor these services under cost-cutting programs to be created in the 1990s to maintain the elderly in

their own homes and reduce the expenses of nursing homes.

Corporate and Public Facilities

Office buildings, hotels, factories, and apartment complexes will have exercise- and skill-development spas including swimming pools, running tracks, exercise machines, and space for free weights, exercise, and aerobics. These spas will be supervised by professionals and will provide comprehensive assessments, program prescriptions, periodic evaluations, and program redesign. Industry will finance most of these facilities because insurance companies will agree to lower fees on comprehensive health coverage for employees on monitored fitness/skill programs. In addition to the advantages provided by decreased insurance rates, health promotion and fitness in the work place will also reduce absenteeism, increase productivity, decrease injuries, and aid in recruitment of employees.

Hospital Wellness Centers

Today's preventive health or wellness center is usually part of a prescription entry program in which a physician recommends specific exercises as part of a patient's rehabilitation. The visit to the center may be for a single lesson or exercise, a periodic schedule, or a continuous program. In some cases, clients may be encouraged to carry out exercise prescriptions in local spas or home fitness centers, with hospital specialists visiting once a week to oversee their programs. This approach to rehabilitation will expand and will include extensive preventive counseling.

Tomorrow's hospital wellness centers will open their doors to persons other than those referred by physicians; these centers will, in fact, assume responsibilities for designing preventive health maintenance programs for the public and for their own medical and health care employees.

Young people are showing greater sensitivities to individual wellness and are taking responsibilities for the well-being of their bodies. Snyder (1982) stated:

In the year 2000, we will be paying almost as much attention to prevention—studying and anticipating problems that could happen in order to keep them from happening—as we currently do to treatment—attending to what has already occurred. (p. 26)

THE SPORT MANAGER

The sport manager of the future will organize, represent, supervise, and deliver sport and fitness services in whatever fashion and environment ultimately develops. Employment opportunities appear to be positive as society places an even greater emphasis on personal health and quality lifestyle, as seniors demand active lives, and as business and industry and their insurance carriers participate in fitness and skill development programs.

You should be cognizant not only of the range of roles in the area of sport management but also the employment skills requisite to each of these roles. Sport managers are currently employed to supervise hospital wellness, corporate fitness, hotel, and public agency programs. As the need for these agencies increases, so will the opportunities. Sport managers who also have an interest in physiology and biomechanics will play major roles in the personal fitness and skill consulting industry as it evolves. They will assist people in creating home, apartment, and hotel exercise centers and will play significant roles in the design and planning of the social, interpersonal mass centers of the extended future. These specialists will also be involved in the

transition of technology to reality, such as the use of robots for game play, movement analysis and elite athlete programming, and in the creation of weightlessness programs. Sport management professionals with interests in physiology, biomechanics, and skill progressions will also oversee skill acquisition.

Sport managers will be employed by corporations and city and state governments wishing to stage events; on occasion sport managers will be employed by companies whose sole responsibilities are to raise funds and stage events. These events may be of the Olympic style existing today, may replicate rural events of years ago, may be competitive, may be "fun games," may pit industry against industry or city against city, or may be executed in space. Such events may also be incorporated into existing agencies such as amusement parks, tourism institutions, business and industry programs, and specific recreational pursuits such as skiing and boating. Possessing sport management skills, in addition to the intuitive capacity to anticipate what clients will want, will ensure your success in this area.

Opportunities with elite athletic organizations and professional teams will also expand as new organizations emerge and as the responsibilities of existing institutions, particularly schools, transfer to these organizations. For example, sport managers will assist scientists in putting together proposals that meet the needs of the professional team owners; serve as brokers to raise money for research; ensure that the results of research are placed in the hands of instructional technologists; and serve as intermediaries between physiologists, biomechanists, psychologists, and owners/coaches. There will also be an increase in professional athletics staff and a greater opportunity for sport managers to serve as player agents and representatives. Sport managers will continue to play significant roles in the media and in journalism as professional athletics remains a major interest to sport spectators. Whether your career is driven by the age of information or the age of light, you will contribute to all facets of society.

Contemporary economic experts recognize sport as big business, and sport and physical activity will continue to play important roles in future societies. We have every indication that sport, as we know it today, will continue to grow and that new programs and activities, some beyond the limits of our imaginations, will develop.

Successful sport managers will be sensitive to trends and events, will welcome change, will anticipate the needs of society, and will develop new programs when requested. They will not only welcome and embrace change, they will recognize timing of program delivery as an element of the change process. Sport management will be a challenging and exciting career if you are sensitive to people and the world around you, eager to dream, and willing to be a diligent planner and a demanding evaluator.

LEARNING ACTIVITIES

1. Identify and list video and computer programs that simulate sport and physical activity and examine two or more of the programs in detail. Outline a system for creating a new program of your choice.
2. Locate journals and books on topics such as environmental and economic futures. Prepare a paper discussing the potential role of sport in these futures.
3. Obtain and share with the class video and publication resources from the World Future Society, 4916 St. Elmo Avenue, Bethesda, MD 20814.
4. Obtain speakers from the World Future Society, which has branches in many cities throughout the country. The World Future Society headquarters can identify the chapter in your area and will provide you with the names of officers.

REFERENCES

Badzik, S.K. (1982). Videotex: Blessing or bane for the "boob tube"? In H.F. Didsbury, Jr. (Ed.), *Communications in the future* (pp. 120-132). Bethesda, MD: World Future Society.

Bezold, C. (1982). Health care in the U.S. *The Futurist*, **16**(4), 14.

Cetron, M., & O'Toole, T. (1982). *Encounters with the future: A forecast of life into the 21st century*. New York: McGraw-Hill.

Cornish, E. (1986). The bathroom: The glamour room of the future. *The Futurist*, **20**(4), 1.

Frank, R. (1984). Olympic myths and realities. *Arete: The Journal of Sport Literature*, **1**(2), 155-161.

Garfield, C.A. (1985). Peak performance. *Women's Sports and Fitness*, **7**(10), 12.

Henderson, H. (1986). The age of light: Beyond the information age. *The Futurist*, **20**(4), 56.

Parks, J.B., & Olafson, G.A. (1987). Sport management and a new journal. *Journal of Sport Management*, **1**(1), 1.

Perelman, L.J. (1986). Learning our lesson, why school is out. *The Futurist*, **20**(2), 13.

Stine, G.H. (1985). *Handbook for space colonists*. New York: Holt, Rinehart and Winston.

Snyder, R.D. (1982). Health hazard appraisal, living longer through preventive medicines. *The Futurist*, **16**(4), 25.

Toffler, A. (1980). *The third wave*. New York: Bantam Books.

Zanger, B.K. (1984). Sport management curriculum model. In B.K. Zanger & J.B. Parks (Eds.), *Sport management curricula: The business and education nexus* (pp. 97-109). Bowling Green, OH: Bowling Green State University, School of Health, Physical Education and Recreation.

Index

About the Editors

Dr. Janet Parks chairs Bowling Green State University's sport management division. Dr. Parks is a founding executive council member of the North American Society for Sport Management, a member of the National Association for Sport and Physical Education  Task Force on Sport Management Curriculum, and a coach with 13 years' experience. She is also the coeditor of the *Journal of Sport Management* and a frequent consultant to sport management programs. She received her doctorate from Middle Tennessee State University in 1977.

Beverly R.K. Zanger helped initiate and design Bowling Green State University's sport management program. She is an assistant professor in the sport management division of the university's School of HPER. Ms. Zanger is a founding executive council member  of the North American Society for Sport Management, for which she serves as archivist. She has over 40 years' teaching experience, 25 years' coaching experience, and experience in business and management. She received her master's degree in education from Bowling Green State University in 1969. Ms. Zanger and Dr. Parks also coedited *Sport Management Curricula: The Business and Education Nexus*, the first book on sport management curricula.

About the Authors

 William L. Alsop completed his bachelor's degree at the University of Corpus Christi (TX). Following 5 years of coaching in Montgomery County (MD), he completed both his master's degree and doctorate in physical education at West Virginia University. After becoming a member of the staff at West Virginia University he was responsible for the development of the Department of Sport and Exercise Studies with the Sport Management Program housed in that department.

 Robert L. Callecod currently serves as director of the Bowling Green (OH) Parks and Recreation Department and is a part-time associate professor of health, physical education and recreation at Bowling Green State University. His research and teaching responsibilities are focused on leisure services marketing and sport and recreation facility design. He served for over 10 years as director of marketing research for the Hennepin Parks System in Minnesota and he has been a marketing consultant for the Nordic and Alpine skiing industries. He received his doctoral degree in parks, recreation and leisure services administration from the University of Minnesota; a master's degree in landscape architecture from the University of Illinois; and his bachelor's degree in business administration from Knox College.

 Allan Chamberlin has been the sports information director for the Mid-American Conference since 1983. His duties include handling media relations, editing publications, and compiling statistics and records. He earned his bachelor's degree from the University of New Hampshire, majoring in nonfiction writing. He was assistant sports information director at the University of New Hampshire for 5 years and sports information director at Bowling Green State University from 1979 to 1983.

 Annie Clement is professor of health, physical education and recreation at Cleveland State University. She holds bachelor's and master's degrees from the University of Minnesota, a doctoral degree from the University of Iowa, and the J.D. from Cleveland State University. She has been a coach and teacher at the secondary and collegiate levels and has held the administrative positions of department chair, academic program coordinator in the vice-president's office, and associate dean of the College of Education. Her publications include the texts *Law in Sport and Physical Education* and *Equity in Physical Education* and several book chapters. Currently, she is on the editorial review boards of *The Physical Educator*, *Future Focus*, and *The Journal of Sport Management*. In 1988 she served as president of the National Association for Sport and Physical Education (NASPE).

Joy T. DeSensi received her bachelor's degree from West Liberty State College (WV), her master's degree in education from Memphis State University, and her doctoral degree in education from the University of North Carolina at Greensboro. Currently an associate professor at the University of Tennessee at Knoxville, her teaching and research focus is in the areas of philosophical and sociological foundations of sport and physical education, sport management, and pedagogy. She is actively involved in a variety of professional organizations at the state, regional, national, and international levels and has served the North American Society for Sport Management as treasurer and member-at-large. She was a member of the Founding Executive Council of NASSM.

David L. Groves is a professor in the School of Health, Physical Education and Recreation at Bowling Green State University. He has published extensively in the fields of psychology, business, and leisure and has practical and consulting experience in these fields. Dr. Groves is the originator and editor of *Visions in Leisure and Business* and has also served on many editorial boards and held positions in many professional organizations.

Dorothy V. Harris is professor of exercise and sport science at The Pennsylvania State University, where she is also coordinator of the Graduate Program in Sport Psychology. She has served as president of the North American Society for Psychology of Sport and is active in the International Society of Sport Psychology, the American College of Sports Medicine, the Research Consortium of AAHPERD, and the Association for the Advancement of Applied Sport Psychology. A renowned speaker, author of over 50 articles, and author or editor of seven books, Dr. Harris was awarded the first Fulbright Research Scholar Award to conduct research in sport psychology in Vienna, Austria.

Mary Jo Kane is an assistant professor in the School of Physical Education and Recreation at the University of Minnesota. She has taught courses in sport psychology at both the undergraduate and graduate levels. Her research interests focus on social/psychological aspects of female sport participation, and she has published several articles on attitudes toward female athletes before and after the passage of Title IX. In the applied area, Dr. Kane has most recently worked with such psychological techniques as stress management and imagery. She is an avid sport enthusiast who spends her leisure time both watching and participating in a variety of sports.

JoAnn Kroll is director of University Placement Services at Bowling Green State University. Prior to joining Bowling Green State University she was the program officer for business, industry, and government at Kent State University Career Planning and Placement Center. She is a coauthor of *Junior/Senior Employment Seminar Workbook* and "Career Planning and Placement," a chapter in *Student Affairs Functions in Higher Education.*

James W. Lessig, a graduate of Bowling Green State University, is currently the commissioner of the Mid-American Conference, one of only nine Division I-A conferences in the country. He has held the position of athletic director at both Bowling Green State University and the University of Kansas. He also has held a variety of other collegiate administrative positions. He has coached basketball at the high school, college, and professional levels.

 David O. Matthews received his bachelor's and master's degrees from the University of Michigan and his doctorate in education from Western Reserve University. He has served as director of men's intramurals at Bowling Green State University and as director of campus recreation at the University of Illinois, where he is currently a professor of physical education. Dr. Matthews has chaired the AAHPERD Intramural Advisory Committee, won the National Intramural Sports Council Service Award, and served as president of the North American Society for Sport Management.

 John McCarthy is a graduate of the University of Notre Dame. He received his master's degree in philosophy and theology from the Aquinas Institute in River Forest, IL. After serving as a Catholic priest from 1964 to 1970, he taught theology, basketball, and tennis at the College of St. Thomas (MN). Following advanced studies at Harvard, he became involved in the club industry as a tennis pro, club manager, club owner, and regional and national association manager. He received a master's degree in business administration from Boston College in 1987 and is currently the executive director of the International Racquet Sports Association.

 Mary Kennedy Minter has been a college faculty member for the past 15 years and has taught organizational behavior, communication, and management. She has taught at several postsecondary institutions including Buffalo State University, Eastern Michigan University, Central Connecticut State University, and Colorado Women's College. She received her master's degree in organizational communication from Purdue University. She has also held full-time positions in training

and development for business and industry, including work for Blue Cross of Michigan, Edwards Brothers Book Manufacturing Company in Ann Arbor, MI, and Humana Hospital in Denver, CO. In addition, she has developed and conducted programs and workshops on such topics as management by objectives, long-range planning, interviewing, and training of instructors.

 Robert L. Minter is currently dean of and professor in the School of Management at the University of Michigan–Dearborn. He was previously dean of the School of Business, Central Connecticut State University; division head of administrative sciences, College of Business Administration, University of Denver; and administrator of management and professional development programs at Detroit Edison Company. Previous professorial appointments have been at Eastern Michigan University, State University of New York at Buffalo, Cornell University, University of New Hampshire, and Purdue University. Dr. Minter has published in numerous journals and is coauthor of a book titled *Perspectives on Administrative Communication*.

 Robert Moomaw is a professor in the College of Education at Bowling Green State University, where he teaches courses in counseling and career development. He has authored articles about occupational prestige, vocational rehabilitation, and student personality characteristics. A licensed psychologist, Dr. Moomaw is also engaged in private practice.

 Crayton L. Moss is assistant professor and athletic training program coordinator of the Sport Management Division of Bowling Green State University. He completed his doctoral studies at the University of Kansas, with an emphasis in exercise physiology. He was awarded a patent for his methodology and instrumentation for skeletal muscle testing. His main professional responsibilities are in the areas of assessment, measurement, evaluation, and rehabilitation of sport injuries.

Catherine A. Pratt is an assistant professor in the School of Journalism at The Ohio State University in Columbus, OH. She has worked in broadcast promotion and public relations and has hosted a sports television show. As a member of the radio/television/film department of Carl Byoir and Associates in New York City, she worked with professional athletes, training them for radio and television appearances. She has a doctoral degree in mass communication from Bowling Green State University.

E. Louise Priest is currently the executive director of the Council for National Cooperation in Aquatics and editor of the *National Aquatics Journal*. Formerly she was the assistant national director of Water Safety for the American Red Cross. She is the author of the American Red Cross *Adapted Aquatics* textbook and supportive materials and has written many articles on aquatics for various publications. She is a master clinician of AAHPERD and is recipient of the AAHPERD Aquatic Council's honor award and service award. She is listed in *Who's Who in the East* and in *The World Who's Who of Women*. She has been a professional in the field of aquatics for 25 years.

Richard J. Quain earned his bachelor's degree from St. Cloud College (MN), his master's degree from the College of St. Thomas (MN), and his doctoral degree from the University of Missouri–Columbia. During his career, he has been an amateur and professional umpire, a teacher, a coach, a sporting goods manufacturer's representative, president and owner of a cash grain brokerage firm, an assistant professor of sport management, and owner and manager of a summer collegiate baseball team. He has held leadership roles in the National Youth Sport Coaches Association and in the North American Society for Sport Management, of which he was a member of the Founding Executive Council.

M. Joy Sidwell is coordinator of sport management field experiences in the Sport Management Division of the School of Health, Physical Education and Recreation at Bowling Green State University. A pioneer in the development of the discipline of sport management, she also teaches history and philosophy of sport and supervises practicum and internship students. She has been a faculty member at Mount Holyoke College and is a member of the North American Society for Sport Management.

Eldon E. Snyder is a professor of sociology at Bowling Green State University. His areas of specialization include the sociology of sport and leisure. Dr. Snyder earned his graduate degrees from the University of Kansas with additional graduate work at the University of Colorado and the University of Southern California. He has taught and coached in Kansas secondary schools, at Kansas State University at Emporia, and at Bowling Green State University. He is a regular contributor to professional journals and is the coauthor of *Social Aspects of Sport*.

David K. Stotlar has a doctorate in education from the University of Utah and teaches on the faculty of the University of Northern Colorado in the areas of sport management and sport law. He has published over 35 articles in professional journals and has written several chapters for physical education and sport textbooks. He has made numerous presentations at international, national, and regional professional conferences. Dr. Stotlar has served as a consultant to school districts, sport professionals, attorneys, and international sport administrators. He was selected by the USOC as a delegate to the International Olympic Academy in Greece, and he has conducted management seminars for the Hong Kong Olympic Committee, the National Sports Council of Malaysia, the Singapore Sports Council, the Bahrain Sport Institute, and the government of Saudi Arabia.

 Michael D. Wolf is president of International Fitness Exchange, a New York City–based consulting company that performs a wide range of services for a diverse clientele. After receiving his doctorate in physical education from the University of Texas at Austin, he served as assistant professor of physical education at New York University and as research coordinator at Nautilus Sports/Medical Industries, Inc. He is a contributing editor for *Fitness Management* and *SELF* magazines and has authored six books, his most recent work being *Nautilus: Building a Hard Body* (1987).